WITHDRAWN FROM
KENT STATE UNIVERSITY LIBRARIES

Modern European History

A Garland Series of Outstanding Dissertations

General Editor
William H. McNeill
University of Chicago

Associate Editors

Eastern Europe
Charles Jelavich
Indiana University

Great Britain
Peter Stansky
Stanford University

France
David H. Pinkney
University of Washington

Russia
Barbara Jelavich
Indiana University

Germany
Enno E. Kraehe
University of Virginia

MODERN EUROPEAN HISTORY

Conflict and Crisis
Romanian Political Development, 1861–1871

Paul E. Michelson

Garland Publishing, Inc.
New York and London 1987

Copyright © 1987 Paul E. Michelson
All rights reserved

Library of Congress Cataloging-in-Publication Data

Michelson, Paul E., 1945–
  Conflict and crisis : Romanian political development, 1861–1871 / Paul E. Michelson.
    p. cm.—(Modern European history)
    ISBN 0-8240-8029-7 (alk. paper)
    1. Romania—Politics and government—1821–1866. 2. Romania—Politics and government—1866–1914. I. Title. II. Series.
DR244.M53   1987
949.8'02—dc19   87-27222

All volumes in this series are printed on acid-free, 250-year-life paper.

Printed in the United States of America

CONFLICT AND CRISIS:

Romanian Political Development, 1861-1871

For J. T. M.

"There is a divinity that shapes our ends,
Rough hew them how we will."
           Shakespeare, **Hamlet**, V.ii.10

TABLE of CONTENTS

	Table of Contents	page 5
	Preface	page 7
	Abbreviations	page 10
	Map: Romania Between 1856-1878	page 11

Part I: **Introduction**
Chapter 1 Prolegomenon   page 15
Chapter 2 Romania in the 1860's   page 26

Part II: **Romania under Prince Cuza, 1861-1866**
Chapter 3 The Political Scene Under Prince Cuza   page 37
Chapter 4 The First Phase: Conflict and Crisis   page 51
Chapter 5 The Second Phase: Internal War and Revolt page 71
Chapter 6 The Third Phase: Interim Government   page 102

Part III: **Romania under Prince Carol, 1866-1871**
Chapter 7   The First Phase: The National Coalition   page 129
Chapter 8   The Second Phase: Non-Party Government   page 147
Chapter 9   The Third Phase: Liberalism in Power   page 160
Chapter 10 The Fourth Phase: Liberalism's Fall   page 177
Chapter 11 The Fifth Phase: Conflict and Crisis   page 190
Chapter 12 The Sixth Phase: Abdication Once More   page 201

Part IV: **Conclusion**
Chapter 13 Romania in the 1870's   page 217

Part V: **Notes and Appendices**
Notes   page 229
Appendix One: A Note on Names and Orthography   page 311
Appendix Two: Money and Monetary Units   page 312
Appendix Three: Prime Ministers, 1862-1871   page 314
Appendix Four: A Note on Sources   page 315

PREFACE

The foundation of this study is my dissertation, **Conflict and Development in Romanian Politics, 1861–1871**, completed at Indiana University in 1975 under the direction of Professor Barbara Jelavich. Research for the thesis was conducted in Romania and London, 1971–1973, and Bloomington, 1973–1974, with the assistance of grants from the International Research and Exchanges Board [IREX] and the Fulbright-Hays Fellowship Programs. Some additional research for this study was carried out in 1982–1983 in Romania under further grants from IREX and Fulbright as well as a sabbatical leave from Huntington College.

The present work improves on the original thesis in several ways. First of all, it is based on an additional decade of study and consideration of Romanian politics and historiography. This has, I think, particularly improved the first three chapters. A number of points about which I was less certain in 1975 seem much clearer ten years later. Secondly, a number of important works have appeared in the interval that bolster contentions and elucidate matters dealt with in this study. I will mention only the two most significant here. One major study is Gerald J. Bobango's **The Emergence of the Romanian National State** [1979]. I was able to use a draft version of the dissertation which is the basis for the book; the present work is much the richer for being able to draw on the finished product. The second important study is Apostol Stan's **Grupări și curente politice în România între unire și independență (1859–1877)** [1979], the major arguments of which are, in the main, supportive of and congenial to my own findings and conclusions. These works have enabled me to be a good deal less tentative about political development in this era. There are numerous other recent studies that have been utilized below to strengthen the original thesis; these are, of course, now included in the notes.

This is not to imply that this study has been completely re-written. In particular, the narrative sections have remained relatively unchanged. And, while the interpretive sections have been greatly strengthened, the essential findings of the original study, by and large, still stand. Some effort has been made to eliminate as much as possible of the "dissertationese" of the original version; the final product is, I think, more readable and more tightly organized.

The archival and printed materials used in preparing this study are listed and described in the notes and Appendix Four. Because of the considerably greater amount of serious scholarly work available on the Cuza era (1859-1866), Chapters 1-5 use more secondary sources than those that follow. This is reflected in the notes. Documents cited from archival sources are originals unless otherwise indicated.

On the always tendentious questions of orthography, the reader should see Appendix One. All dates in this study are given in Old Style, which was twelve days behind the Western [Gregorian] calendar during this period.

In the course of nearly twenty years study of Romanian history and culture, and in four years of work in Romania itself, I have had the benefit of generous cooperation and assistance from innumerable colleagues and friends, and I am indebted to many people. It is almost invidious to single any of them out, but specific acknowledgement must be made to the following: Barbara and Charles Jelavich for their warm interest and support as well as their insights and teaching of East European history; Gerald Bobango, Cornelia Bodea, Grigore Chiriță, the late Constantin C. Giurescu, Apostol Stan, Glenn Torrey, and E. Garrison Walters for their advice, assistance, and encouragement of this particular study; Radu A. Sterescu for his inestimable aid in obtaining printed materials; and Gretchen Buehler for her conscientious efforts to teach not-always willing historians something about the Romanian language, culture, and civilization.

To the librarians, archivists, and personnel of the Arhivele Statului, the Biblioteca Academiei, the Biblioteca Centrală de

Stat, and the Institutul de Istorie N. Iorga, all in București; the Arhivele Statului, the Biblioteca Centrală Universitară, and the Institutul de Istorie și Arheologie A. D. Xenopol, all in Iași; and the Public Record Office in London, go my appreciation and thanks. To the personnel of IREX, the Fulbright programs, the American Embassy in București, the Consiliul Național pentru Știință și Tehnologie, the Academia de Științe Sociale și Politice, and Huntington College, grateful acknowledgement is made of essential support for my research sojourns in Romania and elsewhere.

Finally, to my wife, Jean, and my sons, David and Paul-Philip for their willingness to support me in travel, research, and writing: thanks are not enough, but maybe Daddy can spend a little more time with you—until the next project, anyway.

Huntington, Indiana
11 February 1987

ABBREVIATIONS

Archives:

    PRO London: Public Record Office, London

    A. S. București: Arhivele Statului, București

    A. S. Iași: Arhivele Statului, Iași

    BAR București: Biblioteca Academiei, București

    BCS București: Biblioteca Centrală de Stat, București

Other:

    A.R. MSI: **Academia Române. Memoriile Secțiunile Istorice**

Part I: INTRODUCTION

"You shall be yet far fairer than you are."
Shakespeare, **Antony and Cleopatra**, I.ii.18

Chapter 1

Prolegomenon

"But men may construe things after their own fashion,
Clean from the purpose of the things themselves."
Shakespeare, **Julius Caesar**, I.iii.34

This study provides the first general description and analysis in English of modern Romanian political culture as it developed in the decade following the complete unification of the Danubian Principalities of Moldova and Muntenia. Why Romania? Why Southeastern Europe? All during the 19th century, the Eastern Question kept European diplomacy in constant turmoil. This turmoil not only resulted in numerous outbursts of violence; it led in the end to Sarajevo and the outbreak of the Great War in 1914. In addition to the continuing decline and weakness of the Ottoman Empire—which certainly lay at the heart of the question—the emergence of various Southeast European peoples (long under Ottoman tutelage) into their own nation states and the continuing rivalries of the Great Powers for territory and dominance added fuel to the fire. The Romanian Principalities of Moldova and Muntenia because of their crucial location at the mouth of the Danube and at the juncture of the Russian, Habsburg, and Ottoman empires were an important and integral part of the Eastern Question. Once they gained complete unity in 1861, the Principalities' internal development became a significant factor in European diplomacy since instability or disorder in the new state would furnish the pretext for external intervention and upset the delicate equilibrium established by the Congress of Paris in 1856.[1]

The double election of Alexandru Ioan Cuza in 1859 as prince of the two Principalities had provided the Romanians with a single ruler for the first time in the modern era along with an internal autonomy guaranteed by the Great Powers, but it was only two years later that the actual administrative unification of the two Principalities became a reality. The dramatic story of the Romanian national emergence has long attracted considerable attention, both within Romania and without.[2] The process of nation-state building in 19th century Europe, the patterns of nationalist movements and their development, and the international ramifications of these processes and events have been [correctly] seen as having more than local or regional significance. At the same time, studies of such matters have been encouraged by the relative abundance of documentation, especially that generated by the ever-busy diplomatic personnel of all concerned.

The less dramatic story of Romanian internal development, despite its obvious importance, has been comparatively neglected. Analysis of this development is made more difficult in many ways by the nebulous nature of the problems encountered, the unpredictablity of source materials, and the relative untidiness of internal politics as compared to international affairs. It is apt to involve more heated controversy and intrinsic prejudice. Such history is no less significant or unworthy of the historian's attention for all of that.

The present work moves on to the next stage of the study of Romania in the modern era: concentration on internal processes and systems development. The external problem of union, which had created in the 1850's a "national coalition" comprising most Romanian political activists, was resolved by the events of 1859-1861. The Romanians now turned toward internal debate, the coalition disintegrated, and modern Romanian political life began. It was during the intense struggles which followed that the basic foundations were laid for the indigenous political culture, institutions, and groupings which were to dominate this important but little known Southeast European state for much of the next century.

The analysis which follows is divided into four parts: the first outlines the Romanian situation in 1860, at the outset of its modern political history. Some attention is given to social and economic matters as well as to description of the political environment and groupings.

The second section, covering the last five years of the native Prince Cuza's reign, focuses on the gradual escalation of political conflict within the newly formed nation and the resulting crises which eventually led in 1866 to the forced abdication of Cuza. The primary issues and problems around which political constellations formed and reformed are highlighted along with analysis of the progress made in dealing with these questions.

This is followed by a third major section, covering the first half decade of the reign of the foreign Prince Carol I, which focuses on the placing of a non-native prince on the Romanian throne in 1866, the institutional arrangements which were then established, and the subsequent conflicts and crises which led to the near-abdication of Carol in 1871. Stress is given to problems and issues which appear to have been formative in the emerging Romanian political system.

The fourth and concluding section of the study reviews the major trends and tendencies of the period under discussion, sketches the main outlines of the directions established in this formative decade, and evaluates the results, largely through a number of comparisons and contrasts between the final years of Cuza's reign and the beginnings of Carol's rule.

In addition to elaborating on the situations created by the breakdown and restoration of the emerging Romanian political order, by the formation and evolution of political groupings and actors within that framework, and by the patterns of political culture which were being established in this significant epoch in Romanian history, the study also discusses some key problems related to the political development of the new state. These include such matters as regionalism, elite formation, the Jewish question, and the viability of the constitutional structures established at the beginning of modern Romanian history.

It should be emphasized, however, that no attempt is made here to present a comprehensive history of Romania in the period under consideration; only those issues, events, and persons which seem relevant to unfolding the story of Romania's internal political system and structure are included.³

Before we turn to this development of Romanian politics in the mid-nineteenth century, a few preliminary remarks on politics in general and political conflict and crisis in particular are necessary. Politics is a common human activity that spans the five millennia or so of recorded human action and is intimately connected—sometimes for better, but often for worse—with the unfolding of that record. Indeed, at one time it was considered to be the basic subject matter of history. It is right that the history of politics' place has been put into better perspective by recent developments in historical studies. Certainly it would be absurd to claim that political history should be the only focus of the historian's work.

It would also be absurd to neglect national political history or relegate it to some supposed dustbin of historiography. Such history continues to hold its value by providing an elementary grasp of the past of a country and a people, and by furnishing what remains the most usable framework for other analyses. The very real deficiencies of the existing body of historical [and other] studies on Romania clearly demonstrate the drawbacks of trying to proceed with allegedly more sophisticated analyses in the absence of basic chronological, political analyses. Indeed, ironical references found in Romanian historiography to basic political studies as "mere factology" are more likely to be alibis for the substitution of opinion, presumption, and ideology for empirical evidence than real pleas for any actual or potential movement toward deeper appreciations of the Romanian past and present.

On another—more positive—front, there are those who have pleaded for broader, area-wide historical analyses rather than "national" political studies. Certainly the day will arrive when the former will be obligatory. However, it seems clear that we are yet far from the point where such studies can be meaningfully pursued because we know far too little about far too much.

It is, thus, both remarkable and noteworthy that only recently has the political development of modern Romania been given even the most elementary treatment. The complexities of modern Romanian history, the vicissitudes of the gradual emergence of Romanian historiography in the last century, and the imposition since 1948 of a quasi-Marxist approach to the Romanian past account in part for this phenomenon.[4] It was as late as the mid-1960's and early 1970's that extended [if not always satisfactory] studies of pre-World War I Romanian political life began to be published.[5] And it was only in 1983 that the first comprehensive study of parliamentary history in Romania made its appearance.[6] The situation is much improved over what it was a decade ago when initial work for the present work was first completed, but as will be indicated at various junctures below, many key matters still remain to be elaborated.

Given the existence and importance of governments and politics in history and given that governments both possess and exercise force or power, the question which logically arises is "who will exercise that force and under what conditions?" Politics will be considered here as "the process which ceaselessly aims at forming, developing, obstructing, shifting, or overturning the relationship of domination."[7]

Central to this process are political groupings, which raises the next problem, that of political parties. Attempted definitions are myriad, ranging from the liberal conception of a party as a grouping which shares a core doctrinal commonality to the Marxist approach of party as a function of social class. These definitions generally lack universality. In this study, the approach of Maurice Duverger's classic **Political Parties** will be followed, which defines a political party as a structured community of interests or aims.[8] Universal enough to encompass the criteria of other definitions (including the liberal and the Marxist), this definition helps bring some understanding as well as some clarification of the problem by stressing the importance of permanent organizational structures and of concrete communities of interests in the formation of true political parties. Groups, factions, and so forth, which do not have such organization and community cannot legitimately be called political parties under this definition. The failure of the Romanian political system to foster true parties and the consequences of this failure are a major emphasis of our study.

Crises seem endemic in modern political development and substantial efforts have been made in recent years to organize and clarify their role in the functioning of political systems.[9] "Crisis" in this study will refer generally to any significant threat to the existing political regime or system and specifically to sequences of events which led to an important change (either institutionally or in terms of the process) in the way political life was conducted in Romania. Such threats may or may not have been apparent to the participants, may or may not have been real, and may have been of widely varying dimensions. This is not to say that political leadership and development should be conceived of "merely in terms of crisis management,"[10] or that analysis of the problems governments face should consist only in a description of what governments do in a crisis situation.

Grew and his collaborators have identified five types of crisis which are important for political development: crises of identity, legitimacy, participation, penetration, and distribution.[11] In the study which follows, the second (the establishment and legitimation of a new political order in Romania) and third (the various questions concerning political parties and voting) will receive the primary attention. The others have some relevance to the time period under consideration, but are mainly significant in the Romanian drama either earlier (identity) or later (identity once more; penetration or the development of bureaucratized state mechanisms; and distribution or questions concerning societal arrangements).

And what of conflict? Harry Eckstein, Ralf Dahrendorf, and others have suggested that analysis of a society can be helpfully focused on conflict within that society.[12] Because of power and because of the inherent uncertainty of human affairs, it is crisis and conflict that characterize societies, not concord and harmony. "Because we do not know all the answers, there has to be continuous conflict over values and policies. Because of uncertainty, there is always change and development," Dahrendorf points out. As a consequence of this, the "structures of power in which the political process takes place offer an explanation not only of how change originates and what direction it takes, but also of why it is necessary...Power produces conflict, and conflict between antagonistic interests gives lasting expression to the fundamental uncertainty of human existence, by ever giving rise to new solutions and ever casting doubt on them as soon as they take form."[13]

By focusing on political conflict in the new situation created by the definitive union of the Romanian Principalities in December of 1861, this study also concerns itself with the problems involved in the breakdown and restoration of political order. Analyses of revolutions, their causes, and their results have produced reams of description and discussion ever since Edmund Burke and Thomas Paine assumed opposing positions during the French Revolution. Much of the modern history of Eastern Europe has been seen as a succession of revolutions, successful and otherwise, against a series of foes within and without. A great deal of information, much confusion, and very little systematic analysis has been produced as a result. The concept of "internal war," developed by Harry Eckstein and others, is used in this study to suggest one way of clarifying a complex and confused subject.

The term "internal war" is defined as "attempts to change by violence, or the threat of violence, a government's policies, rulers, or organization."[14] An internal war has four major phases: preconditions, precipitants, a course of events, and outcomes, both short and long run. Eckstein notes that these phases have been given curiously unequal treatment, with the preconditions (more loosely, "causes") given most of the attention while the long run effects (the restoration of political legitimacy, social consequences, the costs, and factors leading the recurring struggle and conflict) are practically ignored. By consciously focusing on the internal war construct, our analysis of the Romanian situation attempts to give balanced treatment to each of these phases.

Eckstein's suggestions for inquiry and clarification of the problem of internal war are also helpful in eliminating some of the arbitrariness connected with discussion of preconditions or causes.[15] One major suggestion is that significant preconditions fall into two classes: those which make for internal war (ineptness of elites, disorienting social processes, subversion, and the resources available to insurgents are the primary ones) and those which work against it (diversionary mechanisms available to the rulers, facilities of the incumbents, feasibility of concessions, and effective repression are operative here).

Finally, as we consider the outcome of internal wars, a number of problems need to be considered. In the short run these include the re-establishment of order; the reorganization of the political structure, if any; and the consolidation of their objectives by the successful rebels, if any. In the long range, other questions come to the fore: What consequences did the internal war have on the society beyond its immediate effects? Was the legitimacy of the new order established? What were the consequences of how it was established, especially in regard to the subsequent stability or instability of the political order? What other long range effects were observable (economic, institutional, social, and the like)? Were the supposed gains worth the costs?[16]

All of the above is not to argue that other approaches to the subject under consideration are invalid; it is only to argue that the one just sketched appears helpful in elaborating and understanding the development of the political process in Romania in its formative stages.

Before we turn to this process, two final preliminary steps remain: this chapter is completed with a brief, highly selective chronology of significant dates and events in Romanian history between 1856 and 1871 to help the reader place the analysis. (Additional data on the cabinets which held office between 1861 and 1871 is given in Appendix Three.) The following chapter describes the Romanian setting in the 1860's in which our story takes place.

CHRONOLOGY IN BRIEF
[All dates given in Old Style]

February–March 1856	Congress of Paris ends Crimean War; The Romanian Principalities are placed under European protectorate
July–August 1857	Osborne meeting between Napoléon III and Queen Victoria. They agree to partial union of the Principalities
September 1857– December 1858	Meetings of the Divans Ad-hoc in Moldova and Muntenia
May–August 1858	Great Powers meet as the Paris Conference concerning the future organization of the Principalities
August 1858	The Convention of Paris is issued establishing the "constitution" of the Principalities
December 1858– January 1859	Election of Assemblies in Moldova and Muntenia
5 January 1859	A. I. Cuza is unanimously elected Prince by the Moldovan assembly
24 January 1859	A. I. Cuza is unanimously elected Prince by the Muntenian assembly
March–September 1859	The Paris Conference acknowledges the double election of Prince Cuza
26 October 1860	University of Iași founded
20 November 1861	The Ottoman Empire recognizes the internal unification of Moldova and Muntenia
11 December 1861	Cuza issues a proclamation that "Union is achieved and the Romanian nationality founded"
22 January 1862	Barbu Catargiu government
24 January 1862	First meeting of the unified Parliament; București is named capital
May, 1862	Conservative agrarian bill is debated
8 June 1862	Assassination of Barbu Catargiu

24 June 1862	Nicolae Kretzulescu government
11 October 1863	Mihail Kogălniceanu government
17 December 1863	Law on Secularization of the Monasteries
12 February 1864	Army Reorganization Law
13 April 1864	Assembly rejects Agrarian Reform law
16 April 1864	Judicial Organization Law
2 May 1864	Cuza dissolves the Assembly
10-14 May 1864	Plebiscite ratifies new electoral law and increased executive power
16 June 1864	Ottoman Empire recognizes right of the Romanians to change internal laws without prior approval, including Cuza's "coup"
4 July 1864	University of Bucureşti founded
14 August 1864	Agrarian Reform Law promulgated
2 December 1864	Penal Code is promulgated
4 December 1864	Civil Code is promulgated
26 January 1865	Constantin Bozianu government
27 July 1865	Romania adheres to the international telegraphic convention
15 August 1865	Bucureşti uprising
11 February 1866	Forced abdication of Prince Cuza; Princely Lieutenancy composed of Lascăr Catargiu, Nicolae Golescu, and Nicolae Haralambie is established
11 February 1866	Ion Ghica government
18 March 1866	Agricultural contract law
1 April 1866	Romanian Literary Society established [precursor of the Romanian Academy]
2-8 April 1866	Plebiscite approves Prince Karl of Hohenzollern-Sigmaringen as prince under the name of Carol I
9 April 1866	Election of a Constituent Assembly
10 May 1866	Carol I is crowned prince
10 May 1866	Lascăr Catargiu government

1 July 1866	New constitution promulgated
15 July 1866	Ion Ghica government
30 July 1866	New Electoral Law promulgated
11 October 1866	Ottoman Empire recognizes Carol I
1 March 1867	Constantin Crețulescu government
22 April 1867	Monetary Law promulgated
1 August 1867	First meeting of the Romanian Academic Society
5 August 1867	Ştefan Golescu government
25 November 1867	First Postal Convention [with Russia]
1 May 1868	Nicolae Golescu government
17 July 1868	Army Reorganization Law
22 September 1868	Offenheim-Strousberg railroad concessions
16 November 1868	Dimitrie Ghica government
19 October 1869	Bucureşti-Giurgiu railroad opened
January 1870	Cuza elected to parliament
2 February 1870	Alexandru G. Golescu government
20 April 1870	Manolache Costache Epureanu government
7/19 July 1870	Outbreak of Franco-Prussian War
8 August 1870	Ploeşti uprising
18 December 1870	Ion Ghica government
10 March 1871	Anti-German riots in Bucureşti
11 March 1871	Abdication Crisis
11 March 1871	Lascăr Catargiu government
16 March 1871	Dissolution of Parliament ends dynastic crisis

Chapter 2

Romania in the 1860's

"There is a tide in the affairs of men, which, taken at the flood, leads on to fortune; omitted, all the voyage of their life is bound in shallow and in miseries. On such a full sea are we now afloat, and we must take the current when it serves, or lose our ventures."
Shakespeare, **Julius Caesar**, IV.iii.217

The Romania with which this study is concerned was a considerable contrast to that of today.[1] From a legal point of view, there was no "Romania" at all in 1860, only the "United Principalities of Moldavia and Wallachia," which were under the protectorate of the the Great Powers of Europe and which owed allegiance to the Ottoman Empire.[2] The "constitution" of this infant state was a cumbersome instrument devised by the Great Powers meeting in congress in Paris, through a convention issued in August of 1858.[3] The Convention provided for each Principality to have separate but parallel institutions, including two princes, two ministries, and two legislatures. A central commission, to meet at their mutual border at Focşani, and a joint court of appeals were created to handle affairs of mutual interest and concern. The United Principalities were thus "united" mainly in name, a compromise that was not at all satisfactory to the Romanian nationalists whose efforts and agitation had prodded the Convention of Paris into being in the first place.

The Convention of Paris also gave some rather emphatic directives concerning social and political affairs in the Principalities. The key provisions were in article 46, which abolished social distinctions and privileges and which called for an immediate reform of agrarian relationships. These "radical" steps were counterbalanced—one might even say negated—by the establishment in the Principalities of an electoral system which placed political power in the hands of the mostly conservative landholding segment of Romanian society, the very group most disinclined to make substantive agrarian reforms.

Politically speaking, the Romanian "political nation" was composed only of the propertied and educated. The electorate established by the Paris Convention was an exceedingly narrow body of less than 4,000 voters, whose franchise was based on wealth and position. One result, it has been pointed out, was that there was an approximately equal number of voters and upper-level bureaucrats.[4] Under this system, the vast majority of the population, mainly peasants, did not count and, as a result, will not figure very greatly in this study. Though on occasion their interests and demands "intruded" onto the Romanian political stage, their importance to politicians, other than demagogically, was small.[5] It was not until the 20th century that the peasantry would become a political factor of more than rhetorical or latent significance in the Romanian political equation.

The single chamber assembly chosen by this restricted electorate was, as one might expect, dominated by the rich and land-owning. It had the right to initiate, consider, amend, and reject or ratify legislation. The power of the assembly, was, however, balanced by that of the prince. The prince in fact governed with a ministry which he appointed, but not necessarily from the membership of the Assembly. This failure to limit ministerial choice to assemblymen was a significant factor in the weakness of the parliamentary system which subsequently developed in Romania. The prince had the right to initiate, sanction or veto legislation. He could also call and dismiss the Assembly as well as govern in its absence.

The third branch of Conventional government in the Principalities, the judiciary, was very similar to that which had existed previously: judges were nominated by the government and approved by the Assembly. In practice, they fell more or less under the prince's control and did not constitute an alternative center of political power or balance in the system.

Though the prince shared power with the Assembly, he had wide opportunities to act apart from it because of his latitude in foreign policy, because he was commander-in-chief of the army, and because of his control of ministerial and other appointments. To limit his power somewhat, all acts issued by the prince had to have a ministerial counter-signature. In practice, this did little to restrict the prince. The first prince under this system, Cuza, exercised powers that were a good deal stronger and broader than those envisioned by the Convention, especially in the face of continual Assembly obstruction to his reform proposals and due to ministerial instability.

From a geographical point of view, Romania was composed of two principalities, Moldova and Muntenia, which comprised an area of 121,000 square kilometers and had a population of 4.6 million.[6] Moldova, with a population of about 2 million, had as its capital Iași, with a population of nearly 70,000.[7] It was divided into fifteen județs [counties]. The population density of Moldova was 42 per km^2. Two of these counties were on the left bank of the Prut River, a portion of the so-called Bessarabian area of Moldova seized by Russia in 1812 and partially restored by the Treaty of Paris in 1856. The rest of Moldova was bounded on the northeast by the Prut, on the north and northwest by the Carpathian Mountains, and on the south by the Danube and the Milcov Rivers. Its port city, on the Danube, was Galați.

Muntenia was the larger of the two, with 2.6 million inhabitants and seventeen județs; its capital, București, which became the national capital in 1861, had a population of 140,000. (The two capitals were the only cities with more than 40,000 people. Another seventeen towns had populations larger than 10,000; with an urban population of less than 18% of the total, Romania was predominantly rural.) The population density of Muntenia was, however, less than that of Moldova at 31 per km^2. Muntenia was bounded on the north by the Milcov River,[8] on the west and northwest by the Carpathian arc, and on the south and east by the Danube River. Its main port city was Brăila; except for the northern (Chilia) mouth of the Danube, Muntenia was landlocked.

From a religious point of view, the Romanian population was relatively homogeneous. 95% of the people were Eastern Orthodox;

3% were Jewish. From a social point of view, it is much more difficult to make precise statements about the Romania of the 1860's. The very important subject of social classes has not as yet received the necessary attention for non-empirical, generalized notions to be replaced with solid information. In very broad terms, Romania had three main social classes: the boiars (land holders, quasi-nobility), the middle classes (commercial, artisan, religious, and professional workers), and the peasantry. In Moldova, the population broke down as follows: boiars, less than 2%; middle classes, about 19%; peasantry, 70%.[9] For Muntenia, the breakdown was similar: boiars, less than 4%; middle classes, 20%; peasantry, 75%.[10]

An examination of the population by profession shows the relative underdevelopment of the country.[11] Of 974,000 heads of family, 648,000 were engaged in agriculture (67%). The small merchants, artisans, functionaries, and other so-called middle class groups included 155,600 heads of family (16%). In this group, two segments were surprisingly large: governmental functionaries, totaling 22,800 heads of family, and "religious people," amounting to 18,450 heads of family. On the other hand, the free professions (doctors, lawyers, engineers) comprised only 838 heads of family.

Agriculture was the mainstay of the economy as can be seen from the above. What little trading and commercial activity there was was largely in the hands of non-ethnic Romanians. In Muntenia, Greeks, Serbs, Armenians, and others dominated the shopkeeper classes. In Moldova, these jobs were generally held by Jews. (It should again be noted that owing to the lack of serious investigation to date, these generalizations need to be taken cum grano salis.)[12]

Virtually no significant industry existed in the Romania of 1861. This was paralleled by a nearly complete lack of indigenous banking institutions (the lack of banks until 1884 created a serious capital formation problem for Romania). And except for the tiny portion of land north of the Danube Delta reclaimed from Russia in 1856, Romania was land-locked; the region between Muntenia and the Black Sea known as the Dobrogea became part of Romania only after 1878. The Danube, with its Moldovan port, Galați, and its Muntenian port, Brăila, provided a potentially important trade artery. There were no railroads in 1861, and the road network was both rudimentary and poorly maintained. In other words, the entire infrastructure of economic development—industry, banking, and communications—needed to be built.[13]

In the area of education, things were equally deficient. The economist and statistician D. P. Marțian's review of the Romanian situation in 1860 pointed out that Romania spent 8.6 million lei on education for its 4.5 million population. This he compared to the equivalent of 95.2 million lei spent by New York for 3.5 million people and 68.6 million lei spent by Indiana for 1.1 million people. The conclusion? Either Romania was drastically behind in education or else the American states "need to enlighten their populations more than we do..."[14]

Other problems coupled with lack of education were land abuse and lack of conservation. Though the Romanian economy was predominantly agrarian, almost nothing was being done to foster better farming techniques or the most basic rural primary education.[15] It would be a long time before even the slightest attention would be paid to such matters in a systematic manner.

Marțian also criticized his countrymen for a lack of the kind of entrepreneurial spirit needed for economic development and for a general lassitude concerning work. He calculated in 1865 that over 150 work days a year were lost to holidays (not including local holidays), many of them in prime work seasons. Given the weather and so forth, most Romanians probably had only 115 actual work days a year. The efficiency of work on these days was such (because of fasts, illness, and the like) that in the end, one could count on perhaps 58 days of all-out work a year.[16] It is not at all surprising that in such circumstances and facing such problems the political institutions and finances of the new Romanian state were somewhat unstable.

Politically and culturally speaking, the two Romanian Principalities had had long and proud separate existences prior to 1859. They had formed independently in the 13th century, produced a noteworthy medieval culture and outstanding rulers in 14th and 15th centuries, but had fallen by the 16th century under Ottoman control, first indirectly and then directly (though never completely assimilated into the Empire as Serbia, Bulgaria, and Greece were). As a result, it was only in the mid-19th century that Moldova and Muntenia were able to unite under a single ruler and to regain a significant degree of autonomy.

Thus, despite the fact that the ethnic composition, language, and, to a large extent, institutions of the two Principalities were basically similar, they had coexisted separately for more than five centuries. Their educated classes possessed, moreover, a highly developed sense of regional pride and identification which was continually reflected in the cultural and intellectual traditions centering in their respective capitals.[17] Though by the 19th century, the reasons for the separate development of Moldova and Muntenia had largely vanished,[18] the traditions of each remained as real factors in their relations and growth.

Temperamentally, the two provinces also had important differences. The Muntenians were seen as more pragmatic, more influenced by French-style liberalism, less traditional. The Moldovans were considered, in contrast, more cultured, their boiar class was stronger, and they were less prone to social experimentation. Not unnaturally, each regarded the other with some suspicion, albeit "within the family." One of the primary problems after 1859 would be to foster a greater unity in order to avoid any incipient tendencies toward separatism.

The Romanian nationalist program, established by the 1857 Divans ad hoc elected in both Principalities at the direction of the Great Powers, had had as its main points four simple aims: union, autonomy, a foreign prince, and a representative, constitutional government. These goals were derived in good measure from the revolutionary proclamations of 1848 and provided, in a sense, the basis for much of the political activity that ensued in Romania, both internally and externally. The nationalists' reaction to the system of "unity" established by the Convention of 1858 was a calculated evasion. They responded to the stipulation that each Principality elect a native prince by choosing the same man, Alexandru Ioan Cuza, first as Prince of Moldova on 5 January 1859, and then as Prince of Muntenia on 24 January 1859. The powers were annoyed, but sufficiently unreconcilable in their individual aims to take any effective action.

The contradiction between actual and desired unity dominated Romanian development until 1861; the contradiction between the ideal of agrarian reform and the interests of those who were supposed to carry it out was crucial thereafter. In addition, there was the clash between Romanian interests and those of the Great Powers. Though for all practical purposes, direct Ottoman and Russian influence in the internal affairs of Romania was eliminated after 1859, the fact remained that its politicians always had to act under the external constraints imposed by a hostile Ottoman Empire, a suspicious Habsburg Monarchy and an expansionistic Russian Empire. If provoked too far, or if internal "disorder" should reach too high a level, these powers would not hesitate to seize on however feeble a pretext to intervene in the Principalities and undo everything achieved by the Romanians during the fortunate conjuncture of events in the mid-to-late 1850s which had led to the initial emergence of the first Romanian national state.

Thus, by 1859, the Romanians had made significant strides, though they were not free of external constraints and dangers. They had recovered from the unsuccessful revolutions of 1848, they had overcome an apparently very unfavorable geographical situation between three not-always friendly empires, and they had established the nucleus around which they hoped a future unitary Romanian national state would emerge.[19]

The environment created by the Crimean War and its aftermath and the emergence of Napoléon III as the political arbiter of Europe had presented a variety of opportunities which the Romanians astutely seized. There was, of course, nothing inevitable about their emergence nor was it the product of accident or external magnanimity. In the end, it was simply the human actions of the Romanians themselves that "made Romania." In the process of creating their own national state, the Romanians demonstrated what a small people can achieve, despite the pretentions and aggressions of their larger neighbors. It is to the internal development of Romanian politics subsequent to the Union of 1859 that we now turn.

PART II:

Romania under Prince Cuza, 1861-1866

"This is the state of man:
today he puts forth the tender leaves of hope;
tomorrow blossoms, and bears
his blushing honours thick upon him;
the third day comes a frost, a killing frost."
Shakespeare, **King Henry VIII**, III.ii.353

CHAPTER 3

The Political Scene Under Prince Cuza

"Let the end try the man"
Shakespeare, **Henry IV, Pt. II**, II.ii.52

What were the basic elements involved in the internal political situation that confronted Prince Cuza as he attempted to lead his new realm? An untangling of the problem of political groups and parties is, of course, central to our analysis of political development in the emerging Romanian state. The first major question is this: on the basis of the definition sketched previously, were there actually any political parties in Romania during the rule of Cuza? Were there permanent or semi-permanent structured communities of political interests or aims in 19th century Romania? Clearly, in this strict sense there were not. Such a conclusion, unhappily, is contrary to the presuppositions of most previous attempts to deal with the political parties in Romania, especially A. D. Xenopol's classic **Istoria partidelor politice în România**.[1] Xenopol's error is easy to identify. His argument is that since parties are based on personal interests [which may be true enough and does not conflict with our definition], Romanian personal interest groups were in fact parties. This is a clear non sequitur.

Xenopol (and many others) makes this mistake because he fails to consider the crucial question of organization, an essential to real political parties. Finally, he makes the mistake of confusing the absence of parties with multi-partism; however, "a country in which opinion is divided amongst several groups that are unstable, fluid, and short-lived does not provide an example of multi-partism...rather it is still in the prehistoric era of parties."[2] Xenopol, himself, admits in the end that "a true political Babel" existed in this period.³

Of course we should not be surprised that there were, strictly speaking, no political parties in Romania: since "In 1850 no country in the world (except the United States) knew political parties in the modern sense of the word."⁴ This will make our analysis somewhat more complicated, but not impossible. It may be objected that under such a strict definition, political parties never or seldom existed in modern Romania. This, for better or worse, was in fact the case.⁵ Political development, however, does not necessarily require parties or imply their formation. A lack of parties might result in instability or a peculiar evolution. It, in turn, is also a product of that evolution. Finally, judgment should probably be reserved as to whether or not the absence of parties is a positive or negative influence in the development of a particular people.

Why did political parties not yet exist in Romania? The most important reason for the fragmentary nature of the emerging Romanian body politic, apart from its very youthfulness, was its extreme exclusiveness based on a voting system according to wealth. Under the system imposed by the Congress of Paris, the 2 million people of Moldova were represented in 1858 by 1,397 eligible voters; the 2.6 million people of Muntenia by 2,482 voters.⁶ Because of overlapping eligibilities, the number of effective voters was probably no more than 700 for Moldova and 1,000 for Muntenia.⁷ A striking example of this narrow franchise was the election of a certain Vl. Stoica in 1860 from the judeţ of Ismail; the electoral college "being composed of a single voter who, forming the electoral bureau as president, secretary, and electoral body, elected himself 'with a majority of one vote, that is unanimously.'"⁸ Such a restricted franchise meant that the interests and ambitions of those who had the actual votes could be represented fairly directly, obviating the need for parties, programs, campaigns, and the other trappings of parliamentary politics.

As a result, real political power during the whole of Cuza's reign was in the hands of a very small number of men, perhaps no more than twenty-five.⁹ Politics within this elite "became the object of transactions without repercussions among the popular masses."[10] In addition, the homogeneity of interests of this select group was sufficiently high to further minimize the necessity for organized centers of political activity, despite the fragmentation that existed. The problem of union had led prior to 1859 to the formation of a kind of "national party" out of the diverse political elements in the Romanian Principalities. Though with the tacit union achieved by Cuza's double election, the nascent national party had soon dissolved; none of these elements—groupings, personality cliques, and individuals—can seriously be called a political party.

However, while there were no political parties in Romania at this time, it is undeniable that there were factions and groupings participating in a very complex swirl of political relationships and activities. How can we describe these factions and groupings? Are we justified in using the liberal-conservative spectrum that many take for granted in discussing modern politics? The answer, on the face of it, is "no." The liberal-conservative antinomy simply does not travel very well or usefully from its French origin. It also implies the existence of a kind of political continuum which is a gross misrepresentation of reality in virtually every case.

Furthermore, we all recognize that such terms vary considerably in regard to time and place, viz., a liberal in 19th century Britain is something rather different than a liberal in the 20th century United States. There is even some agreement that "left" and "right," "liberal" and "conservative," are reasonably unhelpful as identifiers.[13] On the other hand, everyone seems to use these unhelpful, misleading terms. And we search for commonality of aims, approach, or even mood among political groupings. We also want short-cut ways of pinpointing relationships between the actors on our political stages. Finally, there is the fact that the media—in 19th century Romania, this meant the press—tend to label and simplify. Politicians under Cuza and Carol were, in fact, given in the press of their day the labels "conservative" (also "the whites," "the right") and "liberal" (also "the reds," "the progressives," "the left"). Because of this inconvenient historical happenstance, I feel compelled in this study to retain "liberal" and "conservative" as means for identifying two general groups of people in Romania whose political outlooks were more or less congenial. This is done with powerful misgivings and the greatest reluctance, and with emphatic caveats against taking this usage to imply more than terms of analytical convenience and local custom.[14]

This leads, next, to the problem of delineating the essential characteristics of the Romanian conservative and the Romanian liberal. The terms "nationalist" and "unionist" do not distinguish between conservative and liberal in Romania since both generally adhered to these ideas. The basic distinction is between those people who believed that the system established by the Congress of Paris in 1858 was more or less satisfying, with the possible exception of not providing either complete union or a foreign prince, i.e., the conservatives; and on the other hand, those people who saw this system as but a mere stepping stone to a fully unified and independent Romania and who favored, to varying degrees, social reforms and the introduction of liberal [in the European sense] constitutional institutions into the emerging state, i.e., the liberals.[15]

Another way of stating this is that the conservatives were those who wanted to preserve the post-1861 Romanian status quo generally, while allowing for some very slow, evolutionary change. These people were almost always on the defensive. On the other hand [dare we say "left hand"?], the liberals were those who saw the Union of 1859 only as a starting point for further rapid, far-reaching, and even radical changes. They were always almost on the offensive.[16] An additional distinction was that during the revolutionary year of 1848, most of those designated below as conservatives had not participated while most of those who will be labeled liberals in this study had and had been exiled.[17]

Within these two categories, of course, one finds all possible variations. And, in addition, there were those in the hypothetical middle: some, for example, who favored the radicals' goals, but who deplored their methods and tactics; others who favored a moderate degree of change, but rejected the conservatives' methods and attitudes.[18] Finally, it should be emphasized, class differentiation is simply irrelevant here. The Romanian political elite was basically drawn from the landholding and educated segments of society. There is, as yet, no demonstrated correlation in 19th century Romanian politics between class and political doctrine, though, naturally, there were those whose political activities supported their economic and other interests.[19]

Prince Cuza under this scheme was a liberal. He and his closest associates were, largely, nationalist activists from Moldova who had been participants in the events of 1848. They believed that certain changes, especially land reform, were urgently needed to stabilize the position of the Principalities and to prevent a peasant uprising. Cuza, despite his activities in 1848, was not a partisan of radical or extreme views, but rather, was a moderate.[20] On the question of civil liberties and the wholesale adoption of liberal (i.e. French) constitutional institutions, Cuza and his allies showed general "benign" disinterest, especially given the reaction such liberties and institutions would provoke on the part of the conservative empires which surrounded Romania on all sides. The main members of the Cuza faction were Mihail Kogălniceanu, Costache Negri, Vasile Alecsandri, Nicolae Kretzulescu, General Ion Em. Florescu, Dimitrie Bolintineanu, and Ion Strat. The moderate views of these men was well within the prudent traditions of the Moldova from which most of them hailed.[21]

The most outstanding of the Moldovan liberals was Mihail Kogălniceanu, and in his views we see most clearly the tenor of their beliefs. By temperament a conservative, by education a traditionalist and evolutionist, Kogălniceanu was a democratic nationalist, but not a radical. Rejecting all idea of revolution ("when revolutions begin, civilization ceases"),[22] he was in the mold of the reformist, prudent Prussian liberalism of Hardenberg and Stein, which he had, as a matter of in fact, absorbed as a student at the University of Berlin. (Kogălniceanu referred to the University of Berlin as his "second mother" and cited specifically the influence of Savigny, his teacher, and Hardenberg.)[23] In 1860, following the Union of the Principalities,

Kogălniceanu circulated a "Profession of Faith" in which he declared his adherence to constitutional government, civil liberties, electoral reform, separation of powers, ministerial responsibility, and other liberal positions. However, he made it clear that the preservation of union and the nation took precedence over all other concerns.[24]

It was nationalist imperatives more than social radicalism that influenced Kogălniceanu's advocacy of agrarian reform; his call for "the emancipation of the peasantry through their complete takeover of the land now in their possession, this however with a full and complete compensation in advance of the landholders."[25] This was, in Kogălniceanu's case, a direct heritage from Hardenberg, who is quoted.[26]

Though Cuza, Kogălniceanu, and others of their associates often had French educational experiences, moderate, statist, German influences remained the more characteristic. This fact does a good deal to explain their seeming radicality in pushing land reform, while evincing considerably less enthusiasm for the legislating of liberal institutions, such as ministerial responsibility and the freedom of the press. Their liberalism was one which emphasized equality, social amelioration, and, above all, state unity, rather than an individualist concern for liberty.

It was precisely the adoption of liberal institutions and the defense of individual liberties that constituted the primary focus of the men grouped loosely around Ion C. Brătianu and C. A. Rosetti. Mostly Muntenians, mostly 1848ers as well, the Brătianu-Rosetti group included Ion's brother, Dumitru; the Golescu brothers (Nicolae, Ştefan, Alexandru C., and Radu); Eugeniu Carada, and Anastasie Panu (the only non-Muntenian). They were more organized than any other group, even beginning to take steps by 1861 to establish a national "club" to promote their ideas and set up local organizations, rudiments of the kind of activity that would have led to a full-fledged political party had it continued and had it been broader based. They also published a newspaper, which was Romania's most successful. However, their focus was primarily on urban centers and did not extend much outside of Muntenia.[27] Given their weakness in

Moldova and given the paucity of urban areas in Romania, even this most organized of groupings would fail to coalesce into a political party.

It is comparatively easier to establish the viewpoint of the Brătianu-Rosetti group owing to the existence of Rosetti's **Românul**, Romania's most widely circulated newspaper, and to frequent programmatic speeches in parliament and at street rallies, which **Românul** faithfully reproduced. "Liberty is one of the most characteristic attributes of the indigenous peoples of Europe," Brătianu wrote in an 1860 review of the events of 1859 in Romania.[28] The movement toward liberty, both individual and national, is described as a constant of European political history: Europeans have "liberty in their blood, in their souls." The driving force behind all of this is the French Revolution, "The Great Revolution" whose Declaration of the Rights of Man provided "the political decalogue of the new world" of post-1800 Europe and made possible the gains of the Romanian people in the 1850's.

An assembly speech of 1861 by Brătianu and the program he and Rosetti published in the same year[29] are representative of the conclusions derived from such ideas. They consist in three main points: 1) electoral reform to widen the franchise, 2) constitutional guarantees of the separation of powers and civil liberties (especially freedom of press and assembly), 3) speedy modernization and organization of institutions of finance, commerce, education, and national defense. All of these were couched in highly nationalistic terms. From these desiderata one can see that the Brătianu-Rosetti group indeed differed little from its French mentors.

And, indeed, the formative milieu for these men was in fact the radical Paris of the 1840's, the world of Michelet, Quinet, Lamartine, and Mickiewicz, of Masonic lodges and student revolutionaries. Where Kogălniceanu regarded the University of Berlin as his "second mother," Brătianu and Rosetti wrote "France raised us and taught us. The spark which warms our country we took from the French hearth."[30] Where Kogălniceanu abhorred revolution, Brătianu wrote enthusiastically, "If I were forced to define revolution, I would say that it is a cataclysm which swallows the old order of things and at the same time a creation which gives birth to another, newer and higher than the first."[31] Though they had given up, at least temporarily, the idea of republicanism,[32] the Muntenians wanted a weak or even a figure-head ruler, a situation in which the prince "ruled but did not govern."[33] Rosetti, especially, had an extreme distaste for any ruling figure, believing that princes tended toward dictatorship while encouraging the people to think—erroneously—that their happiness or that of the country depended on some single individual.

In another area, Rosetti and Brătianu's impulsive nationalism comes into sharper focus. This was the problem of irredenta. The union of Moldova and Muntenia in 1859 had left outside of Romanian rule the largely Romanian-inhabited provinces of Transilvania and Bucovina (both under Habsburg control) and former Moldovan territories between the Prut and Nistru rivers (under Russian domination, except for three small southern judeţs along the Danube). As a part of their nationalist convictions, the Muntenian liberal group believed quite strongly in the unification of these provinces with the now autonomous Principalities. Though at this time there was virtually no room to maneuver on these questions, through the maintenance of previously developed connections, the Brătianu-Rosetti group was closely associated with other European nationalist leaders (such as Mazzini and Garibaldi) and seldom missed an opportunity to manifest their irredentist views or show their contempt for the conservative empires. Not surprisingly, therefore, they were regarded as dangerous demagogues both within Romania and without.[35]

This is not to say that Cuza actually opposed irredentist or revolutionary action, only that he wanted such to be done covertly or not at all. He merely preferred to postpone discussion of these matters until a time more favorable for action. His ally, Kogălniceanu, moreover, was no stranger to irredentist intrigues, especially in regard to Transilvania. He stood somewhere between Cuza and the Muntenian liberals. Cuza's caution on this matter was an irritant to the latter.[36]

Radical as they were on questions of institutions, nationalism, and individual liberties, the Brătianu-Rosetti group was somewhat more reticent on social issues. There, as in the question of republicanism, their views were conditioned by nationalism.[37] They believed that the agrarian issue because of its explosiveness and divisiveness was a matter best left until more political maturity had been achieved along with the proper institutional development. However sincere this might have been, it sounded very much like a rationalization.[38]

It is obvious that these two groups, liberal though they might be, were destined to be at odds because of their significantly differing orientations and temperaments. The liberal emphasis of each was precisely in those directions most suspect to the other. Cuza, on the one hand, genuinely alarmed the Brătianu-Rosetti cohort with his autocratic attitude toward liberal constitutionalism, his personal role in government, his prudent foreign policy on irredenta, and his persistent interest in social reforms.[39] The Muntenian liberals, on the other side, were viewed by Cuza and his partisans as lost "in a vague utopia borrowed from a bizarre melange of ideas of the first French Revolution and of modern socialism...[and based on] a considerable reshuffling of the map of Europe."[40] Cuza felt that the Muntenians' positions were likely as compromising to the continued maintenance of Romanian union as those of the conservatives.[41]

The differences caused by this disparity of aims were further aggravated by the discordant personalities, temperaments, and milieus of the two groups. The Cuzist liberals came from the more traditionalist, contemplative, agrarian-dominated Moldovan society. The Brătianu-Rosetti liberals were the product of a more innovative, aggressive society whose focal point was urbanizing București. Their schooling, both abroad and at home, was quite different in tenor. It was no coincidence that one rarely encountered a Moldovan radical or that the events of 1848 in the two Principalities had varied so widely in course and tone. These differences of attitude, which should, of course, not be exaggerated, were not the product of any inherent diversity, but the natural outcome of the centuries of separate political and cultural development of the two regions. The most proximate factors were the Muntenians' greater access to nineteenth century Western forms and educational influences, and the Moldovan's greater cultural and political heritage.

Furthermore, though both groups were based on the property-holding sector of Romanian society, the influence of the fledgling middle classes on them differed. The Moldovans were virtually unaffected by the Moldovan bourgeoisie, which being largely Jewish had no political rights. The Muntenian middle class, in contrast, was both a part of the developing Brătianu-Rosetti base and an influence on it. The resulting agrarian-urban contrast has some usefulness, perhaps especially with regard to the land reform question. Loosely speaking, we may say that the Brătianu-Rosetti group was more concerned with the development of a modern, urban society which they regarded as the wave of the future.[42] The Moldovan liberals on the other hand had no real interest in the city (Iași and other centers had very large Jewish populations and commercial interests) and wanted to make the sturdy Romanian peasant of their imaginations the basis for a strong Romanian society. On the other hand, neither group was well-organized or extensive enough to be able to ignore the other. If we add to all of this the natural personal ambitions of these men and their sometimes highly-inflated, highly-sensitive egos, it is no wonder that the liberals were often fiercer foes toward each other than toward the conservatives.

In the discussion which follows, the Brătianu-Rosetti group will be referred to variously as "the Muntenians," "the Muntenian liberals," or just "the liberals," while Cuza and his partisans will be identified as "the Moldovan liberals" or some reference which associates them with Cuza. This somewhat clumsy device avoids the more usual and completely misleading practice of referring to the former group as "the radical liberals" and the latter as "the moderate" or "democratic liberals." This will also help us avoid implying a variety of things about Romanian politics of the time which are simply not true, including organized parties and ideological consistency.

In addition to the Cuza and the Brătianu-Rosetti groups, there were several other men who must be mentioned in this discussion of liberals. The enigmatic Muntenian, Ion Ghica, scion of a princely family, was a highly capable politician and multifaceted man. Well-educated in the West, he had been one of the most radical 1848ers, but was now very much in the mold of classical English liberalism. He was basically in accord with the moderate ideas of both major liberal factions discussed above and opposed to radical land reform and irredentism. Despite his skills and his reasonable, pragmatic but consistent liberalism, Ghica won at most the following of a minuscule clique. The principal reason for this failure was his inability to shake persistent suspicions that he wanted the Romanian throne for himself.[43] His close associates were the Moldovan D. A. Sturdza, who shared Ghica's ideas, but whose antipathy against Cuza was much greater because of a moralistic pique, and the Muntenian Ion Bălăceanu. A third figure sometimes allied with Ghica was Al. G. Golescu, a cousin of the Golescus mentioned previously.

The Romanian conservatives, as previously defined, were those who believed that the adjustments made in Romania's political structure by the Divan ad hoc programs and the Convention of Paris were sufficient. The reasons why various individuals adhered to this point of view need not greatly concern us here except to note that they varied widely, ranging from a simple reaction to the proposals of liberalism to a purely personal propertied stake in the status quo, to temperamental predisposition to ideological conviction. The number of pure reactionaries was small. The ideological conservatives generally harbored certain convictions about the dangers of grafting "foreign" institutions onto the delicate organism of state and the necessity for institutional forms to coincide with social and cultural foundations, ideas that later became hallmarks of Romanian conservatism.[44] The more pragmatic conservatives were not opposed to change as such; they felt that firm, measured steps were necessary to advance the Romanian state while avoiding any kind of foreign intervention.[45]

The conservatives, in general, regarded themselves as the natural ruling class of Romania, though in principle they had given up the throne in favor of the foreign prince that was yet to come and had agreed to the abolition of rank. Both of these represented considerable concessions. To go beyond this (as I. C. Filitti does in a number of articles) and claim that the Romanian conservatives were really classical liberals is absurd as their intransigence on the electoral and agrarian questions surely showed.[46] Representative of conservative sentiment toward other sectors of Romanian society is this exchange in the Romanian parliament in 1868:

A Voice: "But aren't the plebeians the nation?"
P.P. Carp: "No! The nation is us, its representatives; never do I want to say that the nation is those masses gathered on the streets..."[47]

The conservatives' concession in accepting the Paris system is, in hindsight, not very surprising in that it seemed to concentrate political power in their hands. The narrow franchise gave them, as wealthy land holders, consistent majorities in the assembly despite repeated elections and electoral finagling by the government. In spite of this strength, the petty rivalries of the conservatives, who even less than the liberals formed organized groupings, rarely allowed them to present a united front.[48]

The leading conservatives during Cuza's reign were Barbu Catargiu, Apostol Arsache, Grigore M. Sturdza, C. N. Brăiloiu, A. C. Moruzi, Gh. Știrbey, Lascăr Catargiu, Petre Mavrogheni, Dimitrie Ghica and M. C. Epureanu (these latter two sometimes wavered toward the moderate side). Barbu Catargiu was their acknowledged leader and a man of powerful political oratory presence. His assassination in 1862 near the start of our epoch was devastating to Romanian conservatism for more than a decade, the fact of his death means that he enters into our study only very marginally. The conservatives were stronger in Moldova than in Muntenia; this made them, if anything, that much more opposed to their fellow Moldovans Cuza and Kogălniceanu. It also made them very suspicious and hostile toward București and București-based politicians.[49]

Romanian conservatism remained for a long time an informal proposition. They did not organize, they had no platform, they had no powerful press organ. In fact, Barbu Catargiu actively opposed the formation of any formal political grouping on the grounds that to do so would give tacit endorsement to party politics and legitimacy to the liberals.[50] Only on direct threats to their position, such as electoral or agrarian reform, did they unite, giving their efforts a decidedly negative cast. While they had indeed surrendered certain prerogatives, they were not about to give up one square inch of land or an iota of effective power.[51] Their only other rallying points were their undying contempt for the parvenue Prince Cuza, who had taken a place that should have gone to one of their own, and their mixed feeling of disgust and fear of the Muntenian liberals, who they saw as lunatics and ideologues bent on despoiling the country.[52]

In addition to the ideological and pragmatic conservatives, there was a moderate conservative grouping composed of Basile Boerescu, George Costa-Foru, Constantin Bosianu, and Christian Tell. They were uncomfortable with the radicalism of the Brătianu-Rosetti group. On the other hand, they were alienated from the mainstream of Romanian conservatism by their advocacy of a considerable number of reforms, particularly of a legal and constitutional nature.[53] This is not surprising given the fact that most of them were lawyers. Though their very moderation sometimes is a temptation to see them as neither conservative or liberal, they were in this period certainly not liberals while at least in temperament, they were conservatives.[54]

Such were the basic Romanian political groupings in 1862. There were some contemporaries of the period under discussion who would have rejected this very general attempt to bring some semblance of order into a chaotic political situation. These pessimistic observers of the Romanian political scene saw the political struggle as simply a means of getting money, prestige, and or power.[55] In the words of the Romanian national poet, Mihai Eminescu: "Our parties are not called conservative or liberal; rather they are men with bureaucratic posts (the governing party), and men without such posts (the opposition)."[56] In the end, these critics rejected the claims of Romanian politicians in favor of the thesis that Romanian political groupings had no principle save that of opposing one another.[57]

Such cynical observations were far from isolated and are not without their merit as one surveys Romanian political development. It would be unrealistic, however, to take these views too seriously, because they are the expression of a Romanian political position in themselves.[58] And, careful consideration of the character of Romanian political leaders tends to demonstrate the basic good faith of most of them (if not always their wisdom, capability, or consistency). Despite an unfortunate habit of Romanian historiography, both old and new, of picturing Romanian political figures as either unbelievably "good" or unreservedly "bad," these men were not unlike other men. They possessed some commendable and some uncommendable characteristics, but very few of them were without redeeming features.

A more telling contemporary criticism of Romanian politicians may be this: "If we studied a little the history of the Romanian parliament, we would say from the unhappy evidence that we have never had the habit of serious discussion...Instead, we have had perpetual struggle without result."[59] Pointless debate was one of the obvious problems of the Cuza era, owing partly to the fact that Romanian political groupings were almost exclusively parliamentary, with no real existence outside the assembly.[60] This, coupled with the failure of actual parties to develop, led to the problems P. P. Carp was complaining about. And, the absence of real parties, discussed above,[61] further exaggerated the "interior" character of the groupings which did exist. From this overview of the political scene under Prince Cuza, we now turn to the crises and conflicts which characterized this era in Romanian history.

CHAPTER 4

The First Phase: Conflict and Crisis

"In time we hate that which we often fear."
Shakespeare, **Antony and Cleopatra**, I.ii.18

The double election of Alexandru Ioan Cuza in 1859 marked an important success for Romanian efforts to gain complete control over the political destiny of their country. At the same time, it laid the basis for the future complete unification of the two Principalities into a single entity. Under the system erected by the Convention of Paris, government proved to be virtually impossible.[1] The dual cabinets, dual legislatures, and all the other duplication required to maintain separation between the two provinces produced an internal deadlock. The cumbersome nature of the procedures devised in Paris for resolving differences between the two legislatures coupled with a lack of expertise on the part of Romanian parliamentarians further impeded activity.[2] The fact that there was little real organization among the diverse groupings that comprised the Romanian political system added to the confusion. As a result, between 1859 and 1861, when the first united government came in, there were nine cabinets in Moldova and eleven in Muntenia, while most major legislative actions lay smothered in conference (only six joint laws were enacted in the entire period).

After vain years of trying to rule in these chaotic conditions, Prince Cuza and his associates turned to diplomatic channels and, with the tacit support of France, were able to bring the "United Romanian Principalities" into official existence on 11 December 1861.[3] It is at this point that the development of the modern Romanian political system may be said to begin. During the struggle for union, the diversity of aims that existed among Romanian political leaders was generally obscured. Once the basic international arrangements were made to insure the existence of

Romania as a political entity, these diverse aims came to the fore.

The constitutional situation created in Romania by the definitive union of 1861—through the Sultan's issuance of a firman amending the Convention of Paris arrangements—needs to be briefly sketched. From the very start of Cuza's reign it had been seen that the Convention of 1858 was an inadequate instrument, and a special commission had been established to draw up a replacement. The same problems that had disrupted internal political development between 1859 and 1861 prevented commission deliberations from achieving any success. Cuza's new arrangement with the Sultan brought an end to its work. Though the Sultan affirmed specifically that the firman of 1861 applied only to the lifetime of Prince Cuza, the Romanians took it as a final consolidation of the two Principalities, transforming the act of 1859 from one of personal union into a charter for national unification.[4]

The unitary regime established by Prince Cuza neither abrogated nor displaced the Convention of Paris, but was rather an amendment of it to reflect the reality of a single ruler and administration. The chief provisions of the firman abolished the dual institutions and permitted the Romanians to unify legislatively as well as administratively and judicially. The capital of the newly unified country was located at București, and the prince established his official residence there. The two assemblies were prorogued and reconvened in January of 1862 as a single national assembly. A single prime minister was chosen along with a single cabinet. The Principalities were now unified in fact and in name. However, the new system did not alter at all the electoral regime established by the Convention of 1858 nor any of its provisions for social reform. (Both of these issues, which provided much of the political fireworks after 1861, are discussed more fully below.) The "constitution" of Romania, thus, continued to be an awkward composite, though more efficient than the 1858 Paris document alone. The stalemate between Cuza and the assembly lessened slightly, in that between January 1862 and May 1864 33 measures were enacted into law; on the other hand, the underlying problems of the Convention had only been ameliorated, not resolved.[5]

The struggles of 1859-1861 had already given birth to numerous divisions and rifts among the Romanian nationalists. The emergence of political groups in the Principalities had also begun as part of the era of the formation of the Romanian national state.[6] The clarification of the situation brought about by the Union of 1861 marks a convenient and suitable starting point for our study of political development.

The establishment of definitive union in 1861 was a noteworthy success for Prince Cuza. It now seemed that development within a more stable political order was possible. Ironically, the major result was increased political turmoil. The problems inherent in the peculiar working of the dualist system and the tenuous nature of the Principalities' international position had served to moderate and obscure the real nature of conflict between Cuza and the parliamentary factions. The achievement of union now brought these struggles to the forefront. As the facade of unity among the Romanian nationalists fell once and for all, crises and even more serious developments were sure to follow. It is to an examination of these events that we now turn.

It should be noted, however, that the second half of Cuza's reign was not just unrelieved disorder and conflict as this strict focus on political developments might suggest. Many steps of considerable significance for Romanian development were taken during this period; these will be mentioned where relevant. But it is important to remember that this study does not seek to give a history of the Cuza era, which has been done ably elsewhere. Rather, it concentrates on tracing Romanian political developments which led to a situation of "internal war" and the overthrow of Cuza. Its aim is to outline the essential elements of the emerging political system, explaining the formation of the anti-Cuza coalition, and clarifying Cuza's ouster. This, in turn, will lead into an analysis of the subsequent evolution of the Romanian political system, which forms the third part of our study.

At the start of Cuza's rule, the political situation was clear only in the barest outline. The three main groupings—Cuza and his supporters, the Brătianu-Rosetti liberals, and the conservatives—were in evidence and their relationships were roughly delineated. The Cuzists and the Muntenians viewed each other guardedly, as discussed above. They were unified as 1848ers, as reformers, and leaders of the Romanian unionist activities. But they were temperamentally and pragmatically incompatible. Brătianu had had high hopes initially for a Cuza-led, Muntenian-run regime and had taken it on himself to address a lengthy memorandum to Cuza in 1859 full of advice.[7] Cuza seems to have ignored most of it. Suffice it to add that the Muntenians' conduct in office between 1859 and 1862 tended to confirm in Cuza's mind his suspicions of their political irresponsibility. In return, Cuza's refusal to support the liberals when they aroused foreign ire and his casual attitude toward censorship, caused the Brătianu-Rosetti group to resent the prince as lacking in principle.

As for the conservatives and the Muntenians, there was even less sympathy between them. All of the doubts that Cuza and his associates harbored about the Brătianu-Rosetti group were greatly magnified in the eyes of the conservatives. Barbu Catargiu publicly attacked them as hatemongers and brawlers and privately thought they were disciples of Louis Blanc and Proudhon, if not actually utopian communists.[8] As for the liberals, the conservatives were little better than regrettable remnants of the old regime. As Brătianu wrote to Cuza in 1859, in a plea for challenge as soon as possible to the Conventional arrangements: "to conserve the present institutions and to maintain in power the men of the past—wouldn't this be synonymous with maintaining Romania in the state of weakness of the past and to leave it thus at the discretion of foreigners."[9] There appeared to be little reason for their relationship to change—the conservative majority had no need of any cooperation from the Muntenians; the latter shared no interests with the former. It was Cuza's misfortune to alter this situation.

Things were no better between Cuza and the conservatives,

who held a generally negative view of the prince. In the first place, they regarded him as an upstart whose possession of the throne was a happenstance and in any case a temporary event not to be taken seriously. This contempt manifested itself in a number of ways, e.g., Radu Rosetti relates that his family had a jackass which they named "Alexandru Ioan I," while various other family acquaintances owned "an extraordinarily ugly" three-legged dog and a pig, both named "Cuza."[10]

The conservatives followed a more or less obstructionist policy toward Cuza's reforms, varying this at times with support for certain radical proposals whose passage or emphasis they calculated might induce the Porte or powers to intervene against Cuza.[11] Cuza reciprocated conservative defiance, though owing to the conservatives' legislative numbers, he made numerous attempts to mollify them. To get various reforms underway, however, Cuza eventually had to resort to "non-parliamentary" or minority governments. This was one of the few things that united the conservatives, making such cabinets shortlived and causing constant reshuffling. Kogălniceanu aptly characterized the conservatives' policy as one of "nici eu, nici tu," ("if not me, then neither you,").[12]

The electoral situation, which favored the conservatives, slowly came to be seen by Cuza and his associates as the Gordian knot that must be cut if any reasonable government were to be possible.[13] Dissolution of the assembly was no real solution to the intractability of the conservatives because they were generally returned to office. The limitations of the franchise were made worse by the early development of what became a long-standing Romanian electoral tradition: the use of pressure and fraud to affect the outcome. In the words of Kogălniceanu, "elasticity of the electoral law" permitted considerable abuses.[14] Thus, non-conservatives of all stripes spent considerable time between 1861 and 1864 agitating for electoral change, with the Muntenians, as usual, hinting darkly of impending "convulsions and catastrophes" if the conservatives did not allow some modifications.[15]

What shape these reforms should take was unclear. The

Muntenians wanted a larger inclusion of the urban groups which supported them, but did want some property or educational requirements for the vote. Their obvious aim was to replace the conservatives in controlling the assembly. Cuza in the meanwhile seems to have favored universal suffrage along the plebiscitary lines sketched out by Napoléon III. The conservatives, of course, resisted such ideas tooth and nail. On the one hand, they feared "communism" or "anarchy" from the Muntenians; on the other, they feared some kind of manipulation of the masses against them on the part of Cuza.[16] Before 2 May 1864, no solution had been achieved.

Dissension between Cuza and the assembly had surfaced soon after his election. One of these problems was the provisory nature of his tenure, viewed as a stop-gap measure dictated by the refusal of the powers to allow the election of a foreign prince. This idea was shared by all, including Cuza himself;[17] it weakened him whatever he did, because if he tried to strengthen his rule it would be protested as trying to establish a dynasty, and if he didn't try to rule he would be attacked as weak and ineffective. This was another element of instability in an already unstable situation, providing one more issue for Cuza's opponents to utilize against him.

A second and more serious problem arose when it became apparent that Cuza intended to take a wider than ceremonial interest in the administration of his new realm, though it is a myth that his election owed to his supposed innocuousness.[18] After the initial euphoria wore off, the opposition began to resent Cuza as a ruler; the conservatives because they scarcely conceded him the right to the throne, the liberals because they had wished for an English-style decorative prince. Cuza soon hit on the alternative of trying to steer a course between these two hostile camps. The unhappy result was that he made "two foes in place of one."[19]

In light of the difficulty of working with the conservatives whom he regarded as obstructionist and the Muntenians whom he regarded as irresponsible, Cuza might have tried to form a party of his own. Could this have been done, the course of events would have been otherwise. Unfortunately for Cuza, his group was but one more faction and numerically among the smallest. While it is true that he had considerable popularity among the peasantry and the army, neither was a direct force politically since the one lacked the franchise and the other was not involved in the assembly.[20] The political situation facing Cuza was a dismal one in which he had few allies and many potential enemies. The two factions rebuffed by Cuza's policies did not yet see one another as allies, but the basis was laid for a short term alliance against the mutual foe. In the meanwhile, the chief benefactor of the conflict between conservative and Muntenian liberal was Cuza, who was able to cement his own personal regime and begin to push through the kinds of reforms that he deemed essential.[21]

The main battle of 1862 between Cuza and the legislature was over the agrarian problem which long plagued Romanian public life.[22] Our concern in this study, it should be noted, is with this issue as a political football, not with agrarian reform per sea or with the problems caused by the many arcane historico-mythical elements of the question. The agrarian question, briefly put, was the issue of how to deal with the state of rural discontent, unrest, and imbalance that prevailed in Romania. That an undesirable situation existed is unquestionable. The position of the Romanian peasant had been generally declining in the nineteenth century. The movement in 19th century Romania from a system of tradition-based agrarian relationships, enforced by custom and informal agreement, to a system of legally-prescribed relationships, enforced by law and contract, as a rule worked to the disadvantage of the peasant. Traditional arrangements had left hazy the question of ownership of the land and the peasant's tenure on it. Attempts at codification led to resentments, while lack of precise definitions left wide scope for abuses and exaggerated claims for rents and land control by proprietors. The transition taking place in Romania from a traditional to a modern society further aggravated the situation. Thus it was that the Convention of Paris, the "constitution" of the new state, called specifically in its article 46 for an immediate reform of agrarian relationships in Romania.

Two other factors combined with the Convention mandate to make the agrarian question a significant issue at this juncture in Romanian politics. One was the increasing restiveness of the rural populace, which seriously threatened public order.[23] Given the delicate international status of the newly formed Romanian state, it was recognized that such disorders had to be avoided.

Prince Cuza, himself, was the third reason for the emergence of the agrarian issue. Obviously, the enactment of a reform could serve to reduce the political power of his conservative opposition. Much more significant as influences, however, were Cuza's strong personal sense of justice and prudence. Believing strongly that the deteriorating condition of the peasantry was both morally unacceptable and harmful to the interests of the state, Cuza insisted that the situation be ameliorated through reform. The difficulty was the shape of such reform.

In January of 1862, Cuza had appointed the conservative leader Barbu Catargiu as the first prime minister of the United Principalities. He either hoped that some modus vivendi could yet be achieved between his program of moderate reform and the conservatives or he hoped that the conservatives would overreach themselves and allow him to pursue extra-legal options. The first hope was soon dashed. Catargiu's appointment sparked a march of irate peasants on the capital. The new prime minister, a strong-minded and decisive politician, responded by seizing the occasion to weld his forces into a more cohesive body. He crushed the peasant outburst with armed force and immediately proposed his own, conservative resolution of the agrarian question.

The agrarian law proposed by the Catargiu government amounted to a dispossession of the peasants from the scanty plots of land that they were presently working and forcing them to lease even the land on which their houses stood. To obtain additional land, the peasants would have to negotiate with the proprietor who was recognized by the law as owning all the land of his estate by right. These measures were intended to resolve the agrarian problem by giving the landowners an undisputed legal upper hand. Thus backed up by the power of the state, the boiars hoped to definitively put the peasants in their places.

Mihail Kogălniceanu, a historian and lawyer by training, was the spokesman for the Cuzist opposition to the bill. He argued that traditionally it had been understood that the land was owned by the community. Furthermore, the peasant possessed historical claims on the use of certain pieces of land. The Catargiu bill ignored or violated these ancient rights of the peasantry in favor of the boiars who were transformed thereby from proprietors in the medieval sense into owners in the modern sense. Aside from numerous historical and juridical considerations, Kogălniceanu pointed out that the proposed legislation not only made the lot of the peasant worse—thus violating the intentions of the Convention of Paris—but also was likely to convert the peasantry into a dangerous enemy of the fledgling state. Fierce debate continued for weeks along these lines. The situation was further polarized when the Muntenian liberal faction resigned from the assembly to protest the Catargiu government's handling of the peasant march. The fact that Catargiu had also pushed through a more stringent press law in March was a further reason for symbolic protest and more.[24]

On 8 June, events took a new turn. Responding to an illegal liberal rally [i.e., mob action] planned for București, Prime Minister Catargiu concluded his speech by declaring, "I would prefer death to...allowing the breaking of any of the institutions of the country."[25] A few minutes later, as he left the parliament building, Catargiu was shot and killed by an unknown assassin. This killing was a unique event for Romania at that time. Both Cuza and the Brătianu-Rosetti group stood to benefit from the removal of Catargiu from the scene, but no conclusive evidence ever was made public against either.[26] The conservatives, deprived of their only effective leader, responded by summarily voting the Catargiu agrarian law. Cuza refused to ratify it. With this moment passed the last chance of cooperation between Cuza and the conservatives.[27]

The death of Catargiu, however, did not mean the accession to power of the Brătianu-Rosetti group. Rather, Nicolae Kretzulescu, a Muntenian partisan of Cuza's, became prime minister following an ineffective interim conservative government. He directed his efforts toward the consolidation of the various dual institutions now rendered obsolete by union. As time passed the liberals became increasingly hostile toward the ministry. They came to believe that the Kretzulescu cabinet was only a vehicle for a strengthening of Cuza's power—and a diminishing of their own. Cuza, no doubt apprehensive about the course which events had followed in 1862, had apparently concluded that he could not entrust the Brătianu-Rosetti group with any power (as he had earlier) and abandoned the policy of using them to counter-balance the conservatives. "If I succeeded in annihilating the boiars by means of the revolutionary party," he told the Austrian consul in October, "I could not easily rid myself of the latter."[28] Once this policy became evident to them, the Muntenians began to seek to oust the ministry, if not Cuza himself.[29]

Miniature coalitions continued to form and reform. In late 1861-early 1862, some tentative discussions took place between the Muntenian liberal faction and Kogălniceanu's Moldovans. These foundered on the agrarian question, on which Kogălniceanu's position was more radical, and on the methods of the "reds," which disturbed Kogălniceanu.[30] Ion Ghica and Dimitrie Ghica discussed a moderate plan of joint action in 1862, but which did not go beyond the memorandum stage. Ion Ghica then shifted toward the Muntenian liberals and by 1863 was a contributor to their **Românul**.[31]

One surprising result of these events was the tentative appearance of a detente between the conservatives and the Brătianu-Rosetti group.[32] Their initial goal was the fall of the Kretzulescu government; each believed that Cuza would then turn and call them to power. Thus, they launched a concerted attack against the ministry when the special session of the chamber opened in November of 1862.[33] This was done by voting to include in the budget the prospective income of the dedicated monasteries. These monasteries were religious foundations existing within Romania with considerable incomes resulting from their extensive landholdings. Their purpose in the medieval era had been social as well as religious, as they provided schools, hospitals, presses, and the like. As a measure of security against depredations, these monasteries had been dedicated or placed under the protection of various powerful Orthodox institutions within the Ottoman Empire, especially on Mt. Athos. By the nineteenth century, the need for this kind of protection had ended; however, the Greek monks had come to regard the monasteries' income as their private preserve and most of the revenues were diverted abroad. Since the monasteries controlled more than twenty-five per cent of the total area of the country, this meant a considerable loss for the Romanian state. From 1859 on, all Romanian factions agreed that this situation must be ended. Timing was another matter, since the Porte and the Russian government sustained the rights of the Greek clergy. The chamber's action in 1862 was, thus, unacceptable to Cuza and the government because of the diplomatic difficulties involved.[34]

At the same time, the Cuza government was entangled in the ticklish Serbian arms question. The Serbs at this time were attempting with Russian aid to bolster their military position vis-à-vis the Ottomans. On 10 November 1862, rumor spread in București that 500 wagons of arms and munitions had crossed the Russian frontier heading south. Immediately, the Porte demanded to know what role the Cuza government had in their passage. It is now known that Cuza was in full complicity with the shipment, but his response was, first, to simulate ignorance of the matter, and then to adopt delaying tactics at every hand. On 20 November, he finally confirmed that the arms were headed for Serbia, but refused to sequester the shipment on various technicalities. By the time these were resolved, the caravan had vanished across the Danube into Serbia. The powers, except of course Russia, were furious, but unable to act.

The conjunction of the Serbian question and the chamber attack on the monasteries question caused Cuza to assume even greater power. On 1 January 1863, he announced that he was taking personal responsibility for the government.[35] This action was interpreted by the Brătianu-Rosetti group as a further evidence of Cuza's autocratic tendencies, though Kretzulescu remained prime minister. In retrospect, Cuza's action was perhaps a mistake, but the circumstances were mitigating.

The rebuttal to Cuza's act was not long in coming. Anastasie Panu, a leader in the struggle for union and a liberal, proposed an amendment to the chamber's usual response to Cuza's message opening the legislative session.[36] This proposal, signed by thirty-two deputies from both liberal and conservative factions, became a sounding board for the calling into question of Cuza's entire reign, especially for the violation of the constitution. The key point was the role of the prince. As Ion Brătianu saw it, in a long speech of 11 February 1863, "There are two camps: those who want a constitutional government and others who want a personal government." Brătianu further attacked the supporters of Cuza for hypocritically trying to shield him from responsibility: "whoever administrates is the one who must be responsible."[37] The liberals and conservatives had differed sharply, but now they both objected so much to Cuza's policy that they united against him. Though the amendment and the subsequent debate were not really the products of any organized effort, the backing they received from the two previously inimical groups marked the beginning of the anti-Cuza coalition.

The collaboration of the two groups which stood at opposite ends of the Romanian political spectrum promptly brought the criticism from Cuza's partisans that such a coalition was "monstrous."[38] Ion Brătianu's response was twofold: firstly, "when we saw the peril at our door, the doors of Romania, we forgot all...and when we saw that the Right placed itself on the national ground we did not ask where they came from; we extended a hand..."[39] Secondly, he reminded his critics that this cooperation was no more of a "monstrosity" than that which had produced the double election of Cuza in 1859.[40] And, in fact, the coalition was a perfectly logical outcome of political developments during Cuza's first four years. Both groups wanted power; both were blocked from that power by the differing aims of Cuza as well as his very person. When the coalition also raised the issue of a foreign prince once again, their intentions were evident.

Acrimonious debate[41] on the Panu amendment led to its adoption by a 52 to 5 margin with 50 abstentions. Cuza responded by refusing to receive the amended message, and his advisors began to lay the ground work for a possible coup against the assembly. The chamber passed both a Rosetti-sponsored motion of no confidence in the government and a declaration that no taxes should be paid until an official budget was ratified. Cuza thereupon closed the assembly. Relations between the government and the assembly had completely broken down. It is from this point that Cuza's personal rule really began.

The closure of the assembly transferred the conflict to an extra-parliamentary plane. The government moved to the offensive: General Nicolae Golescu and Colonel G. Adrian, both liberal activists, were dismissed from the army; Ioan Albescu, the managing editor of **Românul**, was given a three-month sentence under the restrictive press law; and new court action was begun against other liberal publicists. The opposition, mainly the liberals, responded to governmental pressure with a tax strike—an action quickly broken when the government impounded the furniture of several leaders for public auction. (Rosetti's furniture was, in fact, actually sold at auction.)

Press attacks continued against Cuza. In June, Ion Ghica published an article that was extremely critical of "the men in power" and their "blind and monomaniacal preoccupation" with authoritarian government.[42] Later, Ghica's brother, Pantazi, as manager of the newspaper, **Independinţa română**, was brought to trial for statements in his paper hostile to Cuza.

In May, Cuza assumed direct personal command of the army, just in time to become involved in another embroglio. Early in 1863, a new revolution had broken out in Russian-controlled Poland. Polish exiles had over the years formed a widespread network of agents and sympathizers in Paris, Turkey, and the Principalities to assist in the attempted restoration of Polish independence. Given Romania's proximity to the Polish lands, it was not surprising that many Poles were active there, an activity basically encouraged by all Romanian factions, liberal and conservative. In June of 1863, however, an event occurred that placed Cuza in a highly uncomfortable position. A group of soldiers, under the command of Zygmunt Miłkowski, a leading Polish exile, landed on Romanian territory and asked permission to march into Russian Poland where they would join their compatriots. Cuza refused, fearing Russian retaliation. The fact that Russia and France (Cuza's main supporter) were still on friendly terms was also influential. The Poles attempted to proceed anyway and had to be prevented by force of arms, with numerous fatalities on both sides.

Cuza's action quickly became the focus of renewed opposition attack, both because they supported th Poles and because it furnished a new "cause" against the prince. Russophilism now was added to the catalogue of Cuza's errors, a charge made more plausible by the fact that Kretzulescu's wife was Russian and by the Minister of War Gen. Ion Em. Floreocu's service as aide-de-camp to the Russian General Lüders during the Crimean War. Cuza, on the other hand, had more than a slight suspicion that the coalition, in this case Rosetti, had instigated the affair in order to embarrass him. Neither charge seems true. Since the insurgency had not been authorized by the Polish revolutionary leadership, they exonerated Cuza; on the other side, Miłkowski's extensive diary account reveals no Rosetti influences. The net result was unfavorable for Cuza however.[43]

In August 1863, matters came to a head, following several administrative changes by Cuza to strengthen his position. The prince had been contemplating for some time a coup against his foes, at least since June of 1862. He had even prepared a draft constitution for reaction by the powers. It seems clear that he was now ready to take a "get tough" approach.[44] C. A. Rosetti was arrested "at the express request of Cuza" for instigating disorder.[45] Rosetti, among other things, had been circulating a clandestine, handwritten newspaper directly attacking Cuza, and had been raising funds for the Polish revolutionaries, thus keeping this issue in public view. He had also been using very effectively the foreign news section of **Românul** for oblique attacks on the government. A case in point was the Greek Crisis. When the Greeks ousted their ruler, King Othon, in 1863, **Românul** devoted considerable attention to this happy termination of a "despot's" career.

The trial of the veteran radical did not turn out as Cuza had anticipated. Rosetti's popularity and talent in crowd manipulation turned the trial into a show case for the opposition, giving birth "to street manifestations in his favor with flags, speeches, and ovations." He was easily acquitted.[46]

This open attack on Rosetti was a serious political mistake. Along with subsequent actions that Rosetti felt were directed against his personal welfare and coupled with the long-time suspicions that the liberals had harbored about Cuza's motives, served to make the Principalities' most able publicist an all-out foe of the regime. The skill that Rosetti possessed as one of the most talented Romanian political in-fighters became more and more evident as the anti-Cuza coalition's activities expanded. Ironically, the Rosetti trial gave the coalition a shot in the arm at a time when lack of funds, disorganization, and public apathy had combined to cause deep pessimism in their ranks.[47] The coalition was not yet a disciplined force, but the governmental offensive against all opposition factions was beginning to serve as an integrating circumstance.[48]

Apart from these skirmishes, the coalition took more concrete steps by dispatching abroad, first, Gh. Ştirbey in April, then Eugeniu Carada (a close associate of Rosetti's) in October of 1863, and finally Anastasie Panu in March of 1864.[49] Their purpose was to sound out the powers, especially France. They were charged with finding out whether the powers would intervene, collectively or separately, if the Romanians were to oust Cuza and establish a provisional government. Secondly, they were to try and find out if a foreign prince might be an option externally. In addition, the coalition emissaries were to seek the mutual cooperation of Polish and Hungarian émigrés. These missions, which mark the first really subversive steps taken against Cuza, met with some success, but were made temporarily meaningless by the events of 2 May.[50]

2 May 1864 was the date of the infamous "lovitura de stat" ("coup d'état") executed by Cuza and Mihail Kogălniceanu as the

culmination of the campaign which had been waged since the winter of 1862. The battle entered this decisive stage with the long-sought fall of the Kretzulescu cabinet in October of 1863. To the chagrin of the entire informal "monstrous coalition," Kretzulescu's successor came not from their ranks, but was instead (from their points of view) the worst of all possible choices, Mihail Kogălniceanu. In addition to his undeniable leadership abilities, Kogălniceanu's known antipathy to both the conservatives and the Brătianu-Rosetti group, and his determined advocacy of agrarian reform made it clear that Cuza was fed up with the machinations of the opposition.[51]

The coalition's dismay would have been greater had they known that, except for Kogălniceanu, Cuza and his close advisors were prepared to resolve the political deadlock by resorting to a coup d'état which would permit reform and create a more authoritarian regime in Romania. Kogălniceanu, who still opposed such a drastic step, was in effect the last chance for the opposition to become more conciliatory. The intervention of several issues which cut across factions served to defuse the conflict (the dedicated monasteries, the army law, the communal law). The negotiations just begun abroad by representatives of the opposition were another reason for relative peace as their outcome was yet unknown. Most importantly, there were additional conciliation efforts made by Kogălniceanu.

Kogălniceanu's policy was clearly outlined in a memorandum which he wrote upon his entry to office in 1863.[52] According to this document, Kogălniceanu had been repeatedly asked by Cuza to join the Kretzulescu ministry, but had refused because he favored a confrontational policy toward the assembly. Believing constitutional government at stake and the country on the verge of disaster, the new prime minister insisted that efforts had to be made to reconcile the chamber and cabinet. To do this, he recommended the ouster of General Florescu from the army and refused to defend the arbitrary acts of the Kretzulescu government (especially vis-à-vis the press). Kogălniceanu, further, did not agree with the Cuza-Kretzulescu policy in the Polish question, advocating a more openly anti-Russian and pro-Polish position. Along with his conciliatory attitude, however, Kogălniceanu believed that patriotism also demanded immediate agrarian reform. If the assembly refused to do its national duty, then Kogălniceanu was willing to resort to a decree of universal suffrage. This fell short of the coup that Cuza's other advisors had been developing, but in essence would produce the same result.

Kogălniceanu's efforts almost went for naught at the outset. The usual parliamentary response to the session-opening address from the throne was seized by Rosetti, on 20 November, as a new occasion to blast the regime. Kogălniceanu urged rejection of the Rosetti proposal. On 29 November, Rosetti agreed to retract his draft and promised a new response free of polemic. This about face was not the product of a change of heart by the opposition, but rather resulted from the leaking and sensational publication in a Paris newspaper on 24 November of Cuza's 1862-1863 plans for a new constitutional regime in Romania. Though this coup plan was publicly disavowed by Kogălniceanu, the message was clear to the opposition. **Românul** harped on the issue for weeks, but the Cuza opposition in the assembly beat a strategic retreat and on 2 December even the milder, revised response was voted down.[53]

The "coalition" did not realize it, but reconsideration had come at the eleventh hour. Cuza had determined to go through with the coup on 30 November—if the opposition would provide him a pretext. The hostile Rosetti reply would certainly have been that. The assembly's suddenly cooperative attitude aided Kogălniceanu in postponing Cuza's drastic step at the last minute.[54] Shortly thereafter Kogălniceanu was able to present a bill for the takeover of the dedicated monasteries.

The Cuza government had by this time made the necessary diplomatic preparations. All of the factions in Romanian politics united behind the ministry proposal to secularize the huge monastery income hitherto under foreign control. This popular move further lessened internal tension. In addition, Cuza had decided that he did not want to have to present to the powers both the monasteries bill and a coup at the same time. He therefore temporarily abandoned the latter. The assembly, unwittingly, had a new lease on life.

Once less potent issues were resolved, the Kogălniceanu ministry, perhaps hoping that the assembly would take a more tractable line, proposed a new agrarian reform bill.[55] The raising of the agrarian issue was, however, the one thing that the perennial conservative majority had wished to avoid, and they rose to the challenge by vowing unstinted opposition. The Muntenians, however, did not join in the conservative negation. Following the line established earlier, that agrarian reform must be gradual, the Brătianu-Rosetti group presented their own proposal calling for less radical measures than the government's, but changes nevertheless. In fact, neither the Kogălniceanu bill nor the Muntenian measure was debated by the assembly because conservative attempts to oust the government took the foreground.

What is significant is that the "coalition" which had been forming throughout 1863, rather than consolidating, now appeared to be dissolving. A conservative attempt to muster a vote of no confidence in Kogălniceanu was opposed strongly by the Brătianu-Rosetti group in March. A meeting of opposition leaders called in April by Dimitrie Ghica to discuss the inaction of the coalition was not even attended by Rosetti. Particularly revealing are Dimitrie Ghica's letters to Panu (who was abroad) complaining about the liberals' refusal to back conservative initiatives and about **Românul**'s attacks on the activities of his faction.[56] Ghica characterized the Muntenians' leadership as amateurish (Rosetti), Mazzinian (D. Brătianu) and negligent (I. C. Brătianu). By the end of April it was apparent that the coalition was dead.

What accounts for this defection on the part of the liberals in light of nearly a year of the most bitter confrontation and the annoying presence of Kogălniceanu in the government? One simple explanation is that Kogălniceanu's moderate policy was a success. The generally acceptable conduct of the cabinet thus far was a factor. Press harassment had subsided. The legislative program pursued by the government was congenial to the liberals, though they would have preferred some modifications in the agrarian bill. All of this encouraged the Muntenians to believe that Cuza might soon ask them to collaborate with him. That this belief was not ill-founded is born out by Bolintineanu's report that the cabinet (of which he was a member) and Cuza had even discussed such a possibility shortly before 2 May.[57] A final reason is voiced in a letter from Rosetti to Panu in June of 1864: the liberals simply no longer trusted the conservatives.[58] Thus, while the conservatives were doing all they could to oust the Kogălniceanu ministry, their erstwhile partners in the "Monstrous Coalition" were on the verge of becoming more than covert supporters of the government.

The conservatives forged ahead with a new motion of no confidence. This passed, without liberal support, on 14 April. Cuza refused to accept the motion and prorogued the assembly to 2 May.[59] When the assembly reconvened, it was called upon to vote at once on the electoral reform which Kogălniceanu now saw as the only means out of the impasse. The conservative majority, instead, voted to work in committee, a tacit refusal. In fairness, they had no real choice since a new electoral law would have curtailed their power.[60] Kogălniceanu, thereupon, read a prepared statement dissolving the assembly.

Shortly afterward, Cuza announced a national plebiscite to ratify a new governing "statute" which concentrated power in his hands. The "lovitura de stat" had fallen and the drive of 1862-1864 against Cuza had met total defeat. Three additional years of fruitless effort had convinced Cuza (and finally Kogălniceanu) that 1] a conservative assembly would never allow the kind of development in Romania that the prince believed necessary, 2] that the liberals could not be trusted to govern responsibly, and 3] that government by fusion was impossible. The only option left, Cuza felt, was personal rule.

The blow, when it came, was a surprise to both the liberals and the conservatives despite the years of turbulence which had let up to it. While one might disagree with Xenopol's conclusion that the "lovitura" was "inevitable," its occurrence was not an unlikely outcome of the political circumstances described in the early part of this chapter. The conservatives were especially taken aback that the solution of the agrarian question was now taken entirely out of their hands. The liberals, who had actually long feared a move by Cuza toward more autocratic rule, were jolted from a reverie in which Cuza would call upon them to save the country. In plainer terms, the "lovitura" was a final confirmation of the fact that Cuza did not want to govern the country with either faction. The coalition whose demise Dimitrie Ghica had announced a week earlier would, like a phoenix, rise from the ashes of the defeat of 2 May.

Chapter 5

The Second Phase: Internal War and Revolt

"O, villainy! Ho! Let the door be lock'd:
Treachery! Seek it out."
Shakespeare, **Hamlet**, V.ii.325

With the coup of 1864, the course of Romanian political conflict changed complexion. Whereas the battle had been largely a parliamentary one up to this point, the institution by plebiscite of a new regime which did not include them forced the opposition more than ever into the press, the streets, and dark corners. Secondly, the coup ended all pretense of cooperation between Cuza and the opposition. They were now free to devote their efforts to Cuza's overthrow without having to play parliamentary games.

Cuza was, of course, not unaware of the potential of such organized opposition following 2 May. He therefore took several steps to insure his position including an appeal to the army, suspension of freedom of the press, and a special order to the prefects for daily reports and a close watch on public reaction. However, the possibility of a counter-coup by the opposition was not strong given their mutual distrust, mutual recrimination over the coup, and general disunity They also feared foreign intervention by those powers desirous of seeing the re-separation of the Principalities, especially Austria, Russia, and Turkey. As Rosetti wrote to Panu in June, a counter blow was possible but not feasible.[1]

The discovery in May that two boiars (Constantin Suțu and P. Balș) had been negotiating with the Porte for a restoration of the pre-1859 status of the Principalities served as a further restraint. The plotters, ultra-reactionary and anti-unionist, were not part of the coalition discussed above nor were they representative of anyone but a small minority of discontented Moldovan boiars. However, their actions alarmed both the government and the unionist opposition; the former fearing that they were part of a larger conspiracy, the latter fearing that disorder or minority anti-union appeals would furnish the pretext for foreign intervention or even the dis-unifying of the Principalities.

During 10-20 May 1864, a plebiscite was held to sanction the new regime proposed by Cuza. Certain time-tested "precautions" ensured the correct result, producing a 682,621 "yes"-1,307 "no" victory for the government.[2] A nearly universal male suffrage was instituted, giving the peasants a political voice while a new bicameral legislature was formed. The establishment of a collegial electoral system, similar to that of Prussia, counter-acted the democratizing tenor of the reform however. That is, the peasantry, merchants, and tradesmen (i.e. all those who paid a lesser income tax) voted only indirectly, via delegates, while the wealthier voted directly for deputies. Nevertheless, the reform marked a significant enlargement of the franchise and participation.

The newly-widened electorate voted only for the lower house, the chamber. The upper house, the senate, was appointed solely by Cuza except those few members by right such as the metropolitans of the church. At the same time, the president of the chamber and the vice-president of the senate (the chief metropolitan was president by right) were also named by the prince. Power was further and effectively concentrated in Cuza's hands by the creation of a personally-selected Council of State, which controlled the formulation of laws. Finally, Cuza now assumed the right to rule by decree when parliament was not sitting. In addition, the political inexperience of the new deputies and their general ineptitude further served to make Cuza's new regime a benevolent dictatorship in fact if not in theory.[3] Thus, in a paradoxical fashion, Cuza's new constitution was both more and less liberal than the Convention system. It allowed more participation; it was also more authoritarian. In the end this was the kind of system that would alienate both liberal and conservative. A crackdown on the opposition ensued.

Of the restrictions instituted by the new regime, renewed press censorship was the one that took the heaviest toll of the opposition. After several warnings, Rosetti's **Românul** was suppressed and the publishing society that produced it disbanded. Several other papers were also hit by censorial displeasure. Since most of Rosetti's financial resources were tied up in the society, he was in effect ruined. This double blow, "his ouster from the field of publicistic activity followed by his material ruin did nothing more than turn him more and more against Cuza."[4] In the winter of 1864-1865, the Rosettis were forced by financial difficulties to leave București for Ion Brătianu's country home.[5]

In hindsight, Cuza's press policy was short-sighted and unnecessary. By shutting off the Romanian press, he not only further confirmed the suspicions of the liberal opposition, he also fostered conspiracy, clandestine publications, and recourse to the foreign press. Further, the fact that a bare ten per cent of the population could read[6] coupled with the limited circulation of the press [**Românul**, by far the largest, did not exceed 2,000 copies prior to 1875][7] argue effectively that the press's bark was not likely to produce much bite. On the other hand, Rosetti was now irrevocably in opposition. When the "Monstrous Coalition" re-formed he would be instrumental in all of its activities down to the fatal moment.[8]

Cuza's opponents continued their campaign abroad, though they did not act in concert. Carada and Panu had in fact refused to agree with conservative proposals for countering the coup with demarchés especially at Constantinople. Wrote Carada to Panu in June:

> Secret negotiations with foreigners are not fitting for friends of liberty...I'm not surprised that Dimitrie Ghica asked you. Accustomed to begging all from foreigners, incapable of giving a hand to a really national advance, they [the conservatives] seek escape wherever they believe they can find it. They lost the situation through their knavishness and through knavishness they hope to escape.[9]

Carada concluded that the press and revolution are the only

legitimate means of struggle for democrats.

This tone of recrimination was echoed in a letter from Rosetti to Panu, at about this same time, in which he complained of the fecklessness of the conservatives, especially Dimitrie Ghica. In Rosetti's opinion, the coup was not only the conservatives' fault, but it even was preferred by them to a liberal advance.[10] On the other hand, the conservatives' interpretation of 2 May was that it simply showed the lack of viability in Romania of utopian constitutionalism.[11] Even a little liberalism was too much.

With the press at home silenced, foreign papers and presses became a staple of the campaign against Cuza. The wide acquaintances that the liberals had made abroad were particularly useful in this regard, as they were able to keep a flow of anti-Cuza news going. Among French journalistic circles, especially liberal and émigré, these contacts included Henry Martin and Taxile Delord (of **Le Siècle**), E. Forçade (**La Semaine financière**), as well as old friends Armand Lévy, Paul Bataillard, St. Marc Girardin, and others. They also had contacts through the Jules Michelet-Edgar Quinet circle of liberal nationalist intellectuals, which was very much philo-Romanian, and Michelet's son-in-law, Alfred Dumesnil.[12] At the same time, Paris saw a flood of pamphlets and brochures on such lurid themes as: **Suppression du régime constitutionnel en Roumanie; La France, le Prince Couza et la liberté en Orient;** and **Relation authentique du coup d'état du Prince Couza**.[13]

Following the plebiscite, Prince Cuza journeyed to Constantinople to receive the approval of the powers and the Porte. Cuza's assertion that Romania could act with impunity in her internal affairs now gained official ratification. The "additional act" to the 1858 convention made in June, 1864, specified that "The United Principalities can in the future change the laws which concern their internal administration...without intervention."[14] This re-affirmation of internal autonomy was an important success. It also meant, as the opposition slowly came to see, that logically the ouster of Cuza need not be sanctioned by the powers either.[15]

The formal ratification of the new regime by the powers also caused the opposition to realize that diplomatic avenues were no longer profitable; they began to become aware that they would have to work together, at least until Cuza's ouster. Thus it was that the erstwhile arch-enemies slowly moved toward internal cooperation and organization. The foundations for their cooperation had ironically been laid by the success of 2 May: autonomy meant the opposition need not fear external intervention if they precipitated a change in government, while it was Cuza's new regime that drove them together. As Kogălniceanu noted after Cuza's death, the prince's very successes were what led to his subsequent ouster.

It was in this manner that the anti-Cuza coalition began to emerge in the form that was to result eventually in the coup of 11 February 1866. This coalition, of which incipient forms had appeared prior to 2 May 1864, has gone down in Romanian history as the "Monstrous Coalition." The name is neither particularly apt, nor has it helped historical analysis and explanation of what went on in Romania between 1864 and 1866. Accepting the phrase at face value, an obvious paradox arises: if Cuza was so successful on the one hand and his opponents so "un-naturally" bonded, how do we explain the virtually flawless ouster of the Prince of Union? How and why it ended as it did seems unfathomable.[16] This, in turn, has led to various attempts to "solve" the pseudo-problem thus posed.

Fortunately, the most recent literature dealing with this question has avoided substituting rhetoric and cliches for analysis, with excellent results.[17] First of all, it is clear that the "monstrous coalition" wasn't very monstrous. This emerges as we examine the genesis of the coalition, its participants, and their objectives. When did the coalition form? As might be expected, the collaboration between the various groups involved gradually developed. The conservatives' principal objective had been and would continue to be the obtaining of a prince who recognized their interests. Once they saw that they could not bend Cuza to their will, which was very early on, this obviously implied his replacement.[18] However, Cuza was the "Prince of Union." He could not be replaced as long as the continuation of union was contingent on his person. This was no longer the case after June 1864.[19]

The Muntenian liberals' principal objective had been and would continue to be the pursuit of nationalist aims: defense of union, autonomy, independence, national unification [i.e., the irredenta]. These goals, as well as subsidiary goals such as economic development, could best be achieved, they firmly believed, only if they were in power. By 1862, they had nearly given up on Cuza's calling them to power and had returned to the 1858 Divans ad hoc position of a foreign prince.[20] However, the question of whom that might be remained an open question and an impediment to action.[21]

Thus, by 1864, the major groups and factions not a part of Cuza's chosen circle had converged on a single objective—get rid of Cuza—albeit by very different routes and for very different reasons. Particularly after 2 May, the conservatives realized that they really "needed" the liberals' cooperation to give a "popular" appearance to a forced abdication by Cuza, that the liberals' expertise in conspiratorial activity would now be invaluable, and that the liberals' ability to control and rally the urban rabble of București at will was essential to a successful anti-Cuza coup. The liberals, in turn, realized that collaboration with the conservatives would give them legitimacy in the eyes of many of the Great Powers and that the conservatives' strength in Moldova and outside of the urban centers was an essential complement to their own strengths in implementing Cuza's ouster.[22]

From the preceding, it should be clear that the coalition which eventually resulted against Cuza was not at all monstrous: it was organized to meet specific objectives held by the participants, it was fuelled by a genuine dislike for Cuza on all sides, and it included people from a wide variety of factions, however we describe them.[23] In the end, it was a logical though not inevitable product of the train of events we have been following.

Almost unnoticed in the turmoil of the events leading to the "lovitura" of 2 May was the formation of a "literary" society called "Progresul," in April of 1864. Its ostensible purpose was to defend the constitutional regime; its hidden aim was to fight "despotism" by all means possible, i.e., Cuzism. The membership of this society was largely young and conservative and included many names later prominent in Romanian politics such as G. Gr. Cantacuzino, P. Iatropol, and Nicolae Blaremberg.[24] In addition, there was a very heavy overlap between the membership in this group and a recently established Masonic lodge, "The Sages of Heliopolis." Though the subversive intent of both groups became more pronounced after the coup of 1864, for the time being little that we know about was done other than protest ineffectively and briefly. However, both "Progresul" and the Masonic connection provided seed for the anti-Cuza conspiracy that was to bloom a year later.[25]

The multiple achievements of the Kogălniceanu ministry dominate the remainder of 1864. Rapid changes, especially the long awaited agrarian reform, were the tenor of the times. The rural law of August, 1864,[26] was Cuza and Kogălniceanu's attempt to end years of agrarian hardship and inequities and to establish an independent agrarian populace as the basis for Romanian development. All forms of feudal dues were abolished as were restrictions on the personal liberties of the peasant. The law provided varying amounts of land for each peasant depending on his previous status and holdings, compensation was paid by the government and repayment set at a fixed rate over fifteen years. Mortgages, transfers or sale of this land was prohibited for thirty years, while the obligation of the landowner to provide newlywed couples in his villages with land was discontinued.

Unfortunately, Cuza and Kogălniceanu's well-intentioned reform was neither well-planned or well-executed. Adequate preparations were not made for implementing the reform, due in part to the political desire for speedy enactment. This allowed considerable evasion, violation, and simple neglect to occur. The prohibition of mortgages and the lack of rural banks left the peasant only his services for loan collateral, which quickly led back to a form of serfdom. The revoking of the inheritance grants proved a disastrous road to atomization of the already small plots as the rural population was rapidly growing.[27] However, the seriousness of these problems was not yet fully obvious. The government's position was for the time being strong.

Other reforms followed in 1864 in rapid succession, all by decree as had been the land reform. The courts were reorganized, the metric system was adopted, chamber of commerce was founded, professional schools proposed, a comprehensive education law written (earlier in 1864 the University of București was founded), a complete new civil code compiled on the Napoléonic model,[28] and the church reorganized. These measures, many of which did not immediately take effect, succeeded in counter-acting a good deal of the opposition's propaganda abroad.

In November of 1864, the government held an election for the chamber under its new electoral rules. With Kogălniceanu again demonstrating a technical virtuosity in such matters, the government was able to register complete success. Only seven former deputies were re-elected, none of them from the opposition. Demoralized in their own ranks, suppressed and outmaneuvered politically and journalistically, Cuza's opponents seemed helplessly shunted out of the Romanian political life.

Ironically, just as Cuza was appearing to have won the day, the coalition's opportunity came from a conflict within the prince's faction. Kogălniceanu was an efficient and able administrator, but his forte was not tact. Slowly he antagonized Cuza's close administrative associates, as well as Nicolae Kretzulescu, and the new Cuza-controlled parliament. His patronizing air toward the legislature, owing to its recognized inabilities, was ill-advised, as was a much-publicized trip through the Oltenian region in southern Romania during which he was received as the conquering creator of the agrarian reform. Especially active in the intrigues against Kogălniceanu were the wagging tongues of Prince Cuza's so-called "camarilla." This group of cronies, relatives, and foreign advisors slowly began taking an increasingly larger share in Romanian political affairs during 1865, much to Cuza's disadvantage. Its most notorious member was Cezar Librecht, a Belgian adventurer promoted by

Cuza to director of the Post and Telegraph Department where he amassed an amazing fortune and became a symbol of greed and corruption.[29] Playing on Cuza's own pride, as well as other weaknesses, they convinced him that Kogălniceanu was absorbing entirely too much of the limelight. The clashes led in January 1865, to the prime minister's resignation; Cuza's acceptance of (and connivance at) this event was, it is universally agreed, fatal for his tenure in office.[30]

With the fall of the Kogălniceanu ministry in early 1865, Romania and the reign of Prince Cuza moved into a situation in which analysis along the lines of the internal war paradigm becomes relevant. In Chapter One, the concept of "internal war" was discussed as well as its utility in helping to understand and clarify Romanian political development. The task that arises now is to suggest those factors and events which were the immediate preconditions for the internal war which culminated in the forced abdication of Cuza in 1866.[31]

The first consideration is to sketch those factors which tended to foster a situation of internal instability. The most significant of these is the efficacy or inefficacy of the ruling elite, i.e., division and ineptness in the ruling group. In 1865, a slow process of disintegration and breakdown of Cuza's faction began; the ouster of Kogălniceanu was, as noted, produced by a personality conflict between prominent members of the ruling entourage. This, in turn, alienated Cuza from men who had been his most capable supporters. By the end of 1865, Kogălniceanu, Vasile Alecsandri, and Dimitrie Bolintineanu were all estranged from the prince. The places of these disaffected ministers were, unhappily, taken by the scoundrels of the camarilla. This group had a decided skill for intrigue and personal aggrandizement, but demonstrated considerably less ability to deal with the problems facing Romania. The administration, never very good in the best of times, now became noticeably "deplorable," in the opinion of one contemporary, who added, that "the ignorance and incapacity of functionaries was unbelievable."[32]

An important result of administrative malfeasance, misfeasance, and nonfeasance was burgeoning financial crisis and chaos. The income of the state had grown from about 18 million lei in 1858 to nearly 55 million lei in 1865. Unfortunately expenditures also rose, and a deficit of 2 million in 1858 became a deficit of 8 million in 1865. By 1866, the government found itself faced with an overall deficit of 20 million. Part of these deficits were due to the financial needs of creating and reforming institutions in the emerging state; however, mismanagement, onerous concessions, kickbacks, and embezzlement were largely responsible and were soon notorious. Financial difficulties under such suspect circumstances further lessened the ability of the regime to rule effectively. Not coincidentally, financial disorder and crisis are critical factors in the breakdown of ruling elites.[33]

Another cause for the decline in the position of Cuza's ruling elite was, ironically, the agrarian reform of 1864. The bill was well-intentioned, but poorly conceived.[34] Instead of producing a happy, prosperous peasant class grateful to the benevolent regime, the execution (or mis-execution) of the reform led to discontent, rural strikes, and an eventual decline of the peasant's position vis-à-vis the larger land holders. This unexpected result was the fault of Kogălniceanu's conception of the reform, but by the time the enthusiasm for the reform wore off in the face of harsh new realities, Kogălniceanu was no longer on the scene. His successors reaped the unfortunate consequences of Davies' notorious "J-Curve," when the relative gap between anticipated need satisfaction and actual need satisfaction grew too large.[35]

These problems of the ruling group were aggravated by the decline of Cuza, himself. The prince had shown great energy in important questions, but he never evinced much concern with internal administration. The British consul, John Green, wrote: "The Principalities would be quite as well governed were there no government at all. Prince Couza cares very little for what is passing around him..."[36] His health[37] and personal psychology both deteriorated in 1865, and he began to withdraw in many ways, leaving more and more control in the venal hands of the camarilla. His prolonged adultery with Maria Obrenovici,[38] his strained relationship with his wife, and the death of his mother in May of 1865 all contributed to his malaise. By mid-1865,

Cuza's will to rule was much weakened.

Thus, in the areas which usually contribute most to the fostering of internal war, the Cuza government was showing signs of breakdown at every hand. Bobango's summary is hard to fault: "May 2 temporarily solved the problem of parliamentary obstructionism and irresponsibility, but thereafter neither the prince nor his associates demonstrated the capacity for ameliorating, let alone eliminating, any of the other major difficulties facing the young nation."[39]

Another set of factors that contribute to internal war is disorienting social processes. In Cuza's developing Romania, such processes were certainly active. Relationships between peasants and landholders were not yet settled. The influx of foreigners, particularly of Russian Jewish origin, was slowly coming to be [at least perceived as] a disruptive factor. Despite these trends, and despite a real lack of social harmony in Romania, there was no genuine social reorganization going on in Romanian society and relatively little promise of any in the near future. But, since Romanian politics remained the province of an extremely limited group [Cuza's electoral reform did not significantly alter the body politic except to exclude his opponents], these factors do not appear to have had a decisive effect on the eventual fall of Cuza.

Another factor that contributes to potential internal war situations is subversion. The development of a movement against Cuza has been a prime focus of our study; this description will continue shortly. In view of the attention given below to such activities, it is important to stress that a balanced perspective must be maintained: insurgency is not the only or even the most decisive internal war facet.

Finally, attention should be given to the facilities available to the regime to combat internal war. Of these, only two are important here: the military and natural phenomena. The loyalties of the army are always a prime consideration in any internal war situation. Cuza depended on the army for support; the question was whether the plotters could succeed in winning it (or a substantial portion of it) to their point of view. The Romanian army had had a rather brief modern existence. In

1831, the Russians while occupying the Principalities had reorganized them through the Regulament Organic. As a part of this, a standing army was created in each Principality. The system of training and organization was Russian, and the armies never reached a very high level of proficiency. In 1859, as part of the new organization imposed by the Conference of Paris, these standing armies were reduced to militias; that is, to little more than police forces. Cuza had two major aims: the unifying of the two military bodies and their subsequent transformation into a real army. In 1860, Cuza informally unified the two militias in maneuvers. The same year, a French military mission arrived to upgrade training. In 1862, following the definitive union, the prince was able to complete his transformation of the Romanian military.

Under Cuza's direction the new army was divided into two sections: the regular troops and the militia. The regular army, as of January 1862, had 660 officers and 16,400 soldiers. By 1865, this number had grown to 20,000. The militia was composed of two elements: the grăniceri (border guards) and the dorobanți (territorial militia or gendarmes). The grăniceri were drawn exclusively from the border regions they defended, while the dorobanți were recruited from the remaining villages. There were in 1865 roughly 12,000 grăniceri and 8,000 dorobanți. The army term of service was seven years; the militia's was six, alternating one week on duty with two at home.[40]

Cuza was a military man of long standing and very popular with the army rank and file. He also had the support of most leading officers. Furthermore, all military men were bound by an oath to Cuza as commander-in-chief. His popularity with the army was increased by his rebuffing of an attempt made in 1864 by the assembly to establish a national "civic guard," a measure designed mostly to give the assembly some organized force of its own which Cuza promptly vetoed. Overall, it seemed unlikely in mid-1865 that a conspiracy against Cuza would be likely to gain much military support.

With natural phenomena, it was another story; the weather seemed to be an especially intransigent foe of the Cuza regime.

Among other problems, 1864-1865 saw a severe drought that was particularly devastating for the peasants, while 1865 saw a number of epidemics flourish.[41] These "natural" events did not help the regime; not only did they increase and magnify the normal hardships of the peasants, they also aggravated the fiscal difficulties of the government.

We turn now to those preconditions which act as barriers to internal war. There is much less flexibility in this area owing to inherent limitations of some factors and to the reciprocal relationship that others have to factors in the class already discussed. In Cuza's case, two possibilities—diversions and concessions—appeared to be of low potential. The diversionary possibilities of foreign policy are well-recognized: the effort by the regime here is to focus the gaze of the body politic on some foreign policy "issue" which then diverts attention from internal issues. For Romania, the main "bogey" to be raised was that of foreign intervention. But, as has been shown, one of the effects of the coup of 2 May was to lessen, if not remove, this as an impediment to action against the regime. The threat of foreign intervention, especially by the Porte, could never, of course, be entirely discounted by the plotters. On the other hand, Cuza appears to have had very little interest in creating diversions—or that he even saw the need for them. As for the use of concessions, Cuza had practically no room for maneuver. Concessions had been, in a sense, the subject of the contention in the 1859-1864 period, without result. The only concession that would now satisfy the opposition was abdication into their hands. Cuza could hardly be expected to do that.

There remain one final barrier area that needs consideration in such an internal war situation: the possibility of effective repression. Repression had already been employed, in a sense, through the May coup. This had been followed by shutting down the opposition press, and by eliminating the coalition from the new parliament. The crucial question is the qualifier "effective." It has already been argued that the repression of the press and parliament were actually harmful to the regime; as will be seen shortly, actual armed repression in 1865 was not "effective" either.

The net result of this analysis is to show that, on net, Cuza's position in 1865 was extremely shaky. On practically all counts, the preconditions for an internal war were strongly against him. Yet from the fall of Kogălniceanu to Cuza's abdication more than a year passed. This "delay" is accounted for in part by the still persisting differences between potential members of the anti-Cuza coalition. In June of 1865, however, the various factions that came to compose the anti-Cuza coalition resolved these differences sufficiently enough to begin a conscious, concerted, and eventually successful drive for power. The precise event that precipitated the rebirth of the coalition is unknown. Given the professed fears of the opposition that the prince was going to found a dynasty, Cuza's adoption of his illegitimate son, Sașa, on 11 May 1865, might have been a precipitant.[42]

There is no doubt, however, about when the coalition was formed.[43] On 5 June, a group of conservatives and liberals or all stripes signed a declaration pledging "in case of a vacancy of the throne to sustain through all means the election of a foreign prince from a western ruling family." The signers included: C. A. Rosetti, Ion C. Brătianu, A. Panu, Ion Ghica, Dimitrie Ghica, Gh. Știrbey, C. N. Brăiloiu, and Bibescu Bassarab Brâncoveanu.[44] This document was obviously the product of serious negotiation between the two factions. The significance was threefold: Firstly, it showed that the two groups had, after a long period of on and off cooperation, finally reached agreement; secondly, the declaration specifically made the remaining unfulfilled point of the Divans ad hoc its sole programmatic aim: and lastly, it provided an affirmation and guarantee of the election of a foreign prince on the part of two republicans (Rosetti and Brătianu) and four eligible pretenders to the throne (the two Ghicas, Știrbey, and Brâncoveanu).[45]

The June 1865 declaration, by implication, made it clear that the signers were not going to wait for "a vacancy of the throne," but would do what they could to foster such a state of affairs. The simplicity and convincing nature of the foreign prince proposition was such that the coalition, now truly formed, had a basis for expansion and growth. The policy also had in its favor the declaration of "the nation" by the Divans, giving it thereby a validity unquestioned even by Cuza and his supporters. For the opposition it was valid purely because of the negative experience of Cuza's reign, a point of view Ion Brătianu had already expressed in 1863 when he said, "A Romanian Prince is no longer possible after Alexandru Ion I."[46] Cuza had been unable to please either the Porte or the powers; he had failed to win the respect of the assembly; he had not contained the various pretenders; and he was carrying out a policy that was leading every day deeper into disaster.[47] The opposition believed that Cuza's experience showed that no indigenous prince, however talented, could hope to succeed. Furthermore, they were convinced that no native prince could carry the same weight as a foreign one with European connections in relations with the Great Powers.[48]

Besides these general reasons for Cuza's ouster, the coalition was able to agree on a number of more specific campaign points. Their main complaint was against Cuza's dictatorial acts and tendencies. They claimed that Cuza demonstrated signs of "Caesarism" and that his continued rule would lead to a return to the despotic days of the Phanariot Greeks.[49] It was further charged that Cuza intended to establish a dynasty especially following the adoption of his illegitimate sons. Whether they completely believed these accusations is difficult to tell. We do know that Rosetti sincerely held that Cuza would be forced to resort to more and more desperate expedients as his misrule caused more problems; such expedients would only cause the Porte to intervene and perhaps destroy the fledgling state.[50]

A more telling charge made by the coalition, perhaps their most effective one, concerned the Cuza camarilla. They pointed out how the camarilla's corrupt mismanagement of the country [discussed above] was leading to the precipice of financial disaster. The inevitable result they foresaw would be vassalage to foreign powers or the assertion of Ottoman control. Disgust with the foreigner-filled camarilla had indeed became general as the internal situation became worse.

Aside from these "public" reasons, there was the coalition's personal stake in Cuza's ouster. As has been shown, the coup of 2 May had eliminated both groups from the political life of Romania. Until Cuza was ousted, neither would be able to defend their interests or pursue their political aims. It was thus, for many of them, a question of personal political survival, a factor Cuza seems to have overlooked. It is partly for this reason that Xenopol calls the plot against Cuza more personal then principled. This is slightly unfair, but not entirely inaccurate.[51] To have excluded the bulk of Romania's political elite from the political equation was a serious error by Cuza, however much their own antics had contributed to that end. This is not to say, however, that the coalition was merely a personal reaction to Cuza's reforms. That seems untrue simply because no substantive attempts were made after February 1866, to undo them. One does not, of course, have to accept the coalition's self-glorifying rationalization for their seizure of power either.

Despite all of these factors working in favor of the coalition's primary goal, it must be noted that the coalition was a rather weak one in a number of ways. Mistrust was very high on all sides; as soon as it was convenient, each doubtless hoped to abandon the others and take complete control. Though they all wanted a foreign prince, they all counted on winning such a prince to their respective sides. The collaborators in reality had very little in common as became apparent after they successfully ousted Cuza. But until that time, they would function as a united body.

The newly formed coalition was not merely content to issue a declaration. Immediately after the signing of the June statement, the coalition sent its two most experienced hands west to the European capitals. Ion C. Brătianu went to Paris; Ion Ghica to London, Brussels, and Turin. They met with little success because the powers were reluctant to re-open the Romanian question. It appears likely, however, that both men gained the impression that the powers would not interfere if something happened in Romania. Whether this impression was correct or not is irrelevant since they could act on its validity until shown otherwise by the powers. The anti-Cuza coalition was beginning to prepare the ground for action.

In 1865 Eugeniu Carada returned to Bucureşti. With the assistance, perhaps, of contacts in Paris and Switzerland, he was now responsible for the appearance of a clandestine newspaper, **Clopotul** (The Bell), whose shrill, crude, and scurrilous attacks on Cuza gave the liberals a new voice.[52] At the same time conspiratorial meetings were being held in Bucureşti, Iaşi, and other centers. One contemporary recalls the times as a very "unsettling" ones with the appearance of visitors from Bucureşti at various meetings in Iaşi called for no obvious purpose. All of this contributed to the feeling that the country was sitting "above a volcano."[53]

It was at this tense juncture in July 1865, that Cuza, ill and exhausted, left the country to visit at Ems. We now know that Cuza was not merely taking the waters at a popular spa. He had earlier informed the French of his plan to go west, primarily to demonstrate to the powers that he could not continue and to indicate his desire to be replaced by a foreign prince.[54] When and how were unknown; in the event, his trip was cut short by events at home.

Shortly after Cuza's departure the volcano gave its first shudder. The issuance by the government of decrees at the beginning of August, one proclaiming a tobacco monopoly, the other placing restrictions on street vendors, was manifestly unpopular. On 1 August, **Sentinella Română** (yet another Rosetti-aided production) published an impudent letter from Ion C. Brătianu to the prefect of police.[55] Was the prefect wondering, the letter mused, why Brătianu had come to Bucureşti at a time when normally everyone left the capital because of the heat? The reason was simple: Brătianu had been told that they "were talking about a revolution in Bucureşti." Although, he wrote mockingly, this idea was absurd in a happy land under "such a lawful and fatherly regime, he was fearful that some impetuous folks might go overboard in protest against some act or another of the government's. So, he, Brătianu, had generously come to Bucureşti in order to prevent any such "unfortunate" thing from happening, especially since evolution not revolution was the most appropriate course of action for Romania.

The same day, placards appeared calling for armed action against "privileged thieves." **Clopotul** for 1 August, criticized the election of Cuza in 1859 as "a blunder, madness, or a crime," and announced: "Enough patience, enough misery. The awakening bell has sounded, the hour has come!"[56] The evening of 2 August, the coalition's leaders met, but reportedly could still not reach agreement on Cuza's successor. On the morning of 3 August, a mob formed in one of the market places to protest the new street vending regulations, moved angrily on the nearby city hall, and set fire to its archives. A revolt was on.

The details of the uprising are told elsewhere.[57] It remains here to review the key questions related to the revolt. The first of these involves its nature: was it planned by the coalition or did it occur spontaneously? The foreign press, already under liberal opposition influence, hastened to portray the uprising as a spontaneous uprising against the tyrant Cuza. Ironically, this was the same line followed by those attempting to discredit the anti-Cuza coalition. Such conclusions, however, were deduction or based on hearsay. From the evidence available, the most likely scenario seems to be this: the coalition had been contemplating rebellion, possibly while Cuza was conveniently out of the country. They were, however, unable to agree on the day, the means, or the successor.

On the morning of 3 August, an effort by police agents to provoke the liberal wing of the opposition into rash action coincided with a spontaneous uprising by angry Bucureşti street merchants who were then joined by other malcontents, and even police agents under the mistaken impression that what was happening was all part of a clever plan to catch the liberals in flagrante delicto. At this point, events went out of control, the city hall was attacked, and the government was forced to call in the army.

The troops used the occasion to stage a day-long drunken rampage that left twenty or more dead and scores wounded. Ion Brătianu, Rosetti, Carada, Nicolae Golescu, and C. Brăiloiu were arrested along with more than 600 merchants and artisans (but, interestingly, none of the conservative leadership). That the government had not actually instigated the revolt as a trap and that the liberals (or the anti-Cuza coalition) had not planned this specific uprising were subsequently shown by 1]that the government had not nabbed any of the arrested leaders red handed, 2] was unable to make any kind of case against them, and, 3] eventually (after two weeks detention) had to release everyone.[58]

The second question is: how serious was this whole affair? Many accounts have tended to minimize its importance, allegedly on the basis that Cuza took a casual attitude toward the whole matter. This, as Bobango shows in his excellent discussion, was not the case; the government was quite shaken by the events and a widespread investigation and rooting out of conspiratorial elements followed.[59] An unexpected result was the uncovering of coalition tracks all over the country; also discovered were unconnected separatist activities in Moldova. Such discoveries were certainly alarming to the government. Though it was repressed, the revolt was one more discouraging event for the already depressed Cuza.

Lastly, what were the results of the event of 3 August, apart from the government reaction? Rosetti-Bălănescu wrote to Cuza:

> Here is, in my opinion, the great difficulty of the situation. After the lovitura de stat, all these [the opposition] were buried, ridiculed, and ignored. I am afraid we may give them the significance... that they couldn't find before 3 August...And this significance is fatal not only internally. Foreign countries, almost without exception, are ill-disposed toward us and will find in this new reason for annoyance and demands.[60]

These perceptive words summarize the problem precisely. Externally, the bloody suppression of the Bucureşti mob was widely seen as a sign of injustice and weakness. Particularly in France Cuza's stock went down, while the Porte took the occasion to rebuke the prince for ill-management of internal order. Internally, the results were, as Rosetti-Bălănescu feared, also significant. The bloodshed and looting by the army both disgusted the general population and greatly impressed all opposition politicians. Cuza, thereby, lost support of many who had backed the coup of 2 May and unified the enemy camp.[61]

The solution proposed by Rosetti-Bălănescu to take the wind out of opposition sails proved equally unsuccessful. He suggested an amnesty for the arrested, against whom existed not a shred of real evidence, to be couched in "insulting" terms. This was the course Cuza followed on 30 August.[62] This act, rather than disgracing the arrested, was generally interpreted as a sign of weakness on Cuza's part. Other studies of revolutionary situations indicate that Cuza's action was in error simply because acts of generosity following repression seem to spur on the repressed.[63]

The suppression of the uprising of August was the last spur needed to coalesce the opposition. The "Progresul" group expanded its membership to include I. Gr. Ghica, Th. Văcărescu (both with military connections), and others. Negotiations were begun between "Progresul" and the signers of the June manifesto, and a new secret society was formed uniting all the members of the opposition with Ion Ghica as the key link between the two groups. Each side made certain compromises to the other over the organization of the new government and agreed on the replacement of Cuza with a foreign prince. A directing committee, composed of Lascăr Catargiu, Dimitrie Ghica, Ion Ghica, G. Ghica, C. A. Rosetti, Petre Mavrogheni, Ion Cantacuzino, D. A. Sturdza, and Nicolae Blaremberg, was elected representing every major faction. It now remained to fix on the strategy and then implement it.

The most important lesson of 3 August for the opposition was the realization that the support of the army was absolutely crucial to success against Cuza. The conspirators, thus, began an intensive effort to attract army officers to their cause. At the same time, they prepared to launch another propaganda crusade against Cuza abroad; in November, Ion Brătianu left secretly for Paris to direct this action. Details on both of these efforts are given below. Finally, as a cover for their meetings, the conspirators organized a new "literary" society and undertook to publish a journal, **Revista Dunării**. The list of "editors" and "contributors" to the new review read like a "who's who" not of Romanian literature, but of anti-Cuza politics. Their "program" statement avoided literary polemics in favor of a thinly veiled criticism of the mores and policies of the Cuza regime.[64] Time was beginning to run out for Cuza.

The prince, for his part, apparently reached (in September) his own definite decision to vacate the Romanian throne as soon as was feasible. There has been considerable discussion on this question, but on the basis of the documents available it is reasonably certain that Cuza had genuinely decided to give up his position. Illustrative of this is the 19 September 1865 letter Cuza sent to Napoléon III via private channels. The key passages of this letter were near the end. After admitting that he no longer could control "the intrigues of the parties" or contend with the ill-will of various powers, Cuza told Napoléon:

> I am ready, sire, to descend from the throne... I would be happy, sire, to accept any arrangement which your Imperial Majesty judged favorable to the interests of Romania.... I will re-enter gladly, private life, leaving a throne which I never dreamed of nor sought after.[65]

This seems reasonably straightforward, but there are two difficulties involved: one is that we do not know if Napoléon received the letter or responded to it (it seems to have reached Paris perhaps in late October and may have reached Napoléon by January 1866); the other is that Cuza's remarks seem sufficiently hedged about that Napoléon would be sure to encourage him to stay in office. The first of these is not necessarily a problem in judging Cuza's intentions; the second objection is met by several collateral pieces of evidence.

One major confirmation of Cuza's intention to abdicate was his speech to open parliament on 5 December. After various exhortations to the chambers, Cuza concluded by saying that he remained simply "Colonel Cuza" and that he held the throne "only as a sacred deposit" for the nation.[66] Though this declaration did not explicitly state his desire to abdicate, it was a specific re-affirmation of his adherence to the idea of a foreign prince, as he had made clear to the cabinet in a meeting immediately prior to the speech.[67] The impact of this speech will be discussed shortly.

Another confirmation is found in Radu Rosetti's memoirs. Rosetti recounts the visit to his Moldovan home in December, 1865, by Costica Suţu, a former minister and close friend of Cuza's. Suţu told Rosetti's father, Raducanu Rosetti (who actively disliked Cuza) of having dinner and playing billiards with the prince shortly before. Cuza told Suţu that he had decided to abdicate and also told him of the letter to Napoléon. The elder Rosetti laughed at Suţu's naiveté and replied that Cuza was merely employing a ruse.[68] A similar, but less certain, testimony is given by Titu Maiorescu. He reports that in January of 1866, Dimitrie and Theodor Rosetti (the latter a close friend of Maiorescu's) went to tell their brother-in-law Cuza of their fears that a conspiracy was afoot. Cuza's response was calm; there was, he said, no reason for a secret plot because in two months time he would voluntarily act to fulfill the Divans ad hoc program by abdicating on his own.[69]

Finally, and conclusively I believe, there is the evidence presented by two dispatches from the British consul in Bucureşti, John Green. In the first of these,[70] Green describes a conversation in December of 1865 with Baligot de Beyne, Cuza's private secretary, in which Baligot told him, "the Prince was more and more determined on abdication; that he had hitherto endeavored to dissuade His Highness from that step, but that he no longer did so, as he considered it inevitable." Since Baligot had no ulterior motive at this point for telling Green this, his statements are credible. In the same dispatch, Green reported that Cuza had told him that a foreign prince was needed for Romania. The current situation, Cuza said, would "sooner or later cause a crisis."

The second dispatch dates from just after the ouster of Cuza.[71] Green reports yet another conversation with Baligot on the letter of Cuza to Napoléon and Cuza's abdication wish. Baligot added that Cuza had in fact found a replacement and had planned to abdicate in May of 1866. Green believed that these matters would be resolved when Cuza's papers were published by the new government, an event that never happened since the Cuza papers were kept sequestered by D. A. Sturdza.

Aside from these considerations, there is the evidence derived from studying Cuza's psychology and actions during the last three months of his reign. Given the constant difficulties since August, 1865, his personal problems and health, the mounting opposition and criticism (most of which he regarded as unjust), and his apparently genuine disinterestedness in ruling, Cuza's desire to abdicate was both real and unreluctant.[72] Having achieved most of what he believed he could achieve, Cuza was ready to relinquish the reins when the occasion was ready. The unconcern he showed over conspiracy rumors and the ease with which he was finally ousted confirm this.

Cuza's abdication intentions have been insisted upon both because the question can be resolved with some certainty and because of its implications. Where would a voluntary abdication by Cuza have left the opposition? Obviously such a move would not be satisfactory since Cuza would thereby have retained enormous prestige and influence. The matter became a factor in December, when Cuza's chamber speech made it public. Until then, it obviously did not play any role in coalition-building or formation.

Subsequent to the events of August, two other significant events occurred. As mentioned previously, the Porte had chastised Cuza for the sad conditions in the Principalities which had led to questionable (from the Ottoman Empire's point of view) army activities and general disorder. Cuza's response was a strong affirmation of Romanian autonomy and an assertion that the Porte should mind its own business. The result was a virtual retraction by the Porte. Though the incident seems minor, for the plotters it was another proof that the powers would not interfere in internal Romanian affairs.

The second event was the adoption by Cuza on 4 November

of his second illegitimate son, Dimitrie. Following on the heels of the publication in several newspapers of letters congratulating Cuza, his wife, and the "heir-apparent Prince Alexandru," the matter became more grist for the conspirators' mill.[73] As has been shown above, the intention of Cuza was to resign, not to establish a dynasty. However, the evidence for that conclusion was not available to the public and charges of dynasticism seemed to ring true.

Disgust with Cuza and his camarilla continued to build as matters went from bad to worse. A typical opposition attitude was that of Nicolae Golescu as expressed in a letter to his niece on 25 October 1865: "The Prince was very ill; [Dr.] Davila let some of his blood, but not as much as I could have wished."[74]

On 5 December, Cuza made his speech to the chambers suggesting that he planned to give up his throne. This act had several effects, none of them good. His supporters were more or less demoralized; Bolintineanu wrote, "From his decision to abdicate, he was no longer considered as prince."[75] The once docile chambers, hand-picked by Cuza, began to oppose and challenge the prince; in January and February 1866, they became openly rebellious.

For the conspirators, the speech of December was both alarming and encouraging. If Cuza did in fact abdicate and bring in a successor from abroad, they would remain isolated and unable to continue their campaign. Such an act by Cuza, furthermore, would have wiped out the two points which really comprised the opposition "program." A Cuza abdication would not remove either the financial chaos or the camarilla; the eventual ruin of Romania would still result. Such an eventuality must be prevented, and speed was therefore of the essence.

However, there were other possible interpretations of the speech, and it is probable that the opposition gave these more credence. The first was to regard, as Raducanu Rosetti had, the idea of a voluntary abdication as a hoax, or perhaps a diversion to sidetrack the conspiracy. If one were convinced of Cuza's dynastic or despotic tendencies, this would seem a plausible interpretation. Alternatively, the declaration by Cuza could be seen as a simple admission of weakness. In that case, the opposition could act with even more impunity. Which is what they did. The anti-Cuza conspiracy now moved into high gear. Ion Brătianu's mission to Paris soon proved a success. Working in conjunction with Eugeniu Carada, Brătianu's strategy was simple: by representing Cuza as a tool of the Russians and by demonstrating the disastrous course of the prince's tenure, the conspirators hoped to get Napoléon III and the French public to abandon Cuza to his fate. Apart from this publicity task, Brătianu was also charged with finding a candidate for the throne as soon as it was vacated. The propaganda machine functioned smoothly. In the space of three months, Brătianu was able to publish three brochures that received wide circulation in Paris: **Le Panslavisme; Assemblée élective de la Roumanie; La question religieuse en Roumanie.**[76] The most successful was **Le Panslavisme**, which carefully built the case that Cuza was at least a Russophile if not a conscious agent of Russian expansion. **La Siècle**, a leading French newspaper, published a long front-page review of the pamphlet favorable to the Brătianu charges. At the same time, Brătianu had renewed all of the connections established by the liberals in over twenty years of contact with France.[77]

Cuza was, of course, hardly pro-Russian. His sympathies and his actions were favorable to France. In addition, many of his close collaborators, including his personal secretary, were Frenchmen. As with the charges of dynasticism, the claims were untrue. Yet they had great credibility both within Romania and abroad. Cuza may have taken the matter less seriously than was necessary precisely because of its absurdity. And, though he knew that Brătianu was active in Paris, he was lulled by the conviction that Brătianu was "absolument antipathique au gouvernement de l'Empereur Napoléon."[78]

In addition to Cuza's indifference to these rumors and accusations, the Brătianu mission was abetted by the reports of the French consul in București, Tillos. Somewhat taken in by the reports of Cuza's Russophilism, Tillos sent a series of dispatches to Paris reporting almost daily gains in Russian influence over the prince. Typical was his assertion that "thanks to the government of Prince Cuza, the union is compromised to the highest degree."[79] In such circumstances, Ion Brătianu felt able to report in February the successful establishment of an anti-Cuza sentiment in influential French circles. What success he had on the other issue, the selection of a foreign prince, is not known.

At home, the conspirators were also active; their last task now was to win over the army. The August incident had shown the necessity of army aid. It was also a means for the way out of the impasse. The primary obstacle was the oath of allegiance all soldiers took to Cuza as commander-in-chief. Helpfully, the August events had also influenced the thinking of several army officers. Disgusted by the government's action, they were open to subversive influence. As one of them later wrote, "without 3 August, 1865, we wouldn't have had 11 February, 1866."[80] Several officers were already adherents of Brătianu-Rosetti liberalism, and it was easy to persuade them that since Cuza had betrayed the law and violated his oath by enacting the coup of 2 May and permitting the events of 1865, the army was no longer bound to the oath they had made to the prince. In fact, it now became the serious duty of the army to oust the lawless ruler.[81] This group of officers within the anti-Cuza coalition included Major Dimitrie Lecca, commander of the troops guarding the palace, and Captains Anton Costiescu, Al. Lipoianu, and C. Pilat. Through the efforts of Ion Ghica and Ion Bălăceanu, Colonels D. Crețulescu (the prime minister's own brother) and I. Călinescu were added to the conspiracy.[82] This meant that of the six battalions in the București garrison, four (Crețulescu's and Călinescu's infantry battalions, Lecca's guard battalion, and the engineering battalion) were won over to the plot. There remained only the artillery battalion of Colonel Nicolae Haralambie and the infantry battalion of Colonel C. Solomon.[83]

Solomon was a convinced foe of the opposition and a personal ally of Cuza; he was not a possible convert. Haralambie also appeared to be a devoted supporter of Cuza, but his loyalties were of a military and patriotic rather than a personal nature.

If his cooperation could be gained, the coup would be assured. He was, therefore, approached from several directions. The events of August had been disheartening for Haralambie. When rumors of Cuza's Russophilism began to fly, he had gone to see the prince. His pleas for re-assurance and for action to alleviate the conditions that were distressing the country met with a diffident and jocular response on the part of Cuza. The rather sober-sided Haralambie was quite upset by Cuza's levity and lack of concern.

It was at this juncture that Haralambie was approached by his protégé, Captain Al. Candiano-Popescu. Candiano had been won over to the conspiracy by Major Lecca; he now appealed to Haralambie's patriotism to join the plot on the grounds that only in this manner could the country be saved from sure ruin at the hands of Cuza and his corrupt collaborators. Haralambie was shocked by this proposal, then amazed to discover that Lecca, whom he respected, and Rosetti, whom he admired, were among the plotters. He agreed to discuss the matter with them.

At the same time, Haralambie was contacted by Ion Ghica and Ion Bălăceanu. Assured of the need for army support, he was further impressed by appeals to his own lack of vested interest in the matter and suggestions that honest men such as himself were the key to bringing about Cuza's replacement with a foreign prince before the country foundered or one of the more ambitious members of the anti-Cuza crowd seized the throne himself. The clincher [cherchez la femme!] was supplied when Rosetti got the cooperation of his niece, Sultana Crețianu, who just happened to be Haralambie's paramour. In the end, the crucial convert to the conspiracy was won: Haralambie agreed, with some misgivings, to join the plot, and, additionally, consented to serve as one of the three regents who would act in Cuza's place until the foreign prince arrived.[84]

With the army leadership in hand, the rank and file came easily. The officers and soldiers of the palace guard were reportedly resentful at having to salute Cuza's illegitimate progeny and having to observe the scandalous coming and goings of Maria Obrenovici. The financial crises in the country, caused in part by the widely-known embezzlements of the camarilla, meant delays in pay, lack of equipment and food, and general hardship for the soldiers. Morale was poor and factionalism was rife.[85] To the simple soldier these things, added to the broadly unfavorable picture painted by coalition propaganda, made the ouster of Cuza plausible and even essential. As Candiano wrote later in his memoirs: "On the surface of Prince Cuza's reign, one saw Union, the taking of the dedicated monasteries, the giving of land to the peasants; beneath the surface, however, lay hidden corruption, illegality, cynicism. The country no longer knew what it was to respect the law and had begun even to lose faith in the future."[86] Finally, within military circles, there was even circulating the argument that since Cuza had "served" his seven-year term, he was therefore over-staying his tenure. That this should be a factor is revealing of the sorry state of affairs to which things had come.[87]

> In making the lovitura de stat Prince Cuza had for him the peasants and the army. He had against him the coalition of the old parties represented in the dissolved chamber. The day that the army passed to the side of the coalition, he would be alone because the peasants neither understood politics nor would be able to defend him.[88]

That point had now been reached. As we have seen, even the peasantry was not a possible support, simply because their gratitude depended on a material situation which was poor and declining. And to back up their internal preparations, the coalition had taken sufficient steps to insure that the powers would not intervene in Cuza's behalf. The final act was ready.

Rumors of a revolt continued to flourish. 24 January 1866, the seventh anniversary of Cuza's election, was expected to see some action. Though **Clopotul's** incendiary appearances increased and placards abounded (on the palace walls signs appeared reading "This Palace for rent 24 January," and the like) nothing happened. The conspiracy, now complete at home, was awaiting word from abroad. On 26 January, the British consul wrote, "The consequence of Prince Couza's mismanagement and misconduct are no doubt the rocks on which his system of disorder will be finally wrecked..."[89] Cuza's response was to form a new ministry, still under Nicolae Kretzulescu, but excluding Generals Florescu and Manu, the only really staunch men in the previous cabinet (and among Cuza's few remaining major supporters in the army). This final blunder was enough to ensure the result. When Ion Brătianu sent word that action was imperative, the coalition moved.[90]

The coup was set for the night of 10-11 February 1866. All factions of the conspiracy were notified and previously arranged plans were set into motion. At Rosetti's house, just a few blocks from the palace, a boisterous party began the evening of 10 February as a cover for the comings and goings of the plotters. While the music and partying was going on upstairs, Rosetti's presses were running off the proclamatons of the "new" government. Other groups of conspirators were meeting at the homes of Ion Ghica and Nicolae Blaremberg. In the barracks, the officers nervously awaited the appointed hour.[91]

All was not well at the palace, however. At 7 p.m., a messenger brought a note to Cuza from Cezar Boliac that a plot was in the offing and an assault on the palace eminent. Having heard such rumors for months, Cuza seemed unconcerned, but summoned his security men. None reported any signs of trouble. The prefect of police, Al. Beldiman, set out on a tour of the town to see if there was anything amiss. Cuza also called in the commander of the troops guarding the palace, Major Lecca, and ordered the guard doubled. Lecca, as one of the conspirators, was happy to comply and moved in additional troops loyal to the plot. Prefect Beldiman, a Moldovan who knew București "as well as if he had just arrived from China,"[92] satisfied himself that there was nothing impending, reported this to Cuza, and retired peacefully for the night after ordering the bell ropes cut on church towers as a precaution. The fact is that neither Cuza nor Beldiman thought to suspect the army. Beldiman, by his own account, believed an assassination attempt was possible, but not a coup. Cuza repaired to his apartments, where he was soon joined by his mistress, Maria Obrenovici. She had not noticed the handkerchief signal the soldier escorting her to the palace had made to hidden eyes belonging to the conspiracy.[93] One is safe in assuming that neither Cuza nor Maria took any of the plot rumors seriously.

At midnight, the leaders of the conspiracy, except for Ion Ghica, met briefly to ratify final plans. It is instructive to notice that there were three obvious factions now operating within the coalition: the Muntenian liberals, Ion Ghica and his friends, and the conservatives, all meeting in separate locations. The coup had not yet been carried out and already the "national unity" coalition was beginning to show fissures. A new cabinet was finally decided upon after some tumultuous discussion, the various factions agreed to support Prince Philip of Flanders as the new prince, and a windy proclamation (drawn up by Rosetti) was signed by all present. D. A. Sturdza then departed with these papers to get the signatures of the Ghica partisans who were waiting at Ion Ghica's house. Time passed and Sturdza did not return. Finally, a response came from the Ghica group urging a shorter proclamation as well as Rosetti's replacement in the new cabinet, allegedly because he was unacceptable to the conspiracy's military allies. Ion Bălăceanu, a Ghica confidant, was put in Rosetti's place and the revised declaration was taken to Rosetti's press and printed.[94]

Cuza's bedroom lights extinguished shortly before 3 a.m., and a lookout in the belfry of the Kretzulescu Church opposite the palace signalled to the plotters. Army units began to move into place as the leaders of the plot gathered in the square in front of the National Theatre, near the palace. At 4:30, while they waited anxiously in the cold night air, a group of armed officers burst into Cuza's apartments. Informed that he was deposed, Cuza signed the prepared decree "conforming to the wish of the entire nation" and was whisked from the palace to the home of a Rosetti intimate.[95] He made no attempt to resist. Maria Obrenovici was allowed to dress and was escorted home. Simultaneously, the key figures in the military loyal to Cuza, as well as members of the camarilla were arrested. By 5 a.m., the coup was complete as the conspirators had taken control of the palace and the streets of the capital. Not a drop of blood was shed. Colonel Haralambie, now one of three regents ruling the Romanian state just saved from ruin, looked plaintively from the palace toward the square and asked Rosetti, "Where are the people?" The people were asleep...while the military-politicians' plot was being executed. The pretense that the ouster of Prince Cuza was a "national" undertaking had little basis in fact. Only a few naive individuals, such as Haralambie, took such claims seriously. But, for better or for worse, the reign of Alexandru Ioan Cuza was over.

Chapter 6

The Third Phase: Interim Government

> "Sir, you have wrestled well, and overthrown more than your enemies."
> Shakespeare, *As You Like It*, I.ii.271

The morning of 11 February 1866, an interim government representing all factions of the plot against Cuza proclaimed itself "chosen by the nation" and set to work.[1] The regents[2] were General Nicolae Golescu, a Muntenian liberal, Colonel Nicolae Haralambie, a political neutral representing the army, and Lascăr Catargiu, a Moldovan and a conservative. The new ministry displayed the same evenness: Ion Ghica, the prime minister and minister of foreign affairs, was a liberal, but not a part of the dominant Muntenian group. He was joined by two of his allies, Ion C. Cantacuzino, as minister of justice, and D. A. Sturdza, as minister of works. The conservatives were represented by Dimitrie Ghica, as minister of interior, and Petre Mavrogheni, as minister of finance. C. A. Rosetti, the minister of cults and education, was a leader of the Muntenian liberals, while Major Dimitrie Lecca, the minister of war, was a neutral, but friendly to Rosetti and the Muntenians.[3] Ion Ghica's attempt to seat another of his supporters, Ion Bălăceanu, in place of Rosetti had been thwarted in the end by the indignant Col. Haralambie.[4] The tone of the new government was apparently liberal, but the presence of Ion Ghica and his supporters and the two army men made its overall complexion neutral.[5]

The new regime now summoned the legislature to ratify the cabinet, by the "wish of the nation," and to elect unanimously Count Philip of Flanders as the new ruler of Romania. This docile parliament, it will be remembered, was composed entirely of Cuza's hand-picked men elected in the managed elections of 1865.

Meanwhile, calm prevailed in the capital. The British consul, Green, no real friend of the provisional government, reported that not "a single act of disorder" had come to his attention and that "tranquility prevails."[6] This despite the fact that "Everything was done which stupidity could devise and negligence suggest to produce a counter-revolution, and foreign exertion was not wanting to fan the flame, had there been any inflammable matter to ignite."[7] The same reaction was reported in Th. Văcărescu's memoirs.[8] Most of the population was unwilling to fight for the deposed prince; whether it would give concrete support to the new rulers was unknown. Their bid for legitimacy was yet relatively unproven.

From Cuza, the new government received surprising cooperation in its claim to legitimacy. The abdicated prince made no effort to counter the coup. Instead, on 12 February, he requested permission to leave the country and pledged his support for the regime. He specifically endorsed a foreign prince as the only hope for Romania's future.[9] Cuza's wish for voluntary exile was speedily granted, and he left the country never to return. His calm acquiescence in his ouster was of significant assistance to the provisional government as it left his supporters, including important segments of the army, isolated. The threat of counter-revolution receded; subsequent rumors of plots by Cuza loyalists were of little consequence. As Green concluded, "No one has any longer the right to doubt that Prince Couza's retirement was in conformity with his own wishes."[10]

The act of 11 February seemed to be unfolding smoothly. Beneath the facade of unity, however, there were considerable divisions. Ion Ghica's cabinet machinations even before the coup began were one sign that all was not harmony and cooperation. The factions which had begun to emerge earlier were now operating under the leadership of C. A. Rosetti, Dimitrie Ghica, and Ion Ghica respectively. When it became known that "Prince Filip I" would not and could not accept the throne offered him these rivalries began to flourish much more openly.

Count Flanders, brother of the King of Belgium, as it turned out, had not been consulted prior to his election as prince of

Romania. The Romanians' choice seems to have been based mainly on a rumored Philip candidacy for the throne in 1857.[11] As the grandson of Louis Philippe and therefore an Orleans, there was no real chance of his accepting the throne since Napoléon III would scarcely be favorable to him. The rationale behind the election of Philip appears to have been to assert the new regime's right to select the new Romanian ruler independently of the the powers, to demonstrate the unity of the Romanians, to establish the principle of a foreign prince as a national imperative, and to forestall any action by the Porte and the powers.[12]

The lack of a candidate reopened the whole succession question and produced the seeds of dissention and distrust within the cabinet. The key was Ion Ghica, the prime minister. Ghica's motives and actions during this period are somewhat enigmatic. It is apparent that he wanted to have a larger role in the government than the other partners of the coalition were willing to allow. In fact, following Flanders' unofficial refusal, rumors began to circulate that Ghica wanted the throne for himself. Ghica had supported the election of Philip, so the story ran, knowing full well that the latter could not accept. The resulting confusion and indecision would allow Ghica to step into the void and assume a post he had often wanted and felt entitled to by virtue of his descent from earlier Romanian princes. His good relations with the Porte and Great Britain coupled with the announced preference of all the powers for a native prince made such a scheme plausible.

Ghica's plans, if such existed, were once again repulsed by the action of Col. Haralambie. When the co-regent heard these rumors about Ghica's designs, he immediately raised the matter with the prime minister in the presence of the other regents. Telling Ghica that he would regard such a development as an utter betrayal, Haralambie concluded, "I swear to you in front of God that I will kill you with this revolver," if the rumors proved true. Ghica, "visibly impressed," protested "energetically," against the allegations and tried to demonstrate his bona fides to Haralambie by at once making a telegraphic appeal to Paris asking the French government to name a candidate for the throne.[13] Rumors of a pending Ghica coup ceased.

Why was Ion Ghica chosen as the first prime minister by the coalition in spite of this apparent penchant for intrigue? Why was a man described by consul Green as "insincere, crafty, vindictive, and envious,"[14] given such responsibility in a time of precariousness for Romania? Ion Ghica seems to have been the only man trusted politically (if not morally) by both the liberals and the conservatives in the anti-Cuza coalition. He was not too radical, but he was not too reactionary either. Secondly, and more importantly, there was the fact of his good relations with the Porte. As one who had long held that Romanian destiny could be achieved under Ottoman suzerainty, Ghica enjoyed wide contacts and favor at the Porte. So highly regarded was he that in the 1850's he had been chosen by the Sultan to serve as Prince of the island of Samos, a difficult assignment that he carried out extremely well. Ghica's Turcophilism, indeed, tended to make him somewhat unpopular among the more nationalistic of his compatriots. The primary task facing the interim government was to establish a successor on the throne. This required Ottoman approval, and Ghica was obviously the best man to win the Porte over. At the same time, he was one of Romania's most capable and experienced diplomats, a valuable commodity now that Cuza's ouster and replacement had brought the Romanian question back on the European diplomatic stage.[15]

The abdication of Cuza, from the point of view of the Great Powers, came at a most inconvenient time.[16] While none of the powers had been very enthusiastic over the performance of the prince, the Romanian question was one they preferred to leave well enough alone. Early in 1866, both Britain and France had agreed that Cuza's regime was hopelessly inadequate, but neither could see any more acceptable course than that of trying to maintain the prince in office.[17] Cuza's forced resignation and the election of a foreign prince brought the Romanians into direct violation of the protocols 13 and 22 of the 1858 Paris convention.[18] The troublesome Romanian problem was once more on the table.

The most concerned of course was the Ottoman Empire. In

the first place, she had never been happy over the unification of the Principalities under a native prince. Pressure had caused the Porte to accede to the election of Cuza and subsequent events. It was now obvious to it that Romania was slowly drifting out from under its control. Furthermore, the Porte was not unaware of the possible ill influences the Romanian example might have on its Serbian and Bulgarian lands.[19] It seemed to it that it was now time to take a firm stand and put a stop to the erosion of the Ottoman territorial integrity and authority. The Porte therefore appealed to the sanctity of treaties and the Concert of Europe, hoping that the situation in the Principalities might revert to the pre-1859 situation. Recourse to the treaties was, in the end, its only real option since the unilateral use of force against the Romanians might void these same treaties, which the Porte rightly saw as the main guarantee of its own existence.[20]

As the ruler of a neighboring territory containing large numbers of Romanians, the Habsburg monarchy was also deeply concerned with the developments in Romania. Its minister at Constantinople saw clearly that union and a foreign prince would eventually lead to an independent Romanian state on the lower Danube. This could only be a danger for Austria.[21] In "ordinary circumstances," Austria would not have hesitated to declare strongly in favor of the separation of the Principalities and in support of the Porte. However, because of "menacing eventualities" in Germany and Italy, (i.e. war), the Emperor held "particularly that his government march hand in hand with France," even to the extent of accepting a foreign prince.[22] Austria therefore, from the outset, tried to act in concert with France, while hoping that the Romanians would fail.

The position of Prussia was similar to that of Austria in that it wished to curry favor with France, but different in that she did not face the same national or geographic considerations which restricted Habsburg policymakers. As so often in Bismarck's career, the Prussian leader had a wide variety of options open to him, and it was only a matter of choosing the most profitable. He chose to let the French lead in the matter. Initially, the Romanian problem was a nuisance for Bismarck since it added another factor to his complex calculations with regard to larger aims in Germany. As also happened so often, this unexpected event later turned up on the positive side of the Bismarckian ledger.

Russia found itself placed by the Romanians in a position that was to become an old story in the nineteenth century. The Russian aim was to avoid Near Eastern crises. Though at this point it did not favor the status quo, it always believed that in Southeast Europe any changes would be for the worst. Due to its shaky position in Poland following the 1863 revolt, its lack of a trustworthy major ally, and its demonstrated post-Crimea internal weaknesses, Russia was unready and unwilling to act. Fearing a number of eventualities, including a possible Habsburg annexation of the Principalities, the tsar and his ministers adopted a position of strong support for Ottoman territorial integrity. There were, it is true, a number of positive possibilities from the Russian point of view. These included: a separation of the Principalities which would give Russia the upper hand in Moldova; the winning of Ottoman favor and thus a more favorable position vis-à-vis Austria; or a considerably stronger basis for renouncing the Black Sea restrictions imposed on it by the treaty of 1856 if the Romanians were permitted by the powers to carry through with their violation of the treaty.[23]

Britain's attitude toward the Romanian "revolution" of 1866 was the most open, yet the most complex and confused of all the powers. Preoccupied with internal affairs, it wanted to achieve too many contradictory aims and in the end accomplished very little. Thus, it wanted to maintain the treaties, but also to collaborate with France. It wanted to prop up the tottering Ottoman Empire, but resolutely opposed armed intervention by the Porte, thus tying the latter's hands. It hoped the Conference of Paris would solve all the problems, but did little to expedite realistic solutions by the conference. British policy was at this point in a complete muddle.[24]

France, as noted previously, preferred not to have the Eastern status quo disrupted. It was considered the protector of Romanian nationalism, and in truth it was Napoléon III's determined actions that had paved the way for the union of 1859. But in 1866, his attention was riveted on two other matters: completion of Italian unification and the German question. At the same time, he wanted to preserve an understanding with England, which he regarded as crucial to his foreign policy. France therefore adopted a course of avoiding positive action.[25] This proved to be exactly the policy that the new Romanian regime needed to execute a series of fait accomplis against Europe.

The Romanians had decided that their best course of action vis-à-vis the powers was to argue publicly for the continuity of the Cuza treaty and protocol modifications while privately ignoring the statements and declarations issuing from the chancelleries of Europe. Only if direct armed force were eminent would they abandon this course. This strategy reflected the view of diplomacy voiced by Eugeniu Carada in 1864 after Cuza's 2 May coup:

> Diplomacy occupies itself very little with public law, with guarantees accorded various nations; what it wants is to escape any complications. And my belief is that, in the current case, it will give its approval to the party which has the success of the day; if tomorrow the other party would overthrow the action done today, diplomacy would approve it in turn. The role of diplomacy, in the conditions of today in which nations find themselves, is to be a simple registry, to enter in its book fait accomplis.[26]

In other words, the success of the audacious acts of 1859, 1862, and 1864 had convinced the Romanians of the wisdom of a policy of fait accompli. This was clearly recognized by Austria's experienced Bucureşti consul, Baron Eder, in 1866: "The conduct of Prince Cuza and the negligence of the powers have accustomed the local population to consider treaties, protocols, and conventions as a secondary matter and to regard fait accomplis as the only determinants."[27] Through its provisional government, the Romanians had once more seized the initiative. The question now was, how would Europe react?

The response of the powers to the abdication of Cuza and the presumptive election of a foreign successor was the one that usually occurs when no one wants to act: the matter was referred to committee. The Conference of Paris, consisting of representatives from each European Power, was asked to take up the question of Romanian violations of the Convention of 1858. It began its meetings only on 26 February, thus allowing the Romanians ample time to strengthen their hand. This Ghica did by developing more fully the case which the Romanians would present to the powers, while his agents abroad, especially Ion Brătianu and Ion Bălăceanu, intensified their efforts to find a new candidate for the throne.

The propaganda case that the Romanians were arguing was that the relationship of Romania with the Ottoman Empire was simply not affected by the ouster of Cuza. The events of 10-11 February, including the election of a foreign prince, Ghica argued, were purely internal developments and of no concern to any foreign power.[28] It was to this position that the statements and dispatches of Ion Ghica persistently adhered. At the same time, the usual Romanian weapon of appeal to the European public, especially Parisian, was employed. Another wave of brochures and pamphlets was issued to argue the internal autonomy case and leading newspapers were the recipients of bulky "subscriptions" generously paid for by the Romanian government.[29]

While Ion Ghica was orchestrating external relations, the management of internal affairs fell mainly on Dimitrie Ghica and C. A. Rosetti. The key problem with which they had to deal was lending credence to the argument for legitimacy and continuity of the new regime. Secondly, there remained unsolved the various problems caused by Cuza's misrule which supposedly had made his ouster necessary in the first place. These involved finances, the press, and the constitution. They were also called upon to resolve numerous difficulties that appeared in the wake of Cuza's abdication.

One dilemma facing the conspirators was how to make the

transition to being the "establishment." They were particularly aware of this problem in connection with the army. The conspiracy had spent a good deal of time convincing parts of the army to take an active role in politics and to violate their oaths of loyalty to the chief of state. Now they had to provide a continuing justification for these acts while preventing further use of these "principles." In addition, officers who had not violated their oaths had to be dealt with—to eliminate those who were loyal to Cuza.[30]

Românul served as an effect propaganda voice in this campaign, publishing several laudatory articles on the army's action in February, while promoting the idea that Cuza's ouster had been necessary to save the nation. The army was credited with preventing a certain bloodbath and the breaking of oaths justified by the assertion that Cuza's 2 May regime had been itself a betrayal of legality and of the army.[31]

From the Muntenian liberals' point of view, one of the most important steps that the new regime took was the order of the regency on 16 February abolishing the press restrictions instituted by Cuza.[32] A new era for the Romanian press was opened. For the next decade, Romania enjoyed a freedom of the press that it had never experienced (and would not know thereafter). This had been, undoubtedly, a major objective for C. A. Rosetti.

The financial crisis facing the country in 1866 was acute. Seven years of Cuza's rule had produced a debt of nearly 21 million lei, an enormous sum in proportion to the budget of the country and its means.[33] The credit of the state was nil, the treasury was empty, the budget was an illusion, and all aspects of financial administration were in complete disorder.[34] The new minister of finance, Petre Mavrogheni, proposed to mark a clear line between the past and the present. To this end, a "bank of liquidation" was proposed to consolidate all past debts and deficits. These were to be paid, not from current income, but through means of a national loan, collections of unpaid taxes, revenue from state monopolies, and the repudiation of certain of the more onerous foreign concessions. On 21 February, a national campaign to raise eleven million lei in loans from the populace was launched with considerable fanfare, and in March, the chamber repudiated several concessions with foreign entrepreneurs, including a bank and a railroad project. Both Britain and France were considerably upset by these cancellations, which involved their subjects.[35]

Mavrogheni had hoped to raise enough money to counter-balance the debt, but the measures taken toward that end were insufficient. A deficit of nine million lei remained. However, some of the steps in financial administration were more successful. The careless gathering of taxes was revamped and a number of recently launched institutions, such as the savings bank, were reorganized to produce revenue for the state and not merely the pockets of their administrators. To encourage honesty among the ranks of the bureaucracy, a variety of court actions were begun against those who had abused their positions under the former regime. The foremost among these was Cezar Librecht.[36] The problem of establishing a national monetary unit, one that Cuza had also struggled with, was also brought onto the agenda.[37] This last measure, which was crucial for resolving Romania's monetary chaos, had to wait until 1867 for fruition since Ottoman approval was necessary. In any case, the drift into financial disaster was halted and the basis for a more feasible budget established.[38]

Rather interestingly, the new government continued to conduct business with the assistance of the old Cuza legislature. Not only that, the statute imposed by the "dictatorial" Cuza remained the operating law of the land. The explanation for this moderation is not hard to find. The government wanted, above all, to avoid even the slightest hint of internal turmoil until a foreign prince could be found, lest a pretext for intervention by Russia or Turkey be furnished. In addition, the new rulers had no compunction about using the centralist Cuzist system as a basis for their own activities. **Românul** stated this position clearly in its 21/22 February 1866 issue: "If we disrupt the organization of the country, we would unmistakably also break the statute of Cuza which gives us the right to make any law within without asking sanction from abroad." No doubt this is a rather ironic position for Cuza's opponents to have found themselves in.

The pacific responses of the legislature provided a helpful assist. The ratification of Philip of Flanders' "election" passed unanimously. Subsequent proposals by the government were similarly "successful." Thus, legislation for agricultural contracts, for the reorganization of the army, and for the repudiation of certain concessions all passed easily. At the same time, the Cuza legislature gave its stamp of approval to the budget requests proposed by the new regime.

Especially important was the law on agricultural contracts.[39] One of the problems caused by the land reform of 1864 was an instability of labor supply on properties retained by large holders. The resulting confusion convinced the large holders that they would soon be ruined if no changes were made. Their solution was to propose the establishing of a system of contractual agricultural relations. In March 1866, after a fairly brief debate, a law was passed which required peasants and landholders to make contracts for the working of land. An important innovation of these contracts was that they were specifically to be enforced by the government, with violators being fined, imprisoned, or drafted into the army. And there was no appeal from decisions by the government administrator. The relief of the landholders was obvious.

Some historians have been at pains to see this law as a concrete result of the coup of 1866, and as evidence for the thesis that Cuza's ouster was motivated particularly by upper-class resentment against the land reform of 1864. Such a view is not tenable simply because the drafting of the law occurred before the events of 11 February. Clearly, Cuza himself saw the need for such contracts. More serious were some of the economic effects of this law, though these did not manifest themselves for decades.

The first political problem connected with the new agricultural contract laws occurred when the droughts, plagues, and other disasters of 1865-1866 forced the peasantry into rather one-sided contracts. The law had restricted contracts to five years, but the failure to provide alternative sources of aid, such as rural credit banks, during hard times resulted in the progressive worsening of the peasants' lot. The eventual result was the establishment of a system of rural servitude that is often compared unfavorably with the feudal era. Peasant revolts in 1888 and, on a larger scale, in 1907 were the long run consequence.

At the same time that the contract law was in the works, the government was very much aware that the peasants needed to be reassured that Cuza's ouster did not mean abrogation of the land reform. They were always quick to stress that Cuza's ouster did not imperil land or other reforms, e.g., a circular issued by Dimitrie Ghica to all the prefects denouncing rumors that the agrarian law would be modified: "Tell them that in no word and in no case will the rural law be touched, that it remains irrevocable and sacred in all its parts."[40]

The eventual replacement of Cuza's statute with a new constitution was, of course, one of the aims of the coalition, especially the Muntenian liberals. The conservatives were not particularly enamored with liberal constitutionalism, but they did regard the law of 1864 as unacceptable. Thus, on 16 February, Ion Ghica charged the Council of State with preparing a draft constitution. Real direction of the project fell into the hands of C. A. Rosetti, who promptly revived a liberal project of 1859, one heavily influenced by the Belgian model. This similarity has been responsible for a number of fanciful stories and myths. However, as the work of Angelescu and Filitti [among other historians] clearly shows, the draft was not a mere copy of the Belgian document, but a realistic adaptation of liberal ideas to Romanian conditions drawing upon a wide range of Romanian and foreign sources.[41] By 7 March, the project was ready for presentation to the cabinet. Though the ministry, especially its liberal members, hoped that a new Romanian fundamental law could be in place before the hoped-for foreign prince was actually sworn in, this was not to be. As shall be seen, the debate on the project began only in June of 1866.[42]

On 18 March, more than a month after Cuza's ouster, the

government abruptly dissolved the chamber and prorogued the senate. The alleged motive—that the chamber had become intolerably hostile to the interim government—is simply not born out by examination of the parliamentary debates. The real reason, of course, was that the old chamber, after establishing the legitimacy of the new rulers by collaborating with them and then by voting a new budget, was no longer needed. The fact that the new constitution was now ready for consideration also made it inconvenient for the old body to remain seated. Elections were, therefore, set for 9-17 April. It is significant that at no time did the provisional government refer to this election as being for a constituent assembly; the pretense of continuity remained.[43]

If overt opposition to the new regime was slight, its internal differences were not. Besides the suspicious behavior of Ion Ghica, an intensive struggle was being waged behind the scenes between the conservatives and the Muntenian liberals. Rosetti was the leading instigator of these disputes. The revival of the 1859 constitution was not really to the conservatives' liking, but Rosetti forced the issue. A proposed national guard, once rejected by Cuza, was another favorite topic of the Rosetti group. Its alleged aim was to bolster Romania's feeble armed forces in the event of Ottoman or Russian intervention; its real purpose, the conservatives feared, was that such a force would become largely an arm for liberal agitation.[44]

Rosetti was also the most adamant foe of the Cuzist legislature, which he wanted dismissed. By 18 March, he was able to report to Ion Brătianu virtually complete success in regard to the Muntenian's interim agenda: the chamber was dissolved, the national guard bill had been passed, and the new constitution was ready.[45] At the same time, he was making considerable headway in reorganizing the ministry of education in conformity with Muntenian liberal preferences.[46] The Muntenians clearly had the upper hand at this point. Rosetti was having things mainly his own way internally; Ion Brătianu, as we shall see, was the key agent abroad. Rosetti's aggressiveness was, however, rapidly garnering conservative hostility. In the words of one conservative leader (Gh. Ştirbey in a private letter of 13/25 March): Rosetti and Brătianu "are revolutionaries at heart, they know only the history of France from 1793 to 1800. Both are tainted with revolutionary virus, a virus from which they will never be cured."[47] An open break between the two camps began to build as attention shifted to the election of a new chamber; meanwhile the search for a new prince continued.

Romanian agents abroad were working diligently and determinedly to obtain a suitable candidate for their vacant throne. Efforts in Belgium by Ion Brătianu to change the mind of Philip were unsuccessful. A new candidate had to be found, as the powers and various native pretenders were jockeying for the vacancy.

At last a break came. On 12 March, Ion Ghica sent a desperation telegram to Bălăceanu in Paris committing the provisional government to the support of any candidate that France named for the vacancy.[48] He followed this on 13 March with another telegram to Bălăceanu: "we are ready to establish a fait accompli. Give us the result and the name of the candidate."[49] The telegraphic reply of Bălăceanu on 14 March was, "Do you authorize me to name Carol of Hohenzollern?"[50] The same day from Paris, the provisional government received a second telegram, this time from Brătianu: "Dispositions here good....the candidate of England is Hohenzollern."[51] A new prince had been discovered and the logjam began to break up. Three days later the chamber was dissolved.

Where did the candidacy of Carol of Hohenzollern originate? This has long been a point of contention, both for historians and politicians. Napoléon III has often been credited with first naming Carol.[52] This view must be discounted for several reasons including Napoléon's own denials[53] and his actions through May of 1866. One instance is Napoléon's refusal to even consider discussion of the idea of a foreign prince until after Carol's arrival in Romania. A more telling argument lies in the repeated and completely unsuccessful efforts of both the Romanian agents and the Hohenzollerns to get some sign of Napoléonic support for Carol after the candidacy became public. This would scarcely have been necessary if Napoléon had originated the idea of a Hohenzollern candidacy in the first place.

Where then did the candidacy come from? The key figure behind the nomination appears to have been Ion Brătianu. It also appears probable that the name of Carol was first floated by Mme. Hortense Cornu, doyenne of a Parisian circle of liberals that included nationalist émigrés. Mme. Cornu was both the childhood friend of Napoléon III and an acquaintance of Ion Brătianu. She was also close to the Sigmaringen branch of the Hohenzollern family. Well aware of the Romanian search for a prince and favorably disposed toward the Romanian cause, Cornu is reported to have told Brătianu, "Vous cherchez un prince, prenez un Hohenzollern; ils sont alliés à l'Empereur qui les aime beaucoup."[54] She also assured Brătianu that Napoléon would not permit the Conference of Paris to go "to extremes," that is, to use force in preventing a foreign prince.[55]

This suggestion and this assurance were all Brătianu needed. The problem of filling the vacancy on the Romanian throne could now be solved using the tried and true method of fait accompli. Brătianu's assertion that England backed Carol was pure eyewash since Britain at this point in time was committed against a foreign prince.[56] It is clear from this, and subsequent misrepresentations by Brătianu that he had decided to get Carol to Romania by all means and leave the quibbling over the details for later. Thus, Napoléon III's later protests that Cornu and Brătianu had simply forced the issue appear valid.[57]

By 18 March, Brătianu was in Düsseldorf to begin negotiations with Carol and his father, Karl Anton. Meeting with them on the 19th, he informed them that the Romanians were offering the throne to Carol, "following the suggestion of Emperor Napoléon."[58] Here again the Romanian agent took considerable liberties with the facts.

Karl Anton, Bismarck's predecessor as Prussian prime minister and an experienced politician, was favorably impressed by Brătianu's presentation and by the opportunity that was being offered to his 26 year-old son. However, as Carol was both an officer in the Prussian army and a member of the Hohenzollern family, the Romanian project had to be discussed and approved by the head of the army and family, Wilhelm of Prussia. Such niceties did not deter Brătianu in the least from firing off two telegrams the next day. The first, to Bălăceanu in Paris, read in part: "Doctor Charles accepts the cure without condition. It remains to consult medical celebrities in Berlin and Paris."[59] The second, to București, read: "Carol of Hohenzollern accepts the crown without conditions. He has been put immediately in touch with Napoléon III."[60] These telegrams do not appear in Carol's **Memoirs**, primarily because Carol did not, in fact, decide to go to Romania until two weeks later. Further soundings by Brătianu convinced the Romanian diplomat that all was ready, if not actually signed and sealed. He now returned home to consult with his government and to work out the final steps.[61]

With the refusal of Philip of Flanders having been made official on 18 March and secure in the "knowledge" that Carol's candidacy had the blessing of both Paris and Berlin, the Romanian cabinet was ready to act. On 30 March, they heard Brătianu's first-hand report and published a decree announcing a plebiscite for 2-8 April, to ratify the election of "Prince Carol I of Romania." It was two more days after these bold actions were completed, that the British consul, Green, communicated to the Romanian government on behalf of the Conference of Paris a declaration taking some umbrage over the dissolution of the chamber on 18 March.[62] The Romanians were now two full weeks ahead of the Conference and pulling away.

The Conference of Paris, as expected by the Romanians, had proven completely ineffective in its meetings thus far. The five debates between 26 February and 23 March had developed into extended sessions of shadow-boxing. The only participant with a clear position was Turkey, who urged application of the treaties. This called for the polling of the populations of the Principalities on the question of union and on their selection of a native prince or princes. France, the only forthright defender of the union of the Principalities, took the position that the Conference must deal with each of these problem on the basis of changed conditions in Romania, not the status quo ante. All the powers were agreed, however, that the provisional government in București must not take any independent action. On the other hand, nothing whatever was done to penalize or prevent the Romanians from doing as they pleased.[63] This was exactly the situation the provisional government wanted since it tied Ottoman hands while leaving theirs virtually free. It further served to strengthen their conviction that they could act with impunity.

As the declaration delivered on 1 April [appropriate date!] showed, Conference action lagged several steps behind the Romanians. In addition to the reasons mentioned above, several factors were working toward making the Conference a feckless debaters' assembly. Britain and Austria were unwilling to oppose France openly. They waited for French initiatives which were not forthcoming. The Porte made its case weakly and ineffectually.[64] Russia's Dudberg was ordered by Petersburg to back the Ottomans, but was actually favorable to the Romanians. He therefore continually delayed the proceedings in order to obtain additional "instructions." from home.[65] Italy and Prussia were preoccupied with other matters.

The plebiscite for a new prince began on 2 April with a proclamation from the provisional government to the effect that Carol had been chosen by God and Napoléon III, not necessarily in order of importance.[66] Governmental preparations for the voting were extensive as special commissioners were sent to all districts. The minister of interior, Dimitrie Ghica, sent comprehensive directives to all the prefects concerning their "delicate missions." These involved "going from community to community [where] you will write all the residents...without too much deliberation in the notebook with the word 'for' because only thus can the future happiness of our country be assured."[67]

The next morning, overlooking the fact that the plebiscite still had five days more to continue, Ion Brătianu cabled Karl Anton, "5 million Romanians acclaim as Sovereign, Prince Carol..."[68] The voting, under the efficient supervision of Dimitrie Ghica, ably seconded by Brătianu and Rosetti, gave Charles not 5 million, but a nevertheless healthy 685,969 votes out of 686,193 cast. Though the truth of the matter cannot really be determined from such an electoral process, it is probable that it at least expressed the wishes of the politically active sector of Romanian society. Karl Anton replied the same day.

> Reçu avec vive émotion la nouvelle que vous m'announcer avec tant défusion de coeur. Le fugement sur l'opportunité et la decision de la question reposent maintenant dans les mains du Roi, au quel j'ai soumis de suite votre communication.[69]

Românul hailed the plebiscite as a triumph of the national will even though less than two months earlier it had derided Cuza's plebiscite as ridiculous "in a country where the majority of the nation does not know how to even write and read."[70] The plebiscite was designed to show both the powers and Carol that the Romanian government was determined to have the Hohenzollern prince as ruler.[71] It is not unreasonable to say that these objectives were achieved.

The reactions of the powers to the candidacy of Carol were varied. What was more important, however, was the response of the Conference of Paris. When the Conference met again on April 12, the nomination and election of Carol was not even mentioned. Once again the Romanians escaped any consequence for their clearly illegal actions. The diplomatic aspect of the Romanian problem in 1866 was about to enter its final stage.

Within the country, things were proceeding less smoothly. In Moldova, the unpleasant specter of separation raised its head at a very crucial moment—3 April —just as the plebiscite for Carol was beginning. The separatists were mainly Russophile landholders who were encouraged by the Russian consul in Iași. Given the miserable economic and physical conditions in which the erstwhile capital of Moldova now found itself, given Iași's new status as a political backwater being taken over by Jewish merchants, the separatists' claims against București had some validity. On the morning of 3 April, as the Orthodox faithful and their Metropolitan, Calinic Miclescu, left the cathedral they were joined by several separatist leaders, including Prince C. Moruzi, T. Boldur-Lățescu, and N. Rosetti-Rosnovanu. The group, augmented by the servants and paid retainers of the boiars, coalesced into a small, but belligerent mob and headed for the administrative palace, shouting, "Down with union!" and other inspiring phrases. This somewhat artificially contrived street action was the outcome of several days' agitation by the separatists.

Unfortunately for the cause of the minuscule Moldovan separatist faction, they had been anticipated and outmaneuvered by the central government. Ştefan Golescu, a Muntenian, had been appointed as prefect of the police in Iaşi while two of the regents, Gen. Nicolae Golescu and Lascăr Catargiu had already arrived in Iaşi in anticipation of trouble. With them was yet another Moldovan cabinet officer, D. A. Sturdza, and a couple of battalions of Muntenian soldiers.[72] As the separatist mob advanced on the palace on 3 April, they were met by loyalist troops with fixed bayonets. In the carnage that ensued, the separatists were routed. Conflicting reports placed the total dead between fifteen and seventy on both sides. Their leaders were arrested or fled across the border. Prince Moruzi, it was reported, returned to the Russian-annexed portion of Moldova [often called Bessarabia] where he actually resided.[73]

Apart from the hysterical dispatches some consuls sent about the matter to their governments,[74] the incident had little effect. It, in fact, represented a last, but not terribly serious effort by separatists in Moldova to overturn the Union of 1859. The government's firm action as well as its foresight had prevented a potentially dangerous situation from going too far. It even managed to capture additional support in Moldova from some of those who had previously opposed a non-Latin foreign prince. These men, mostly from Iaşi, were alarmed enough by the manifestation of separatism on 3 April that they now felt they needed to throw their support to the central government.[75]

Apart from the events in Iaşi, the election for the new chamber was producing turmoil. An agreement had been made by the coalition to form a "central electoral committee" which would ensure that each faction received its rightful share of representatives. Mutual trust and respect were not very high, however. In addition, new groups which had not been a part of the coalition now sought their place in the political arena. The major factions of the coalition, as previously mentioned, were the Muntenian liberals, the Ion Ghica group, and the conservatives. The new groups included the "independent liberal Fraction" of Iaşi and a somewhat haphazard Muntenian group led by Cezar Bolliac, Christian Tell, and Ion Heliade Rădulescu.

The independent liberal Fraction was led by Nicolae Ionescu and was composed of Moldovan professors influenced by the late Transilvanian nationalist Simion Barnuţiu. Their beliefs were a confusing amalgamation of liberalism, nationalism, republicanism, bizarre economic theories, and anti-Semitism. They were pro-unionist, but ardently opposed to a foreign prince (as they were to foreigners in general). Though a small group with a political ideology of limited appeal, their leader, Ionescu, was one of the most effective parliamentary orators of the day.[76] The second group to appear, the Bolliac-Tell-Heliade faction, was united largely by hostility toward the new coalition (especially Ion Ghica) and anti-Semitism. Its leaders were chiefly noteworthy for their crankiness. Their role was largely negative; as a result, their influence was somewhat ephemeral.[77]

The claim by **Românul** at the end of March that the elections were for a "constituent" assembly was one of the first clear signs of a breach in the coalition since the conservatives had been careful to avoid any such references.[78] The British consul's reports emphasized the split and the apparent dominance of the radicals under Rosetti.[79] Relationships among coalition members were not improved by the gigantic hero's reception prepared by Rosetti for Ion Brătianu when he returned with Carol's candidacy in hand. Rumors even spread of a possible liberal coup.[80]

The work of the electoral committee went forward, however, with Rosetti's backing. A letter by him to a rural prefect is illuminating. The government, he wrote, had "decided not to exercise any personal influence whatever on the elections." Political decisions must "emanate from the nation." But, because of the Cuzist election law still in force, the government had a duty and an obligation to take the measures necessary to assure a good election. "This committee [the electoral committee], elected in the fullest liberty and after the freest public debate, is in truth the true representative of the will of the nation." The prefect was therefore instructed to give all "moral assistance' possible to the committee candidates so that "the will of the nation will triumph." A list of chosen candidates concludes the dispatch.[81]

Rosetti's professed loyalty to the "will of the nation" did not prevent him from preparing and carrying out various electoral maneuvers and counter-maneuvers.[82] Nevertheless, the election produced a chamber which not only included every major coalition figure, it also included leading representatives of most other factions including the despised Kogălniceanu. Thus, despite the fact that the electoral rules followed in 1866 were identical to those of 1864, the results were completely different.

The assembly which opened on 28 April was generally conservative in tenor. The election for chamber president saw the moderate conservative Manolache Costache Epureanu defeating Ion Brătianu by 76-46 margin; a good reflection of the relative strength of the Muntenian liberal faction. From their point of view, it was encouraging that less than 15% of the new representatives came from the extremely conservative great families.[83] Thus, even though the conservatives had the majority, this majority shared many ideas in common with the liberals. The Brătianu-Rosetti group was thus assured that there would be no reversal of the gains already made.[84]

The ministry opened the new assembly by presenting a fairly comprehensive report on the status of Romania up to that point, department by department.[85] These problems were secondary, however, to the chief job before the chamber which was to ratify Carol's election by plebiscite. After desultory and surprisingly unenthusiastic debate, the election was approved 109-0 with the Iași Fraction of 6 abstaining.[86] The only other significant action taken was to vote the exclusion of Mihail Kogălniceanu from the chamber as a reprisal for 2 May 1864. Though the liberals had hoped that the constitution could be ratified before Carol actually arrived, the wasted debate between 28 April and 10 May precluded it from even being discussed.

Diplomatically, the Romanians had one final coup to execute against the Conference: the actual bringing of Carol to Romania. For Carol and his father, the month of April was one of anxious negotiations with Berlin and repeated soundings in Paris. By the beginning of May, Carol had decided to go to București. His decision was bolstered by numerous assurances from Mme. Cornu that Napoléon III would back him and by Bismarck's encouragement. Both urged taking matters into his own hands. Said the Prussian prime minister, "if Europe see itself faced with a fait accompli, the powers most concerned will protest, but a protest remains on paper and the facts will not be altered."[87]

Carol obtained a leave of absence from the Prussian army and informed Brătianu and Bălăceanu on 29 April that he was accepting the throne and would leave at once for București.[88] He then slipped into Switzerland, assumed the name and passport of "Karl Hettingen," commercial traveller bound for Odessa, and set out across a hostile Austria [the outbreak of the Austro-Prussian war was just around the corner] for his new realm. Arriving in eastern Hungary, he had to wait two days for Danube river connections. On 8 May, who but Ion Brătianu should arrive from Paris as Carol's steamer prepared to depart for Romania.[89] At 4 p.m. that afternoon, Carol stepped off the boat onto Romanian soil where he was ceremoniously welcomed by Brătianu.

The new prince of Romania immediately dispatched a telegram to the regents in București:

> En mettant le pied sur le sol roumain, ma nouvelle patrie...je suis heureux de me trouver au sein de la nation qui m'a honoré de sa confiance, et avant tout j'adresse mes prières au ciel afin qu'il m'aide à remplir avec dignité à la grande et belle mission que la Providence m'a imposee.[90]

On 10 May, accompanied by Brătianu, General Golescu, and Ion Ghica, he arrived in București and was sworn in as "Prince Carol I of Romania." That evening a new cabinet was formed. The provisional government had completed its job.[91]

The powers had utterly failed to prevent the Romanians from getting their foreign prince. What was the consequence of European "involvement" in the Romanian question of 1866? In the end, very little except to immobilize all the powers concerned. The Conference of Paris met to consider the problem ten times between February and June. It issued several directives, which the Romanians simply ignored. It refused to hear the Romanians' case, but prevented the Porte from taking armed (the only effective) action. Ottoman belligerence, ironically, was a key factor in providing "the wedge by which the powers were likely to come to the point of accepting the fait accompli."[92]

The powers' positions have been described above; their division was obvious. The intricacies of the diplomatic situation preceding the Austro-Prussian war of 1866 served to further confuse the picture. The inconclusive and ineffective actions of the Conference of Paris presented what Henry calls "the curious spectacle" of a European congress whose decisions were "systematically ignored."[93] When the installation of Carol failed to "stir the sluggish powers into really effective action" modern Romania was "made.[94] At the same time the Crimean system was shown to have no consistent defender left.[95]

From the Romanians' point of view, the attitudes of the powers and their statements over the next few months of 1866, were, in the final analysis, nearly irrelevant. That is to say that, while the powers' opposition to a foreign prince, the threat of a Ottoman invasion, and Russian encouragement of Moldovan separatism certainly affected and even modified the policies of the provisional government, they did not change them very significantly or divert them from their main goals. It is usually taken for granted that external pressure and influence on the policies of a small country such as Romania are crucial; yet, it can be argued that this was not the case in 1866. The explanation for this, as we have seen, lay in the indecisiveness and division of the powers, in the conviction of the Romanians that a policy of fait accompli would work, and—most importantly of all—in the Romanians' own initiatives and skill. The last point of the Divans program had been completed.

Part III:

Romania under Prince Carol, 1866-1871

"Unthread the rude eye of rebellion, and
welcome home again discarded faith."
Shakespeare, **King John**, V.iv.11

Chapter 7

The First Phase: The National Coalition

"Our wills and fates do so contrary run
that our devices still are overthrown."
Shakespeare, **Hamlet**, III.ii.223

The arrival of Carol and his installation on 10 May 1866, opened a new era in modern Romanian history. The Romanian search for a foreign prince had been terminated and a new constitutional order of the Romanian's own devising could now be established. The first step taken was the appointment by Carol of a new cabinet to replace the provisional government. His choice was to form a virtual "national coalition." The prime minister was a man who had emerged as a leader of the conservatives, Lascăr Catargiu. Besides Catargiu, who was also minister of interior, the cabinet included two other conservatives, Petre Mavrogheni, as minister of foreign affairs, and I. Gr. Ghica as minister of war. The Ion Ghica liberal group retained two of its representatives, D. A. Sturdza, as minister of works, and I. C. Cantacuzino, as minister of justice, while the representation of the Muntenian liberals was increased with Ion C. Brătianu, as minister of finance, joining C. A. Rosetti, who continued as minister of cults and education.[1] In comparison with the interim cabinet, the conservatives seemed to have the advantage.[2] The dominating presence of Brătianu and the value that the liberals placed on Rosetti's education post, however, made the cabinet on the whole a balanced one. This attempted national coalition government was one more try at conformity with the rhetoric of 11 February.[3] Once again, however, only the participants in the ouster of Cuza were perceived as part of this coalition; Cuza partisans, the Iași Fraction, and minor groupings were excluded.

What was the actual state of Romania as Carol began a reign

that was to last nearly fifty years? One of the main efforts of the provisional government had been to prepare an extensive report on the conditions facing the new regime and parliament. This report had been presented to the new chamber on 28 April, and then to Carol on 10 May.[4]

The situation described in the report was in many senses not very promising. Apart from the lamentable fiscal heritage of the Cuza era, Romania was almost totally unequipped to enter the modern world. The heart of any modern government is its bureaucracy. In Romania, owing to the backward condition of education and a certain softness of the Romanian church, the general run of functionary was deplorable—either incompetent, corrupt, or both.[5] This naturally produced an administrative chaos that in turn aggravated the financial difficulties faced by the new regime. The government, therefore, pledged to work for a complete reorganization of the bureaucracy.[6]

Rosetti's report on education reflected these concerns, as well as his nationalist liberal faith. "The church and school are the most powerful organs for the triumph of well-being, justice, truth, and particularly 'Romanianism.'"[7] The schools were functioning, however, only at a most rudimentary level, teachers were too few, and adequate facilities were non-existent. Some 3,000 rural communities had only 1,300 schools, and these were in the most wretched condition of all. The connection between poor schools and other governmental difficulties was plain. Here, again, reform was promised. Unfortunately, improvements depended on financial resources which were lacking and on trained personnel which did not exist.

The financial status of Romania in 1866 has already been discussed. It was, apart from obtaining the recognition of Carol, the key problem for the new regime once its hold on power was established. The efforts made in the financial realm by Mavrogheni and by his successors were essentially positive for the interests of the state. However, inundated by current needs, the new regime did not yet see the necessity for taking actions which would encourage the development of Romania's economy, especially in industry, nor for measures which would alleviate an agricultural decline caused by years of ill-advised state intervention.

The ministry of works, separated from the ministry of interior for the first time, had a more promising report. It was engaged in numerous projects which had favorable implications for other areas. The rail link between București and the Danube, at Giurgiu, was underway. Iron bridges were promised for key roads. The navigation of the Prut to Iași was being explored. On the negative side, all of these measures were obviously dependent on an improved financial situation.

From a military standpoint, it was the government's contention that definite progress was being made. The newly-organized civic guard seemed a success, while the reorganization of the army on a regional basis had improved the provisioning situation and morale. However, extensive funds were needed urgently for new weapons, depots, gunboats, and other military supplies, and the threat of Ottoman or Russian invasion remained real. It must be also said that the government's optimistic view of the army should be tempered by the new regime's continued attempts to justify the army's support and participation in the revolt of 11 February as well as to win the approval of those who had felt such participation was illegal.

Lastly there were the considerable problems created by crop failures in recent years, and by various plagues and epidemics that had affected both people and livestock.[8] The result, apart from the misery caused, was that the peasants lacked sufficient grain even to eat, let alone for paying taxes. These results of natural phenomena were a further barrier to recovery of financial stability and the raising of the people's morale.

In addition to these observations recognized by governmental sources, the Romanian state had other problems as well. Political development since 1862 had served only to make demagoguery and political bombast an accepted mode of action. The reading of speeches and discussions in the **Monitorul** must be one of the most tiresome activities conceivable. Almost every speaker seems impressed by his own significance and intent on working into his endless perorations all the classical, literary, and patriotic allusions he can muster. Many political figures were in fact only men of opposition, men whose forte was to oppose whatever was being presented, rather than offering solutions of their own. Here the limited access to Romanian politics showed its worst face since it not only permitted such performances, it actually fostered them.

Because the franchise remained very limited, political activity continued in the pre-party stage. The liberals around Brătianu and Rosetti once more began to take on some semblances of party organization with **Românul** as their center. However, they themselves were the first to recognize that neither they nor any other group as yet constituted a real political party.[9] The same view was shared by Dimitrie Ghica, a leader of the conservatives.[10] Some effort was made to assert that this lack of parties was a sign of progress, of real national unity. Though this was already a dubious proposition, no one was yet willing to publicly establish otherwise.[11]

On the positive side of the ledger were the achievements of the provisional government already mentioned, the Romanians' unshakable self-confidence, and the promise of the new prince. No matter how bleak the situation might appear, the Romanian leaders remained faithful to their nationalist creed and their policy of prudent daring.[12] Though the Romanian's historically demonstrated ability to bend with vicissitudes is well known, it is equally true that they have always had a flair for the kind of rewardable impudence shown by the successive acts of the 1860's. Such daring has its drawbacks, but if truly prudent it provides a powerful counter to crises of the kind that can be best met simply by having the right psychological attitude.

The new prince was the key to the future. With the selection of Carol, the Romanian leaders were hopeful that a new epoch free from hindrances of the past had opened.[13] The new ruler was the second son of Prince Karl Anton von Hohenzollern-Sigmaringen, born on 8/20 April 1839. In contrast to the ruling Prussian branch of the family, the Sigmaringen Hohenzollerns were Catholics in religion, had close ties to France, and were considered to be much more liberal. Carol's father had in fact been the Prussian prime minister during the short-lived liberal "new era" between 1858 and 1862 that preceded Bismarckian Prussia.

The connections of the Sigmaringen family to France were in large measure responsible for their reputation for advanced political views. Carol's grandfather had married Antonia Murat, niece of Napoléon I's close associate, Joachim Murat. Carol's mother, Josephine, was the daughter of Stephanie de Beauharnais, the adopted daughter of Napoléon I. The Sigmaringen Hohenzollerns were also closely linked to other French families of note including Napoléon III and Mme. Hortense Cornu. At the same time, the family had excellent marriage ties to various European royal lines. Carol's older brother, Leopold, was married to Antonia, the Infanta of Portugal; his older sister, Stephanie, was married to the king of Portugal. His younger sister, Marie, was to marry in 1867 Prince Philip of Flanders (!) and become the mother of the future King Albert of Belgium.

Owing to the culture and intelligence of both his parents, Carol received a first rate upbringing. He appears to have been, even in youth, a serious, somber and methodical person. After secondary education in Dresden, he entered military training as a sub-lieutenant in the Prussian artillery in 1857. Here his education continued under the same careful instruction from his father. When Karl Anton was named Prussian prime minister of 1858, the youthful prince had the chance to become familiar with wider ideas of contemporary German political life.

While he was thus being raised in a classic Hohenzollern mold, Carol also traveled widely, including several visits to Paris where he was warmly welcomed to the court and society of Napoléon III. In 1862, at Paris, he fell in love with Princess Anne Murat, but the possibility of marriage foundered on the stipulation that he become a French citizen and take up residence in France. In 1864, Carol saw action in the Danish war as ordnance officer of Crown Prince Friedrich of Prussia, taking part in the siege and assault of Fredericia.

The twenty-seven year old Carol seemed for the Romanians an ideal candidate for prince. He was reasonably liberal in inclination and idea, yet with a military background and a sense of hierarchy and discipline. He was a serious, hardworking young man with a balanced background and excellent connections. Though lacking in political experience, he had the benefit of first hand observation of his father's activities and the ready, perceptive advice of the former Prussian first minister. All of these qualities and experiences would be useful to and in his new realm.

And despite Carol's seemingly innate severity, which is generally stressed as his most characteristic trait, there must have existed some adventurous inclinations: to become prince of a backward and far away land was not exactly easy. The British foreign minister, Clarendon, was only half-joking when he asserted that no "Xan Gentleman Prince" would "put himself at the head of 2 millions of pauper brigands in order to become a vassal of the Sultan."[14] Disregarding the accuracy of this characterization of Romania, the point is well-taken that an overly cautious young man would not be likely to accept the Romanian throne in 1866. The fates of other European princes who had embarked on such romantic adventures, such as Othon of Greece and Maximillian of Mexico, were not exactly encouraging.[15] This spirit and determination, coupled with Carol's other qualities, were great assets for the young nation.

Carol's status as a newcomer to the Romanian political scene meant that he had little knowledge of the abilities and faults of those with whom he had to work. This dictated that he would play a cautious, learning role the first years of his reign. However, it also meant that he had no political skeletons to hide or liabilities to defend against, a point that was recognized and emphasized by Carol himself in a speech to the army on 24 May 1866. "Do not forget," he said, "that I have come to create a future and not to make a past, which I do not know nor even want to know, the base of my activities."[16] One of his first acts had been to issue a pardon to all political arrestees, including the 3 April rioters. His hands were relatively free for the future.

Carol, of course, was not ignorant of his new country's past nor did he disregard it. He recognized as Romania's two main problems the economic and financial disorder continually plaguing it and the ceaseless political infighting. These were, in his view, precisely the main causes of Cuza's fall.[17] To meet these problems he choose a coalition cabinet in the hope that true national unity might develop, and he chose the Romanian leader who impressed him the most, Ion Brătianu, for the post of finance minister. In addition to these immediate problems, Carol saw as his long range task to establish, by personal example and good administration, moral and financial rectitude in a country utterly ruined by the past.[18] The contrast between Carol and his new realm in these respects was almost complete.[19]

These tasks coincided with the need for firmly establishing his dynasty, as Carol and most politicians of the day recognized. This would be a force for producing the stability Romania needed after so many chaotic decades. Carol's installation and the prestige of his family were a guarantee for the existence of the new Romanian state; on the other hand, if he were to abdicate, Romania might again become a simple territorial pawn suitable for incorporation by one of its powerful neighbors.[20] Clearly there were pitfalls ahead and many serious problems to be faced. However, both Carol and the men of 11 February looked forward to a new order and a new day for Romania.

In establishing a firm basis for a stable new order, one of the most important tasks of the Catargiu coalition government was the ratification of a constitution. It has been said, by A.D. Xenopol, that Cuza and his supporters had focused on equality while the 1866ers emphasized individual liberty. This is born out to a degree by the constitution-building events of 1866. **Românul**, in fact, made it a point of proclaiming in 1867 that the day of 11 February was a "national reclamation from equality in favor of its sister liberty."[21] Such a thesis is, however, only partially correct. While it may have been that the Muntenian liberal contingent of the plot against Cuza favored a dramatic expansion of individual liberties, as did Ion Ghica and his friends, that can hardly be said of the conservatives. Disagreement over the extent such liberties were to be guaranteed by the new system was one of the key points of conflict between the supposed allies as they debated the new fundamental law for the country. As could be expected, the liberals and conservatives split on ideological lines in all questions involving a broad versus narrow constitution.[22] The arrival of Carol added a third point of view to the discussion since the new prince was determined that the document should give the ruler quite specific and definite powers.

The model for the new constitution, as previously noted, was the liberal Belgian instrument of 1831. The essential features of the draft[23] were the following: The United Romanian Principalities were to constitute a single state known as Romania (art.1). Romanian citizens were to have freedom of conscience, education, press, and assembly (art. 5). These liberties were further amplified by other articles. Religion was not to be a barrier to citizenship (art. 6). There were to be no distinctions whatever between citizens before the law (art.8). The death penalty, except for certain provisions of the military penal code, was abolished (art. 15). Property was to be considered inviolable except for very specifically limited reasons (art. 24). Legislative power was to be jointly exercised by the prince and the general assembly (art. 28); both were to have legislative initiative (art. 29). Interpretation of the laws was to rest with the legislature (art. 30); enforcement with the courts. Administration was the function of the prince, operating through the constitution (art. 31). A measure of decentralization was introduced by specifying that local matters were to be handled locally (art. 34); article 90 specifically endorsed "the most complete decentralization of administration." Representatives who became paid government functionaries were declared to cease exercising their mandates (art. 64). The legislature, consisting of a single chamber, was to convene automatically on 15 November of each year for a period of three months. The prince could dissolve it or call it to special session (art. 49).

The person of the prince was declared inviolable and ministerial responsibility was established by the draft version of the new constitution. All acts of the prince, therefore, had to carry a ministerial counter-signature (art. 46). The prince was to name and dismiss ministers as well as to sanction, promulgate, and apply the laws. If he vetoed a law, the chamber could re-vote it; the prince could then sanction the law or call a new assembly. If the second assembly rejected the veto, the prince had to sanction the law. The ruler could issue pardons, money, decorations and military grades, in conformity with certain laws. He named all functionaries and diplomats. He could also conclude conventions with foreign states provided the legislature ratified them. He could not intervene in the judicial process (art. 27). The electoral system was to be established separately as were the legal system, the civil and military codes.

The draft constitution represented a fairly full realization of the Muntenian liberal program. However, with the election of a more conservative assembly to consider the constitution, some of the liberals' prime aims now had to be sacrificed or compromised in order to maintain others; these are discussed below. A number of other changes represented certain stresses neglected by the drafters. Such a change was the addition of the word "indivisible" to article 1 to stress union against any separatist inclinations as might still exist. The other significant change of this nature was article 20 of the final document which emphasized that peasant lands granted by the 1864 rural law were inviolable; this was specifically added to assuage the peasants' ever-present fear that Cuza's ouster would mean a reversal of the 1864 decree.

The first major struggle came over the question of a senate. The draft had proposed a unicameral assembly. The liberals saw clearly that a senate would become the preserve of the conservatives; the conservatives argued the need for a body to take a more contemplative view and to moderate any hasty legislation. They also argued that a single chamber would allow too frequent clashes between legislature and prince; with two bodies, the princely role of mediator would come into play.

The conflict over this measure, as with most of the crucial issues, began first in the cabinet. Here Rosetti and Brătianu met with opposition from both the conservatives and the prince.[24] The debate continued among the ministers until 2 June, when Carol declared himself absolutely in favor of the bicameral system.[25] This was decisive on the final outcome. When the legislative committee to study and modify the draft constitution finally reported on 16 June, their recommendation included a senate as well as a chamber. The liberals, both the Brătianu-Rosetti and the Ghica groups, had conceded, mainly fearing that the other liberal provisions of the constitution, which they regarded are more important, would be endangered if they appeared to be too intractable.[26]

At the same time the liberals agreed to the conservatives' demand for a more restrictive collegial voting system based on income. The original draft electoral law had established three voting colleges—two rural and one urban. This system would have given the rural wealthy a third of the vote, the urban vote would have gone largely to the liberals and the remainder would have been open competition. All the votes would have been direct and all taxpayers eligible. The four college system insisted on by the conservatives effectively disenfranchised the majority of the population. Everyone paying annually less than 80 lei taxes voted indirectly; this included the entire peasantry. They could only vote for a committee which in turn would elect one deputy per district. Direct voters elected 80% of the deputies and all of the senators; the indirect voters had 20%. The election rights for the newly-created senate were open only to the upper groups of the population with incomes in excess of 3,525 lei. Senate candidates had to meet even higher income requirements of 9,400 lei or belong to a special category (generals, former ministers, and so forth).

Though the liberals had tried to establish a wider franchise, they had been reluctant to endorse universal suffrage, since that would lead to a swamping of "intelligence" by mere "numbers."[27] They were thus unable on principle to oppose conservative efforts to extend the Prussian-style college system. The result of the new law was to give real political participation to about 20,000 out of a population of 5 million.[28]

These concessions by the liberals were severe blows to their hopes. Nevertheless, the liberal civil rights of the draft constitution, which were so dear to Rosetti and his colleagues, were preserved. And in face of an obvious conservative edge in the newly elected assembly, they felt lucky, even if betrayed. **Românul**, naturally, fulminated against the changes,[29] but in the end the Muntenian group had to accept the decision of the majority. They also wanted to avoid driving Carol over to the conservatives' side by appearing too radical or too oppositionist.

The draft proposal and the assembly revisions were placed in discussion on 18 June. The debate immediately focused on article 6 of the draft (article 4 of the modification). The original had stated that "Religion can no longer be an obstacle to citizenship." The revision was more cautious; it added "as regards the Jews, a special law will regulate their gradual admission to citizenship."

The government's support of this measure was due to the liberals' interest in promoting civil liberties. The proclamations of 1848 had declared for allowing Jewish citizenship.[30] Such a provision was apart of the liberals' ideology while the conservatives of the coalition saw no reason to oppose it.[31] A second reason for maintaining the clause once public discontent began to mount was the mission of Adolphe Crémieux. The head of the Paris-based Alliance Israélite arrived from Constantinople on 2 June. He was hailed by **Românul** as a stout friend of Romania and was received in secret meetings by the government and deputies. As a powerful French political and financial figure, Crémieux's views carried considerable weight with Romania's leaders. His offer was simple: If the constitution gave political rights to his co-religionists, Crémieux would assure the procuring of a 25 million franc loan at reasonable interest for the struggling state.[32]

The reaction of many Moldovans as well as of several anti-governmental agitators in București, led by Cezar Bolliac and his newspaper **Trompetta Carpaților**, was, as they put it, "an alarm, a fright of the most terrible kind."[33] Violent debate ensued in the chamber with the upper hand clearly going to anti-Semitic sentiment. There was a growing consensus that the proposal be removed from the new constitution. At the height of this discussion, a mob of București rabble, led by Bolliac, surrounded the parliament building, actually drowning out the ongoing debate. The government's spokesman, Ion Brătianu, finally arose to announce, "Gentlemen, the government declares that it withdraws the article regarding the Jews." Prolonged applause followed.[34] Debate continued briefly until the noise of the mob forced the session to adjourn. The crowd then headed back to the center of the city and razed a recently completed synagogue. Guard troops finally dispersed the throng; the police, wrote one observer, were not very active.[35]

Needless to say, this sequence of events did not create a very favorable impression outside of Romania. Carol, who had been out of the capital, rushed back to București. He offered 70,500 lei of his own funds for the reconstruction of the synagogue. Order was apparently restored. The government's retreat allowed the offending item to be removed from the constitution, and the final proposal (art. 7) read "only foreigners of the Christian faith can gain naturalization."[36] For the first time the "Jewish question" had reached major political proportions in Romania. Because of the circumstances, the matter faded away at this point. Rosetti and Brătianu did not feel strong enough to fight the anti-Semites; there is some question whether they even really wanted to. Foreign individuals and groups who might have taken a greater interest in these events did not do so because they had their attention diverted by the Austro-Prussian war.[37] In 1867, the matter again became a central issue, domestically and diplomatically; it will be discussed in greater detail at that time.[38]

Another retreat by the liberals concerned the matter of the princely veto. The draft proposal gave the ruler only a suspensive veto; Carol again strove "with all insistence for an absolute veto."[39] Strenuous debate in the cabinet resulted once more in liberal concessions. When the amendment on this measure came, Ion Brătianu spoke in favor of it for the government, and Carol was given the unrestricted right to refuse legislation. This was an important gain in power for the executive branch.

Despite these defeats, the liberals believed that the new constitution was an instrument they could work and live with. Public and private liberties were defended by the new act.[40]

Press restrictions were completely abolished; though this law was modified in the 1870's and 1880's, it was seen even in the twentieth century as "too liberal."[41] The conservatives also agreed to let the most representative body, the chamber, be responsible for the budget and other financial legislation. **Românul**, though regretting the institution of a senate, hailed the new constitution in its final form as "one of the most liberal in Europe."[42]

Indeed, the Romanians had much to be proud of in the new document and the system it tried to establish. It provided for a relatively more open society that those of its neighbors. It was the product of compromise, but not unilateral concessions. In fact, despite the setbacks the liberals had suffered in its adoption, the constitution of 1866 never was an obstacle to them. As Ion Brătianu noted in 1869, the conservatives were the ones who complained of the act, not the liberals.[43] And by comparison with Russia, Austria, and Turkey, the tiny new state was far advanced on the road of constitutional government. This, too, was a triumph for the liberals: the adoption of a liberal constitution was virtual defiance of her autocratic neighbors. Furthermore, the instrument remained, with slight modifications, the basic law of the land until the turbulent aftermath of World War I made it obsolete.

However, the problem of the constitution of 1866 was not that the conservatives gained too much[44] or that it was too liberal.[45] Rather the problem was simply that it is "not enough to pass enlightened laws; it remained to enforce them and to imbue public opinion and the governing class with respect for the principles they embodied."[46] For example, though the separation of powers principle was upheld in the act, it was also true that the administration had fairly wide powers whose abuse could undermine the whole document. Particularly crucial to this was establishment of a centrally-controlled French-style bureaucratic regime of prefects, sub-prefects, and mayors. These jobs were filled, directly and indirectly, by the ministry of interior in București and gave the government enormous leverage over most political matters including elections. There was, however, the hope that "honest" traditions could be established to prevent these abuses.

On the other hand, the basic compatibility of strong, honest civic traditions and a centralized bureaucracy might be questioned. "Power tends to corrupt," Lord Acton has taught us, and it is difficult to see how the bureaucratic mentality can avoid undermining the kind of initiative and respect for rule of law that are part of building successful (i.e., ethical) political cultures. Centralization in Romania was a result of four factors: the influence of the French model, a fear of incipient separatism, the growing 19th century prejudice toward social engineering and holistic theories of society, and the desire for control of the political environment. D. P. Marțian wrote in 1861, in a plea for more administrative decentralization: "It is fatal that Romanian legislators don't have before them the examples of other peoples than France. In truth, from this country we can learn much but not, however, all we need."[47] Though in the epoch under consideration, this problem was not yet of the first magnitude, it is in this era that the Romanian centralist tradition develops and grows.

The constitutional debates had placed great strain on the coalition. However, Rosetti was optimistic. While he admitted differences in detail, he still believed that the coalition was intact behind Carol. The fact that the new law was voted unanimously by the chamber on 29 June after a month of acrimonious debate was a point in his favor. Both the liberals and conservatives seemed basically satisfied with their efforts; only time would tell if they had succeeded. The powers conferred on the prince by the constitution were great, but both parties believed that they could win Carol to their respective points of view and were not troubled by this. Carol, on his part, was gratified by the changes he had been able to make in the draft, but he was not completely satisfied. A letter from his aide, Werner, to Karl Anton suggested that a "more absolutist regime" would have been more suitable.[48] This, too, remained to be seen.

As with the previous cabinet, finances were a preoccupation. The selection of Ion Brătianu for the post of finance minister showed Carol's desire for an energetic resolution of the fiscal problems besetting his new realm. The 11 million lei loan launched in February had produced only 6.2 million thus far, and all of the financial problems were still current. Brătianu and Carol were also deeply concerned to be able to finance a rapid expansion of the army to meet a possible Ottoman threat.

The solution that Brătianu seized upon was to propose the issuance of 12 million lei worth of unconvertible paper currency in a bill of 26 May. The measure met with an immediate uproar on all fronts, and Brătianu was forced to withdraw the measure. His subsequent resignation was refused by Carol. The measure would probably have only worsened the monetary situation; opposition to it, however, was in good part politically motivated.[49] A major ministerial crisis had been survived.

In place of the currency scheme, various money-saving measures were adopted, including pension reductions, higher import duties, and the sale of various small state properties. These measures were not sufficient and negotiations were begun abroad for a new foreign loan. Since Napoléon III had tied his support of such a loan to the recognition of Carol by Turkey, these negotiations were protracted.

External pressures also had their impact. The arrival of Carol had brought to its highest point the threat of Turkish intervention. Wild reports of Turkish troop crossings of the Danube poured into București.[50] Most alarming were the reports of Romania's agent in Constantinople, Al. G. Golescu. On 2 May, he telegraphed that the British, Russian, and Austrian ambassadors were pressing the Porte to cross the Danube.[51] On 4 May, Golescu reported that "the Ottoman Porte had decided to cross the Danube and send troops to Tulcea."[52] The government had to take energetic, though probably not very efficacious, steps to bolster Romanian defenses.

Carol was discovering that the Romanian military establishment was in deplorable condition at this time, despite the optimism of the April governmental report.[53] The regular army had been divided over Cuza's ouster. Its officer corps was still in disarray. The reorganization of the army into four divisions on a territorial basis had improved the material conditions, but was disorienting. The effective strength of the Romanian army was less than 20,000. Additional levies brought the strength of all forces to about 40,000 as of 19 March 1866.[54] This total was boosted to 45,500 by June.[55] To these numbers could be added the untried and unpredictable mass belonging to the newly created "civic guard."

The poorly-trained and poorly-paid grăniceri battalions were ordered in May to take up positions along the Danube. This proved to be a serious error. Poor morale, conflicting rumors, general dissatisfaction, and a justified belief that the new posting away from their homes was illegal spread throughout the ranks of the grăniceri, and refusals to march soon became outright rebellion.[56] Though the seriousness of this uncoordinated mutiny can be exaggerated,[57] it was nevertheless a real problem for the Catargiu government. Much of May was consumed by careful maneuvers on the part of the regular army and civil authorities to disarm and disband the rebellious grăniceri before blood was shed. Meanwhile, the regime could only hope that the Ottoman threats would remain bluster. Had an invasion taken place during the summer of 1866, the minuscule Romanian forces would have been helpless. By the end of May, the grăniceri were at last successfully dispersed, to the considerable relief of București.[58]

Meanwhile, Carol had to face certain difficulties with the regular army. The government had tried unsuccessfully to mollify those officers who regarded the actions of the military men involved in the ouster of Cuza as oath violating. These officers now forwarded to Carol a protest, asking the dismissal of those who had participated in the revolt of 11 February. Carol was in a difficult position since to endorse participation by officers in politics in violation of their oaths was neither a good precedent nor acceptable to his Hohenzollern discipline. On the other hand, the government and the majority of politicians were men of 11 February. Without them, Carol wouldn't even be there. Carol's response was careful and clever: rejecting what he saw as an attempt to pressure him, the prince asserted the "absolute submission" of soldiers to their oaths to him personally. At the same time, he assured the officers that he had not come to dwell on the past.[59] His firm bearing and tact laid this problem to rest.[60]

These problems, coupled with those of finances, morale, poor training, and the disorganization caused by 11 February rendered Romania's military rather shaky. Fortunately the Ottoman danger never materialized. France, was now exerting considerable influence on the Porte to abandon the idea of invasion and to take up direct negotiations with the Romanians.[61] At the end of May, it was reported that Turkey had agreed to call off preparations for an armed occupation.[62] And on 4 June, Ion Ghica was sent to begin serious direct negotiations with the Porte.[63] When Napoléon III officially received the Romanian agent Bălăceanu in an audience on 21 June, it was generally agreed that France had recognized the new state of affairs in Romania. The Porte had to follow suit. These negotiations were to drag on for several more months, but the danger of Ottoman invasion was over. On 23 June, the masthead of the **Monitorul** carried for the first time the subtitle **Official Journal of Romania** instead of **Official Journal of the United Romanian Principalities**.

Almost immediately the liberal members of the government seemed to get involved in exactly those "radical" activities which the neighboring powers had feared they would. Thus in July, the Hungarian revolutionary, General Türr, secretly visited Prince Carol in București, a meeting arranged by C. A. Rosetti. Later that same month, another Hungarian general, Eber, arrived in București for further discussions with the new Romanian prince. Their purpose was to prepare a possible rising against Austria in conjunction with Prussian aid.[64] Meanwhile, considerable aid and comfort was being given by the liberals to Bulgarian exiles stationed in Romanian territory.[65]

As Carol began his reign, the specter of separation was still real despite the easy suppression of the April revolt in Iași. The citizens of the former Moldovan capital had many legitimate grievances. The new ministry, led by Moldovans, introduced therefore, a sizeable list of measures designed to placate the populace of Iaşi and cut what ground remained out from under separatist intriguers.[66] Considerable administrative decentralization was promised, a relocation of the Court of Cassation [Appeals Court] to Iaşi was pledged, hundreds of thousands of lei worth of transportation improvements were to be allocated for Iaşi, and other fiscal amelioration was to take place. Such promises of aid were doomed in existing financial circumstances. In the end, the Iaşi aid package was the only measure rejected by the parliament. Despite full support by the ministry, the chamber had refused to endorse the move of the appeals court on the grounds that it would cause considerable confusion and delay in legal transactions.[67] In a more subtle vein, there was the fear that many Bucureşti anti-Semites had of having the court in Iaşi because of its large Jewish population.[68]

Catargiu promptly tendered his resignation when the chamber rejected the court transfer, but again Carol supported his ministry and refused the resignation. The bill was re-submitted and again defeated. Before the issue could become the center of a new clash, the chamber was dissolved on 6 July.[69] The chamber had in the meanwhile passed the budget (3 July) and the new electoral law (4 July). Its tasks, except for the Iaşi matter, were completed. Because of the hot weather and the deterioration of debate, the chamber had been on the verge of dissolving itself anyway.[70] Catargiu was determined to see the Iaşi issue through, as he assured the mayor of Iaşi,[71] and therefore a new chamber was necessary. But before he could hold new elections, Catargiu's cabinet itself fell as well.

The "national coalition" had survived a number of crises. It had achieved its primary goals of adopting the new constitution, budget, and electoral law. However, the internal strains on the cabinet proved too great, especially with an electoral campaign looming. When the conservative and the Muntenian factions found that they could no longer cooperate, Carol accepted the resignation of the entire cabinet on 13 July and replaced it with a new Ion Ghica ministry.

Chapter 8

The Second Phase: Non-Party Government

"Whate'er you think, good words,
I think, were best."
Shakespeare, **King John**, IX.iii.28

The restoration of Ion Ghica to power was not exactly a surprise. As early as 22 June, Carol had been sending overtures to him through D. A. Sturdza.[1] Ghica, who was in Constantinople trying to win Carol's recognition from the Sultan, was told that he represented the only real hope for stability due to inter-factional dispute. "I do not see any other way than your arrival and entry into the government. This is also the frank advice of Brătianu and Rosetti," wrote Sturdza. Carol hoped that negotiations with the Porte would soon be advanced enough that others could complete them.

By 15 July, the dealings in Constantinople were indeed such that Ghica could return to București and become prime minister once more. As head of the government, he was in fact now in a better position to conclude this important transaction, one which would place the final seal of success on the plot of 1866. At the same time, Ghica's political neutrality was seen by Carol as a possible guarantee that the first elections under the new system would be precedent-setting for honesty and openness.

The new cabinet was largely comprised of Ghica's associates. There was a scattering of moderate conservatives and four of the ministers were holdovers. The absence of any Muntenian liberals raised a few eyebrows, but Rosetti, for one, thought this unimportant. In his view, the second Ghica cabinet was a continuation of the act of 11 February. There was still no left or right in Romania, he asserted, only those who backed the new constitution and its application versus those who wanted "to return to that which was."² This benign state of affairs would not last long.

The new Ghica cabinet began under the most favorable augurs yet.³ The Romanians had their prince, a new constitution, and considerable internal unity. They had yet to achieve Ottoman approval, but the threat of invasion was gone. As Ghica, himself, saw it, Romanian development had now moved into its first really normal phase, a period in which they could "sustain the edifice we have built."⁴ The need now, he told his subordinates, was to "accustom yourselves to considering the constitution of 1866 as our political gospel and to uphold its prescription unshakeably." By ceasing to perpetuate the lamentable habits of the past, Romanians could build an orderly, lawful, and free society. This, in turn, would produce progress and civilization. At the same time, Ghica promised, his intention was to curtail the pervasive centralism which weighed all and sundry down.

The peaceful note on which the new Ghica ministry opened seemed re-inforced by the season. The heat of summer had led to the usual exodus from București for mellower climes and the usual lethargy of July followed. However, on 19 July, the prefect of police reported to Ghica the news that a group of forty-seven men had met to form a new club called the "Friends of the Constitution."⁵ The group, he said, described itself as patriotic and "liberal." It was, in fact, simply a front for the Brătianu-Rosetti faction. Despite the latter's disclaimers that no such factions existed, it became clear that this new group was intended to be the Muntenian liberals' vehicle in the upcoming elections. At the beginning of August, the new society elected Gen. Nicolae Golescu as president, with C.A. Rosetti and Dumitru Brătianu as vice-presidents. Though ostensibly open to all who supported the constitution, membership was by election only and seemed strangely limited in its scope.⁶ The ploy became more obvious when **Românul** hailed the new group as the champions of constitutionalism, liberty, and public morality and implied that to oppose the society was to oppose all of these fine ideals. Indeed, to oppose it was to be very nearly traitorous.⁷ This device initially was successful in muting criticism both by the conservatives and by the government.

That the Muntenians were now readying themselves to take power is clear from a letter sent by Rosetti to a French friend on 8 August. Significant obstacles remained in the liberals' path, he wrote, but their political situation was excellent, and they had great influence over Carol. The push was being timed for "the coming spring. I believe that we will conquer..."[8] The liberals were giving every sign of beginning to enter the organizational stage of party development.

For the time being, it was the Muntenians' aim to collaborate with the Ghica ministry, at least until after the first elections were over. These were announced for fall, but the date was not yet fixed. Attention had been diverted by Carol's long-awaited trip to Moldova. On 10 August, the prince left București to visit for the first time the other half of his realm; he was to be gone until the 24th. The trip had many purposes. Carol wanted, first of all, to see and be seen in Moldova. He wanted to generate what popular support his very presence might create, while he was getting a first hand view of the problems and concerns of an area already feeling left behind by the shifting of the capital to București. There is no doubt that Moldova was in a dour mood, a mood scarcely improved by cholera and famine, and by restiveness about the steady influx of Galician Jews into the region.[9] In short, there was in Moldova an "absolute lack...of faith in the future."[10] This, Carol could see, did not bode well for his rule. He also was appalled by the lack of bridges and by the poor conditions in general. It was then that he envisioned for the first time the creation of a railroad network to tie his country together and to raise the levels of existence.[11]

The prince's trip was a success. Carol was enthusiastically received, especially in Iași. He was seen as a practical and sensible man who understood his mission and his duty.[12] He reiterated the promises of the various post-11 February governments to do all possible to restore Iași to the pride of its place as the second city of Romania and succeeded in cutting most of the ground out from under separatist elements.[13] At the same time, his own perceptions of the task that lay before him had been broadened and deepened considerably.

Meanwhile, the Muntenian "Friends of the Constitution" effort sparked a conservative counter attack in August. The conservatives' main journalistic vehicle, **Desbaterile**, had appeared more and more sporadically in the summer and finally ceased publication entirely in August. On 13 August, however, a letter appeared in **Românul** announcing the formation of a new "central election committee" to coordinate activities for the upcoming election.[14] Its ostensible purpose was "to arrive at a common understanding in all districts," and all were freely invited to join in the effort. The signers happened to all be conservatives: Lascăr Catargiu, G. Costa-foru, Dimitrie Ghica, Aristide Pascal, M.C. Epureanu, C. N. Brăiloiu, and A. Știrbey. The liberals, recalling the result of a similar committee in the elections of April 1866, made no rush to join the new group. Shortly after that, the signers of the 13 August letter appeared as the directors of a new political journal which surfaced on 18 August, called **Ordinea (Order)**. Their program was summarized by the title of their journal. With the formation of these two groups, one under the guise of defending the constitution, and the other under the pretense of coordinating the electoral efforts in order to preserve order, the coalition of February 1866, had come to a virtual end.[15]

Furious jockeying for position now began on all fronts. The election dates had not yet been set, but the all-important compilation of voter lists was in progress, a key activity that made the actual vote itself later on less important and certainly less suspenseful. Both liberals and conservatives quickly became quite agitated over what they felt were registration abuses on the part of the Ghica government.[16] Both Ghica and Carol were, however, apparently making a sincere effort to conduct an honest election and declarations of stiff penalties for violations were repeatedly carried in the **Monitorul**.

The violence of the campaigning put considerable stress on all concerned. Carol, brought by the coalition to power, wanted to avoid offending any of its factions. (He would eventually recognize the impossibility of this.) The Brătianu-Rosetti group, though they believed both that their position was stabilizing and that Carol was leaning their way, still felt rather vulnerable. The election was crucial to their future plans, a litmus test of how they might fare under the new system.[17] The conservatives, somewhat outmaneuvered at the palace and highly suspicious of the professed neutrality of the Ghica government, were suffering from the essentially reactive nature of their politics. Their approach allowed their opponents to take the initiative.

At the same time, the prime minister, Ion Ghica, who for once was playing above board, was irritated by the criticisms being made of his conduct. He was especially miffed by the attacks of **Românul** and by Brătianu's attempts to manipulate the prince.[18] Finally, there was concern over the strength of non-coalition elements, something that remained an unknown. The possibility that too much conflict among the February coalition would aid the opposition such as the Iaşi Fraction, the Cuzists, and others acted to temper confrontation.

There were other problems for Carol and his government. The cholera epidemic was reaching ever more serious proportions. As an example, the judeţ of Bacău, with a population of 185,000, reported between May and September, 1866, a total of 4,847 people afflicted and 3,308 deaths due to cholera.[19] Additional efforts had to be made to cope with the concurrent famine. In July, all export of foodstuffs was prohibited, prices on certain goods raised, distilling was banned, and massive relief programs launched. The problem was a major pre-occupation of the government throughout the remainder of 1866, filling the pages of the **Monitorul** with notices, appeals, and discussion.

Due in part to the epidemic and to the famine, the fiscal situation of Romania continued to remain perilous.[20] To make these matters worse, France was now making its support for a loan contingent on official Ottoman recognition of Carol.[21] Gaining official sanction of Carol by the Porte, one of the main tasks of the Ghica government, thus became even more critical. The diplomatic aspects of this question, discussed by Riker and others, are outside the scope of this study; its impact on domestic developments is, however, relevant. The most important effect of nonrecognition was to bring the progress begun with the revolt of 11 February nearly to a standstill by the fall of 1866. Not only were a number of important financial matters dependent on it; other activities, such as the scheduling of the elections, were being delayed as a result. Worse, the foes of 11 February were beginning to capitalize on the situation.

The negotiations, begun by Ion Ghica in June, had bogged down over the place of Romania in the Ottoman empire. The Porte wanted it plainly stated that Romania was "an integral part" of the empire. The Romanians asserted that this was an unwarranted usurpation by the Sultan since the Principalities under the terms of the medieval capitulations had never been completely annexed into the Empire. Carol, furthermore, was unwilling to accept any restrictions on his own position except for a purely ceremonial recognition of Ottoman suzerainty.

However, the tedious months of negotiations finally came to an end at the beginning of October when the Porte agreed that recognition and the Romanian relationship to the Empire would continue within the context of "limits fixed by the capitulations and the Treaty of Paris." An exchange of letters on the key issues by Carol and the Porte, rather than an actual treaty, codified the arrangements and the matter was resolved. On 5 October, Carol announced that elections would be held 29 October-10 November. On 9 October, he left for Constantinople to be invested by the Sultan. The twelve-day trip was eminently successful;[22] the last act of the events begun by 11 February was over.

The electoral campaign of the fall of 1866 was both one of the freest and most violent in Romanian history. The Ghica government was true to its (and Carol's) expressed aim of an open, "un-managed" election.[23] Ironically, the repeated publicity given to the necessity for free elections was seen in some quarters as a governmental assist to the liberals.[24] Voting proceeded on the collegial system described earlier which gave the propertied and educated classes a guaranteed 80 per cent of the mandates. Despite some reported illegalities by the liberals in urban areas, and despite an atmosphere of near "civil war"[25] generally, the election results seem to have been a reasonable reflection of the sentiments of the limited Romanian voting public.[26] The results were a huge disappointment and anticlimax for everyone, from the prince on down. The major consequence of this unusual free election was that no group gained a substantial position in the new legislature. Liberals, which included the Brătianu-Rosetti group, the Ghica group, and the Fraction, garnered one-third of the seats; conservatives had won another third; and a third had gone to various non-coalition groups and people: the Cuzists, separatists, and a host of others.[27] The prognosis for anything but chaos in the assembly was not good.

Indeed, this is was the basis for an appeal to the prince by the Muntenian liberals. On 13 November, with the opening of parliament just two days away, Ion Brătianu asked for an audience with Carol.[28] His primary point was that the country would be un-governable with such a fragmented parliament, especially one that contained so many elements hostile to the regime. Just what Brătianu had in mind is unclear; Carol, however, insisted that the new parliament must govern. The following evening, the Brătianu-Rosetti group met and, under Brătianu's urging, agreed to support the Ghica government and to try to make the system work.[29]

The chambers opened on 15 November. Carol gave a rousing [for him] exhortation to action, to measures of economy, and to the forgetting of petty disputation.[30] He pointed out the successes of the last six months: a new constitution had been laid as a base, diplomatic recognition of the prince had been gained, and honest elections had been carried out. Now it was time to get to work on other major issues. Many of the tasks initially addressed under the new prince had yet to be completed, especially those dealing with finances, honest administration, and bureaucratic re-organization.

The parliament responded to this urgent agenda by spending a month discussing and verifying elections. Attempts to oust Kogălniceanu and Rosetti-Rosnovanu on various pretexts failed.

Debate became "more and more outrageous, discussions more passionate and more envenomed than ever,"[31] over matters of less and less import. Only in December did this useless bickering subside. Meanwhile, the budget and other matters stagnated.[32]

New factions seemed to be forming in the parliament on a daily basis. The deputies from Moldova fell into at least four distinct groups: the separatists under N. Rosetti-Rosnovanu; the conservatives under Gr. Sturdza; the Cuzists under Mihail Kogălniceanu; and the Fraction under Nicolae Ionescu. The Muntenian contingent was split into Brătianu-Rosetti liberals; Ion Ghica liberals; conservatives under Dimitrie Ghica; a new conservative group under G. Costa-Foru; and half-a-dozen more factions under Cezar Bolliac and others. The key point to notice is that personalities, not ideas, were still the basis for these groups.[33] Intense infighting and much secret negotiating took place.[34]

While the chambers were wasting time, the Ghica government found itself in other difficulties. Its agent in Paris, Ion Bălăceanu, had been empowered in July to seek a loan abroad to help alleviate the pressing financial needs. Several agreements proposed by Bălăceanu were rejected as too costly. In October, while Carol was in Turkey, Bălăceanu wired a new proposal. When the government did not respond, he closed the deal himself on the tenuous basis of his earlier mandate.[35] The loan, from the Oppenheim group, was for 18,800,000 francs. The interest, to be paid over twenty-three years, amounted to more than 13 million francs, an outrageous amount. Worse, the loan would serve only to cover deficits; it provided no new funds. The cabinet finally decided at the end of October that they had no choice but to accept the loan or see Romania's credit disappear completely.[36] The chamber, in turn, after attacking the government from all sides, voted the agreement because it, too, could hardly do otherwise.

The position of the Ghica government was seriously weakened as a result. Ghica, despairing and feeling undermined by the blunder of his close associate Bălăceanu, offered to resign. Carol's response was to meet with Ion Brătianu on 10 December to ask if he could form a new government;[37] two weeks later he had to admit that he could not.[38] In the interim, Brătianu told Carol that the government was holding itself too rigidly within the constitutional formula.[39] Again it is unclear just what alternatives Brătianu had to suggest. The Ghica government remained in office, but only because a replacement could not be found.[40]

The situation as 1867 opened was, therefore, as bleak as it had been promising just three months earlier: political strife was general, there was no budget, the Ghica ministry was shaky, and, worse yet, Moldova was again restive. Uncertainty was the order of the day. It seemed as if little real change had occurred since the supposedly bad, old days of Cuza.[41] Worse still, France was beginning to show dissatisfaction with its Southeast European protégé.

The decisive and somewhat astonishing triumph of Prussia over Austria in the summer of 1866 had forced a drastic re-evaluation of French policy. No longer was Napoléon III the sole arbiter of Europe and no longer could he afford quixotic support for various national movements. In addition, Paris became increasingly cooler towards Romania as the notion that Carol was "Prussianizing" his country began to circulate. Mme. Cornu, well aware of the possibility that Prussia might try to take advantage of its natural ties to Carol, was at some pains to keep the young prince aware of his obligations to France. She was a constant correspondent and advisor; she actively sought a suitable consort for the as-yet unmarried prince; and she installed the young scholar Émile Picot as Carol's private French secretary. It is Picot's correspondence with Cornu and others that provides us with considerable insight into Carol's early months in Romania.[42] The picture that emerges at this time is that Carol was very eager to maintain good relations with France, both formal and informal, and that he was not particularly eager to increase the influence in Romania of his northern German cousins.

There was, however, one area in which Prussian influence was certain: the army. Here, Picot admitted, the efforts of the

French military mission to Romania had proven generally ineffective. Though they had been working with the Romanians since virtually the beginning of Cuza's reign, the army was simply a "lamentable spectacle...Impossible to imagine anything so sad."[43] The French consul in București, Avril, concurred with this view. His conclusion was that the best means of strengthening the Romanian army would be a complete phasing out of the mission.[44]

Carol was astute enough to see that a withdrawal of the French mission would have unfortunate repercussions. On the other hand, he had seen enough to know that a change was essential. And, as a man thoroughly trained in the Prussian system and convinced of its superiority, he believed that its gradual introduction into Romania was the best course. The policy he adopted, therefore, was to continue to ask for French officers, while at the same time bringing in Prussian military men to advise. This process gradually accelerated after 1867. The net impact on France, despite the caution and justifiability of Carol's actions, was unfavorable and Carol's relationship with Napoléon III began to sour.[45]

In the financial realm, some steps forward were, at last, being taken. Even though the budget proposed by the Ghica government failed to pass and even though Romania had been forced to accept the onerous Oppenheim loan agreement, the activities of the minister of finance, Petre Mavrogheni, receive high marks.[46] Presiding over the fiscal affairs of Romania from February 1866 to February 1867 (except for May-July 1866), he had had time to study carefully what was needed to revive the country's treasury. In addition to the reorganization of finances proposed during the first Ion Ghica ministry, Mavrogheni now proposed further fiscal reorganization, more strenuous efforts to balance income and expenditures, the creation of new sources of state income, and the inauguration of an independent monetary system. The budget proposal, actually voted only after Mavrogheni left office, was greatly successful from the regime's point of view, producing a surplus of 4.6 million lei. The re-shuffling of the finance ministry (also a project carried out by his successors) was effective in introducing control and accountability into the system. Finally, the monetary law proposed by Mavrogheni became the law passed in April 1867, under the liberal regime discussed below. Its basic outlines were due to his work and the credit for the measure belongs to him.

On 15 January 1867, Carol made a second Moldovan trip to counter increasing separatist agitation. Despite the fact that none of the promises made in 1866 had yet been fulfilled, except to transfer the military school (these had included, among other items, the transfer of the appeals court to Iaşi and huge financial investments in civic and industrial improvements), Carol's welcome was as enthusiastic as the first time. His energetic inspection of facilities and forces in Iaşi impressed the populace with his seriousness and good intentions.[47] The question of moving the Court of Cassation was again discussed and Carol re-affirmed his support for Iaşi's request by promising that the matter would be taken up by parliament in March. Carol was anxious to defuse the issue of Iaşi's grievances because it was all the argument that remained for the separatists.[48] The prince's awareness and attention to the problem was, however, enough to partially disarm the last vestiges of opposition. Separatism by 1867 had become a very weak issue because of Carol.[49]

On 30 January, the Brătianu-Rosetti front, "The Friends of the Constitution" held a huge rally. The keynote speech was delivered by Ion Brătianu; it was a blistering attack on the Ghica government.[50] The thrust of Brătianu's speech was that the country needed active, new leadership; the implication was that only his group could muster that leadership. Behind Brătianu's speech was a strategy which he and Rosetti hoped would create the basis for cooperation between all of the liberal factions and lead eventually to the formation of Romania's first real political party.

Clearly the Muntenians were beginning the push that Rosetti had promised in the autumn. This fact was recognized by the Ghica government when its police surveillance reported meetings between Brătianu, Rosetti and others with the Moldovan/Cuzist liberal leader, Mihail Kogălniceanu.[51] The liberals had finally recognized that their disunity only left the field open to the conservatives.[52] The negotiations involved over fifty deputies from the Muntenian, Kogălniceanu, and "independent Fraction" groups and culminated in a program written by Brătianu, Kogălniceanu, Nicolae Ionescu, and Gheorghe Vernescu, and edited by Rosetti.[53] Between 6 and 14 February, Kogălniceanu, Ion Brătianu, and Dumitru Brătianu held long conversations with Prince Carol.[54]

By 21 February, the new coalition felt strong enough to issue its manifesto and to spearhead a vote of no confidence against the Ghica ministry. In the end, the Fraction did not adhere to the program, probably because of its anti-Kogălniceanu sentiment. However, the liberal group was able to muster a 59-56 no confidence vote against the Ghica cabinet. The public motives for the vote were varied--mishandling of the loan, lack of a governmental majority in parliament, and so forth. The political motives were clear; the liberals believed that only they could get the country on the path to progress and growth. In short, they should have the power not Ghica or the conservatives.

The program,[55] besides the already-familiar and hackneyed appeals for honest functionaries and fiscal reform, contained two significant items which undoubtedly attracted Carol's interest. These were: 1) a stress on rapid development of Romania's military capacities and, 2) and an emphasis on the defense "in any circumstances" of the Romanian nationality. This latter point was amplified to say that while "the rights and interests of neighboring states; must be respected, Romania must reach a position where it "can make foreign states respect the rights and interests of Romania." The direct allusion was to Transilvania and the treatment of the Romanian population there by the Habsburg regime.[56]

The liberals' program, which was attractive to Carol, and their newly-found unity in the chamber were sufficient to elevate them into the power which they sought. The second Ghica ministry was over. Four days before his ouster, the prime minister had written in disgust about his current tenure to his ally Al. G. Golescu.[57] Facing "15 or 20 parties" in the chamber, work was impossible. Thirty-two days had been wasted on the

verification of elections; another sixty on the budget. All the
parties were trying to "prove to the Prince that they are loyal
and devoted" while prophesying revolution if Carol did not install
them in office immediately. "I swear to you that I want to
resign..." he concluded gloomily. "Our country has become difficult for honest men."

Ghica's fall was the signal for intensive negotiations for a new
cabinet. These proceedings dragged on until 27 February. The
conservatives in the assembly were unwilling to allow a
straightforward liberal cabinet under Ştefan Golescu, but Ion
Brătianu didn't think a purely liberal cabinet could succeed
anyway.[58] The prince, for his part, insisted on the inclusion of
Ion Brătianu in whatever new ministry was formed;[59] this was
unacceptable to most conservatives.[60] In the end, Constantin
Creţulescu, a moderate conservative [and brother of Cuza's
oft-times prime minister Nicolae Kretzulescu], was prevailed upon
to form a new government with Brătianu. On 1 March, the
Creţulescu ministry took office.

Chapter 9

The Third Phase: Liberalism in Power

"A good plot, good friends, and full of expectation;
an excellent plot, very good friends."
Shakespeare, **King Henry IV, Part I**, II.iii.21

The appointment of the Constantin Crețulescu cabinet on 1 March 1867, represented, despite the moderate conservative character of the new prime minister, a virtual takeover by the Muntenian liberal group. Ion C. Brătianu assumed direction of the crucial ministry of interior; his brother Dumitru became minister of cults and education and, interim, public works; their close ally Ștefan Golescu was named foreign minister. The two remaining posts went to Moldovans friendly to the group; Al. Văsescu became finance minister and Gen. Th. Gherghel, the minister of war.

Crețulescu, Golescu, and Văsescu were basically front men for Ion Brătianu. He was, in Carol's words, "the heart of the ministry."[1] For the first time, the veteran conspirator, diplomat, and political maneuverer had real control of Romania's destiny. What was more, he had the complete cooperation and confidence of Prince Carol, in spite of the unfavorable impression made abroad by the naming of a liberal cabinet. And beside Brătianu stood C. A. Rosetti, his lifelong friend, colleague, and alter-ego; director of the country's leading newspaper, **Românul**; and chief ideologue and organizer of the Muntenian liberals.[2] The ascension to power of Brătianu and Rosetti was a potential turning point for Romanian political development. The Muntenian liberals[3] had begun to form a coherent political community of interests. The question now was whether or not they would be able to expand beyond being just a pressure or interest group.[4] The new cabinet certainly tackled its mission in a way that indicated a search for a broader organizational and ideological basis. It took its inspiration from the 21 February manifesto, geared itself toward certain clear political goals, and abandoned support for the imaginary non-partisan anti-Cuza coalition.[5] The unifying theme of their program was to "defend and advance the Romanian nationality." In this, they were nationalists first and liberals second. This meant that for them the union of 1859 was merely a prelude to the final union of all Romanians into a single entity that included Transilvania, Bucovina, and Russian-annexed Moldovan territories, as well as the Principalities. There were numerous political and cultural contacts between leading Romanians of these provinces with the now-unified Principalities. Though there was as yet little likelihood of such a Romanian unification, the matter was one of constant interest to the Muntenian liberals.

In 1867, the Hungarians managed to establish a new working arrangement with the Habsburg Monarchy. Part of the agreement (The Ausgleich) gave the Magyars complete control over Transilvania, which now disappeared as an autonomous entity within the monarchy. The Romanians of Transilvania (i.e., the majority of the Transilvanian population) were completely ignored in this transaction; it was clear that a process of Magyarization was underway to the detriment of the Transilvanian Romanians and, of course, to the aims of Romanian nationalists on both sides of the Carpathians. The Transilvanian irredenta thus became after 1867 even more of a concern to the nationalists of Carol's new realm and a further incentive toward building up a powerful Romanian state. It is important to keep this preoccupation in mind when looking at Romanian political development.

Brătianu and Rosetti saw the necessity of significant internal development of the Romanian state to make the aid to their Transilvanian brethren meaningful.[6] They therefore stressed a dual task: the army must be strengthened and internal state administration must be bolstered. In this regard the influence of many years study and exile in France was reflected in the liberals' thinking and action. Ion Brătianu, we are told, was "a keen adherent of French political and administrative methods."[7] This undoubtedly implied the showing of a stronger hand by the central government in local affairs and a more high-handed approach toward opposition in the parliament. They also recognized that it was Ion Ghica's unwillingness to be more arbitrary and aggressive that had allowed parliamentary paralysis and his eventual ouster.

The liberals also called for a more definite idea of ministerial responsibility and a more independent judiciary. These planks were orthodox liberalism. In addition to fiscal reform and reorganization, the liberals saw a crucial need for developing the transportation network of Romania, both road and rail, so that more serious economic development could proceed. They also wanted to bring about growth in the agricultural sector of the economy. This could be achieved in part, they felt, through judicious enforcement of the agricultural contracts. Finally, the new program included a pledge to resolve the problem of "vagabonds," a euphemism for illegal Jewish immigrants who were a source of difficulties in Moldova.

The elevation of the liberals to power was not only viewed positively by Carol; it was in many ways for Carol one of a rapidly diminishing number of options for running the country under the 1866 system. As the British consul, Green, put it in commenting on the Crețulescu cabinet, "It may appear strange that I should lay stress on the fact of the late and present ministers being honest men...[but] Prince Charles has now exhausted the supply of that article afforded by the country and must soon have recourse to the usual run of easy-going rogues."[8] Carol had tried as his ministers almost every leader of repute who was acceptable to him. If the liberals' attempt failed, it might mean that Romanian politics would slide back into the fruitless prince-assembly conflict that had produced so many crises and so little development in the young nation's early years.

Carol was thus in a rather difficult position. He believed Ion Brătianu to be his ablest and most forceful minister and that the Muntenian liberal group was his best hope for stable growth.[9] The tenure of the Ion Ghica government had also convinced the prince that a more resolute regime was necessary. Brătianu's group had both determination and program. On the other hand, Brătianu and his friends were widely regarded with hostility abroad. France regarded Brătianu as too radical, a Mazzinian revolutionary if not worse. One of the Napoléon III's collaborators, Victor Duruy, wrote to Carol, "les hommes qui sont bons pour faire des revolutions et pour renverser des governments, ne sont jamais bons pour governer; à chacun son emploi!"[10] A somewhat startling attitude, coming from the camp of Napoléon III!

For Austria and Russia, Brătianu was a radical of the most suspected sort. The allusions often made by the Muntenian group vis-à-vis Austria's Transilvanian Achilles' heel did little to mollify Habsburg opposition. Britain, as a supporter of Turkey, likewise had low regard for the ambitious plans of Brătianu and his colleagues. That left only Prussia with any toleration for the new government. And the policy of Bismarck, if anything, was pragmatic. Since he was trying to open new approaches to Austria and Russia, it is clear that no support would be forthcoming from Prussia either if the Brătianu regime fell afoul of the two neighboring empires.[11] The apparent complicity of the liberals with Bulgarian and other revolutionary actions further alienated foreign regimes. Given this complete lack of external support and the internal weaknesses that the new government had to contend with, one might have thought that circumspection would be their watchword.

Several events occurred to lessen the liberal government's caution. First of all, there was a crisis in the ranks of the conservatives. Their new press organ, **Ordinea**, ceased to appear in February. The cooperation among chamber conservatives also declined. This gave the government more leeway. Secondly the revolt in Crete, the activities of the Bulgarians and Serbians against the Porte and the Ausgleich in Austria provided both distraction for the powers and apparent opportunity for the ministry. The activities and involvements of Romania in the external sphere are not our concern here. What is important is that the conjuncture of events in 1867 caused a lack of caution on the part of the Romanian cabinet.

Not that Brătianu was unaware of his need for allies; one of the first decrees issued by his office was an order designed to systematize the agricultural contract scheme established in 1866.[12] Though the circular emphasized that the contracts let by the landholders should not "profit from the adversity and need of the peasants" nor lead "to impoverishment of the agricultural class," it was obviously both a gesture to appease the fears of the landowning classes and a bid for their support. Secondly, the government made further overtures to the Fraction group of Iași in an endeavor to gain additional support in Moldova. This will be discussed subsequently.

Other energetic moves were taken. On 9 March, the budget was at long last passed. Two batteries of artillery were immediately ordered from Krupp to improve the army, and Col. Krenski, one of the chief architects of the 1866 Prussian successes against Austria, arrived in București on a "visit." Carol remarked in his diary on 9 March that since Brătianu's installation, "more life and liveliness" had been observed in administration.[13] On 13 March, the much-discussed move of the Court of Cassation to Iași was passed by the lower house 75 to 52 with the strong support of Brătianu. This was followed by the approval on 21 March of a new concession, a București-Giurgiu rail link between the capital and the Danube; and a settlement on 24 March of the cancellation of the Godillot construction and arms concessions on terms acceptable to Napoléon III. A bill to reform the army was introduced on 28 March and the long awaited monetary reform, to be discussed below, was voted by the chamber 68 to 6 on 29 March. Carol's commendation of Brătianu's energy was not amiss.[14]

The string of successes registered by the government was snapped on 30 March when the senate rejected the chamber-approved transfer of the Court of Cassation. The defeat was inconvenient for the government, but not really crucial. Brătianu, who had hoped to gain support in Moldova through the move,[15] achieved at least a partial success by having showed his willingness to help Iași. That the conservative-dominated senate had rejected the measure could hardly be his fault.[16] The blame would not fall on the cabinet and the Moldovans seemed to be content with Brătianu's reaffirmation of Carol's commitment to the move: "Iaşi will have the Court of Cassation, but a little later."[17] The measure was then allowed to gradually fade away. The first month of the new ministry had gone very well.[18]

The need for monetary reform, as had been noted, had long been a concern to Romanian financial experts.[19] Because the matter was closely tied to the Romanian-Ottoman relationship and raised symbolically the issue of sovereignty, the issue was more difficult to resolve than originally anticipated. A considerable part of the negotiations over Carol's recognition had focused on this question. Petre Mavrogheni, as minister of finance in the Ion Ghica governments, had devoted a good deal of his time in 1866-1867 to preparing a law for the introduction of an official Romanian monetary unit. This bill was now presented by the liberal government.[20] From the point of view of the government, there was little question about the necessity for a national unit. Until a real monetary unit was established, Romanian financial affairs would be subject to fluctuations and uncertainties.

As a gesture toward France, the new "leu" unit was modeled to conform to the rules of the Latin monetary union.[21] Its nominal value equalled the franc, and it was decimal. The measure was designed therefore to meet both fiscal and diplomatic ends. At the same time as it gave the regime more control over the economy, the new law would facilitate the enlargement of Romania's international economic ties and also mark subtly Romania's existence as a state.[22] The ratification of by the senate on 6 April 1867 of the previously passed chamber bill was a significant step in the development of the Romanian state. The fact that the changeover to the new system netted the government 3 million lei didn't hurt either.[23]

Although Carol professed some disappointment in the record of the chambers, the session that closed on 13 April 1867, had been quite productive, especially in the month after the liberal ministry came in. It seemed as if the liberals' policies and methods were what had been needed.

As previously noted, the Brătianu group's political base was București and Muntenia. In Moldova, though they had scattered adherents, their support was negligible. The Muntenians' very accession to power in 1867 had owed to a realization that more organization was necessary and that cooperation between Muntenian and Moldovan liberals was essential. Once in power, the personality conflict between the Muntenians and Kogălniceanu's Moldovan group proved too great.[24] The Muntenians sought, therefore, to gain support from the quixotic, but increasingly influential, "independent and liberal Fraction" led by Nicolae Ionescu.

One key condition set as the price for this cooperation, however, was an increased enforcement of legislation relating to "vagabonds,"[25] that is to say, laws which could be applied to the growing number of Jews in Moldova. On 7 April 1867, Ion Brătianu issued a circular in very strong terms, urging the prefects to enforce the laws in existence against "vagabonds." According to the minister of interior, Romania was being inundated by "foreigners" with no means of support; prompt action must be taken to prevent a situation damaging to the Romanian nation. The minister of war joined in adding his vigorous support. Though the circular did not once mention the word "Jew," the identity of these dangerous "vagabonds" was clearly understood.[26] Though the order was similar to one issued by Ion Ghica in September of 1866, the circular was most unfortunate since it reopened the Romanian "Jewish" question.[27]

Previously we encountered the "Jewish problem" in connection with the creation of the constitution of 1866. There, an attempt (ironically by Brătianu and Rosetti) to make all Jews in Romania citizens had failed due to mob protests. What lay at the root of this protest? The issue of the Jews in Romania was an exceedingly complex one. Despite the vast literature concerning the matter, there exists no thorough, balanced treatment of the problem.[28] As with most complex questions, there existed some truth on both sides of the controversy; in the end, both sides ignored the other.

The Jewish problem had been a concern for Romanian rulers

on several occasions during the first half of the nineteenth century. From time to time more or less ineffective efforts were made to prevent the illegal entry into Moldova by Jewish refugees from Galicia and Russia. Various restrictions and prohibitions had also been placed on Jews resident in Romania, the net effect of which was to concentrate them in urban areas and to retard or discourage assimilation. These actions and their ill-thought out consequences, in turn, caused the problem to worsen. The Regulament Organic of 1832 added further to the confusion by eliminating, for practical purposes, any distinction between indigenous Jews and immigrants.[29] The Convention of Paris in 1858 renewed the distinction by granting in article 46 full civil and legal rights to all residents of the Principalities. Political rights were, however, specifically reserved only to those of the Christian faith.[30] Under Prince Cuza, the distinction between indigenous (or resident) Jews and non-residents was maintained and strengthened by the wording of the new civil code introduced in 1864 and the communal law of 1864.

The situation in 1866 was, from a legal point of view, the following: those Jews who had been born and raised in Romania were considered as a sort of second-class citizen with civil and legal rights and equality, but no political rights. The remaining Jews were, probably rightly, considered as foreign subjects. The intent of the proposed article six of the constitution was to grant to resident Jews full citizenship. This was the move rejected by the assembly in 1866 under pressure of anti-Semitic agitation by Bucureşti street mobs.

From the Romanian point of view, the problem had been created in this fashion. At the beginning of the nineteenth century, there was in Moldova[31] a small ethnically Jewish population, perhaps 12,000 (two per cent of the total).[32] By 1859, the number had grown to 119,000, or nine per cent of the total Moldovan population.[33] This substantial rise in the Jewish total owed to several factors: first of all, the Jews had a higher birth rate and a lower mortality rate than the Romanians. More alarmingly, while the Romanian Jewish population was growing, the ethnically Romanian population of most Moldovan cities was showing a death rate greater than its birth rate, resulting in actual as well as relative decline.[34] Thirdly, there was a sizeable influx of Jews from Galicia and Russia, most of them crossing the borders illegally. And, as could be expected, many of those fleeing persecution in Galicia and Russia were extremely poor, possessing little or nothing. Their migration into Romania was particularly resented in a time of poor harvest, famine, or epidemic, as was the case in 1865-1867. Their presence made hard times even more difficult, while providing at the same time a convenient outlet for some of the resulting tensions. In addition, penniless refugees crowding into the cities in wretched conditions both served to spread the epidemic, and to foster a situation even conducive to it.[35]

Not only were the Jews beginning to dominate the Moldovan cities (Iaşi was 47 per cent Jewish in 1859, while the urban population of Moldova overall was 35 per cent Jewish),[36] but they were beginning to control more and more of commercial and artisan trade (78 per cent of trades in Iaşi in 1860 as opposed to 43 per cent in 1831), taverns, and market towns.[37] A good deal of this economic advance was alleged to be a result of support coming from wealthy Jewish banks and firms in Łwow, Cracow, and Leipzig.[38] On the other hand, it had to be admitted that the Jews were more educated than 98 per cent of the Romanian population.[39] And it is also legitimate to ask: "How much more backward would Moldova have been economically without the Jews?" It was the conclusion of at least one unbiased contemporary observer (Desjardins) that the Jewish economic impact on Romania was indisputably positive.[40]

Additionally there was the fact that the Jewish sector of the population remained very distinct from the Romanian.[41] They retained their religion, language, culture, and customs, and gave very few signs of wanting to assimilate. Large Jewish quarters sprang up in the major towns; the most noticeable was that of Iaşi. These Jewish "communities" were also in close contact with Jewish organizations abroad, especially the Paris-based Alliance Israélite Universelle under Adolphe Crémieux. By 1867, there were 34 local committees of the Alliance in Romania, mostly in

Moldova.[42]

The Romanian reaction was, thus, very mixed; a compound of ethnic, economic, religious, and social distrusts, fears and differences. It was not in the main, however, a question of religious or even racial intolerance per se.[43] The key aspects were: the enormous growth in the Jewish population which apart from the nationalist feelings such a rise was bound to incur, was a serious problem for a government trying to integrate an already diverse society; the demographic aspects of Moldovan population growth; and the economic domination threatened by the industrious Jewish merchants and bankers, a development which promised to impede the emergence of a Romanian middle class. While a major portion of the Romanian response was comprised of xenophobic and irrational reactions, there were enough real problems involved to prevent a simple resolution.[44]

The Jewish point of view was in the main a legal one bolstered by moral considerations. They rested their case, firstly, on the argument that there were two categories of Jews in Romania: resident and non-resident. The resident Jews were legally entitled to all the rights of Romanians, except political, at least since the Convention of 1858 and the civil code of 1864. Laws restrictive of Jewish rights were violations of these and subsequent acts. It became increasingly obvious that civil and legal rights without political rights were honored more in the breach than in practice. The Jewish minority, thus, sought to have the barriers to full citizenship removed.[45]

As for the status of foreign (non-resident) Jews, this was a matter to concern their respective governments. Here the issue was a little more complicated. The British citizen who happened to be a Jew was not party to the same rights in Romania as his non-Jewish countryman. This was an offense to foreign governments, particularly since Romania was yet regarded as a chattel of the great powers.[46] At the same time, it opened the door to foreign intervention.

Morally speaking, the Jewish communities was argued that unequal treatment of the Jews was wrong. The thrust of the nineteenth century, embodied in Romania's own constitution, was the elimination of arbitrary discriminations. Further, the violence often concomitant with special action against the Jews was deplorable and unacceptable. Romania, as a presumptive civilized state, must not be allowed to carry on the harassment of a particular minority. In fact, it was to be regretted that the constitution of 1866 had failed to remove the barrier to full and honorable citizenship for Jews in Romania. The emphasis, here, was primarily on the problem of religious discrimination or intolerance.

The Jewish argument was reasonable and plausible. It neglected entirely, however, the concern of the government over the countless thousands of destitute Jewish refugees entering the country or the dislocations and other difficulties caused by this entry. Secondly, it obviously did not sympathize at all with Romanian fears that the economic life of the country would fall completely into the hands of non-ethnic Romanians.

Politically, the Jewish question would normally have been a rather secondary issue in this era. That is to say, the main political groups of the day, the groups which had formed the coalition of 1866, had no strong feelings on the matter and would have been content to give indigenous Jews political rights or to ignore the matter entirely. This was shown by the draft constitution of 1866. Unfortunately, there were other elements in the society which placed a higher value on the problem. The Iași Fraction was particularly virulent in its opposition to the Jews as were Cezar Bolliac and his friends in Muntenia. It was a popular issue among the ethnic Romanian rabble of the cities as well, especially those who felt threatened by the Jews economically. Ironically, many of these ardent crusaders for "Romanianism" carried rather un-Romanian-sounding Greek and Armenian names.[47]

It was in these circumstances that Ion Brătianu issued his order of 7 April 1967. Brătianu, incidentally, had no particular anti-Semitic bias, as is often charged. He had in fact been, as a student, a member of a radical circle patronized by Adolphe Crémieux.[48] He had also supported attempts to grant political rights to all Romanians regardless of religion both in 1848 and in

1866. His actions in 1867 were influenced by two considerations: the problem of illegal immigration into Moldova by Galician and Russian Jews, which was a serious one and needed to be dealt with, and, secondly, by his need for political allies. Measures against the "vagabonds" were just the program to win the adherence Brătianu sought from the anti-Semitic Fraction in Moldova. The cooperation of the Fraction was needed to widen the political base of the Brătianu-Rosetti group and to enable them to complete the legislative agenda that they had committed to. And, not coincidentally, the order of 7 April was also popular among the non-Jewish commercial groups which formed an important part of the liberals' support and cut much of the ground out from under Bolliac in Bucureşti. In short, Brătianu's circular was partly designed to deal with what he saw as a very real practical problem regarding illegal immigration and partly a logrolling measure to curry political support.[49]

The Brătianu order of 7 April roused a storm of protest. Though he apparently had intended the measure to be a rather limited one[50] against illegal immigrants, it was widely misinterpreted, both by the police and by their victims. The prefects and local authorities in Moldova took it as carte blanche to arrest, harass, and otherwise persecute any and all Jews in their bailiwicks, whether "vagabond" or not. Local anti-Semitic groups seized the occasion to engage in various excesses.

The Jewish population was, naturally, in great alarm. Protests were immediately sent to Jewish groups and leaders abroad, especially the Alliance, and to the governments of the powers. It was here that Brătianu's real miscalculation entered in. All of Europe saw the matter purely as anti-Semitism, even though that was not really the case. On the other hand, Brătianu and his colleagues seem to have thought that the complaints were directed against individual abuses rather than the whole activity itself. The government's remedy was, thus, not to withdraw the measures but to try and implement them more cleanly.

The subsequent circulars of Brătianu, on 24 April, 7 May, and 20 May,[51] designed to make more specific the actions he wanted (and thus limit abuses by subordinates), and to show the historical precedents for his orders, did little to still the storm that was descending on him. The fact could not be obscured that there was no legal basis for orders directed specifically against the Jews since all the precedents Brătianu had cited had been abrogated by the civil code of 1864 and the constitution of 1866. The only extant laws, those concerning vagabondage, were, on the other hand, being misapplied since several of those who were deported had not had the trial clearly specified by the law.[52]

In May, Brătianu personally went to Iaşi to supervise measures there against vagabonds and illegal immigrants. He also made a very stringent inspection of the Jewish quarter. His recommendations for tighter control over the many private Jewish institutions of the Moldovan capital followed. Specifically, he mentioned the hospital which he deemed a breeding ground for epidemics. He further ordered enforcement of laws which required all children to attend schools which used Romanian as the primary language of instruction and followed the official program.[53] Neither of these orders, the one a reasonable sanitation measure, the other a normal practice in all countries, can be considered necessarily anti-Semitic. Brătianu's timing, however, was ill-advised, and the new orders on the heels of the former merely worsened both the abuses by Romanian authorities and the protests by their victims.[54]

On 11 May, Professor Ernest Desjardins arrived as a personal envoy of Napoléon and Mme. Cornu to investigate the Jewish question. He expressed to Carol Napoléon's strong opposition to the course being followed by Brătianu.[55] His advice was the dismissal of the liberal cabinet. Carol, however, did not yet believe this to be necessary.[56] Though Desjardins' pamphlet, **Les Juifs de Moldavie**, published in July, was a balanced picture of the situation, it was on the whole unfavorable to the minister's action and provided more ammunition against it. It is probable that Desjardins' report to Napoléon III solidified the French Emperor's hostility to the Brătianu government.

Brătianu's efforts in Moldova to prevent administrative abuses of his circulars only produced a strong collective protest by the French, British, and Austrian consuls to Carol on 14 May.[57] The same day, Carol received a note from Napoléon which concluded, "Je ne puis croire que le gouvernment éclairé de Votre Altesse autorise des mesures si contraires à l'humanité et à la civilisation."[58] Convinced by Brătianu that the measures being taken were justified and that those few abuses which had occurred would be investigated,[59] Carol assured Napoléon (and the consuls) that he personally would ensure that any illegal acts or abuses of authority would be met with due punishment. He also affirmed his "solicitude" for the welfare of the Jewish population.[60] Meanwhile Crémieux, of the Alliance, and the Paris press were bringing more and more weight to the attack on Brătianu.[61]

What was actually happening to the Moldovan Jews? The government claimed that reports of violence were highly exaggerated. In mid-May, the British agent in Iași, St. Clair, who was unfavorable toward the government, confirmed most of the minister's claims.[62] Green in București noted that the complaints of the Jews had been "vague reports" and wondered if any hard evidence was available. He also asserted that abuses of police power were commonplace in Romania, that Jew and Christian alike suffered simply by dint of where they were.[63] On the other hand, an atmosphere very dangerous to the Jews in Romania had been created. Given the lawless and violent nature of many Romanian anti-Semites, a massacre could have broken out under such circumstances at any time. Though there were undeniable excesses, arbitrary arrests, police brutality, and the like, there were no known fatalities.[64]

The internal opposition to Brătianu and the liberals was quick to recognize that the foreign attack on the government represented an opportunity to oust their foes from power. Thus at the beginning of May, Carol was presented with a petition from a group of Iași boiars strongly protesting the action taken by Brătianu on the vagabond and Jewish issues.[65] This appeal made little impression on Carol since he believed the boiars' attitude to be hypocritical.[66]

A more serious action was already beginning abroad. The

Romanian diplomatic agency in Paris was staffed by Ion Bălăceanu and P. P. Carp. Both of these men were political opponents of the liberal government.[67] The uproar caused in France by the supposed persecution of Jews in Moldova furnished them with an excellent chance to undermine the Brătianu regime they allegedly represented in France.[68] Bălăceanu and Carp soon had their first major success: they were able to persuade Mme. Cornu that Brătianu must be ousted from office if Carol was to retain French support. As a result, in May, Cornu wrote to Carol that if Brătianu were truly devoted to the prince, he should resign at once. Carol replied that Brătianu had offered to do so, but that he had been refused.[69] The conversion of Mme. Cornu from supporter to active opponent was a serious weakening of Brătianu's position.

The loss of French support, both official and unofficial, opened the liberal government to a wide scale attack on all fronts. The French and British accused Brătianu of anti-Semitism and pro-Prussian leanings; the Austrians and Russians charged the ministry with Mazzinianism. The fact that the Bulgarian revolutionaries continued to use Romania as a base for operations into the Ottoman empire was highly offensive to the Porte (and Britain). Within the country, the opposition charged the regime with being too liberal or too anti-Semitic, depending on the circumstances and individual preferences. By mid-year, the ministry was being maintained only by Carol's refusal to be swayed; its excellent start had now been nearly washed away by external forces. A counter-effort in France by the liberals to portray the whole uproar as a clever Russian intrigue failed to make much headway.[70]

In June 1867, Carol made yet another trip to Moldova. This time he was concerned with calming the situation created by the unfortunate "vagabond" circulars and with ascertaining the true conditions as far as possible. He was reported determined "to put a stop to all persecution,"[71] but because separatism was not yet a dead issue,[72] he had to proceed with utmost caution. But it was not only these continuing issues that brought him once more north of the Milcov: rumors were running rampant over a possible return of Prince Cuza from exile.[73] The former prince's Moldovan supporters were thus emboldened as well.

Once again, Carol's visit to Moldova produced a salutary effect. He visited the poorer part of the Jewish quarter in Iaşi where he saw for himself deplorably crowded and desperate conditions.[74] He continued to feel that the complaints against Brătianu were simply politically motivated. In the end, his assurances to the powers temporarily quieted foreign protests and mollified their representatives in Bucureşti. As Green reported to London, "I feel certain that Prince Charles would lay down his life rather than wittingly be a party to a Jewish persecution."[75]

This proved to be a lull before a storm. On 1 July, a group of ten Jews were taken to Galaţi and then expelled to the Turkish side of the Danube. These unfortunates were returned to the Romanian side on 2 July, where Romanian border guards with bayonets refused to allow debarkation. In the end, the Turks apparently threw their captives overboard with the result that two of them drowned.[76] The report of the foreign consuls at Galaţi placed entire blame for the incident on the Romanian authorities, and the liberal ministry was once again under heavy foreign pressure, especially from France.

Greatly alarmed, Carol's father, Karl Anton, now paid a secret visit to Paris where he held several conversations with Napoléon III. The result was conclusive. Napoléon would not be satisfied, Karl Anton informed Carol, until Ion Brătianu was ousted from the government. "It is regrettable, but that does not change the situation." Despite Brătianu's great ability and patriotism, "it is a high political necessity" that he resign.[77] The recommendation of Karl Anton tipped the scale. On 29 July, Brătianu submitted his resignation to Carol, which the prince's diary notes he received "with great displeasure."[78] Prime Minister Creţulescu and the entire cabinet followed suit. Letters from Carol and Picot to Napoléon and Crémieux apprising them of the change followed.[79] The combined efforts of France and the internal opposition had cut short what had appeared to be a very promising ministry.

The fall of the Creţulescu government brought an easing of

tension in the Jewish question. No real resolution had been achieved as the government had pointedly refused to withdraw any of the infamous circulars, despite a private admission by Carol that they had been a mistake.[80] Nevertheless, something of a calm ensued. On 10 August, Sir Moses Montefiore, the British Jewish leader and banker, arrived in Bucureşti to investigate the problem in response to urgent appeals from various Moldovan Jewish communities.[81] The 83-year-old baronet was too tired and ill to visit Moldova and was in fact warned that the trip to Iaşi was too dangerous. His impressions of the matter, formed in the capital rather than Moldova it is true, were somewhat less hostile to the Romanians than the views expressed by Crémieux and others, but the fact that his hotel was nearly sacked by an anti-Semitic mob and that death threats against him were a daily occurrence in Bucureşti hardly persuaded him of Romania's tolerance and kindliness toward Jews.

However, like the British consul, Green, Sir Moses was favorably impressed by Carol's sincere promises that religious liberty would be upheld and injustice rectified.[82] Carol, thus, continued to be personally undamaged by the Jewish questions, but his search for a suitable government was now open once more. This was getting to be an increasingly difficult task.

Chapter 10

The Fourth Phase: Liberalism's Fall

"Call you that backing of your friends? A plague
upon such backing! Give me them that will face me."
Shakespeare, **King Henry IV, Part I**, II.iv.168

On 3 August, Prince Carol charged Ştefan Golescu, a leading liberal, with forming a new ministry.[1] It was only two weeks later, however, that Golescu was actually able to present a new ministerial list. Obviously, the problems that had brought an end to the Creţulescu government made creation of a new liberal cabinet difficult.

In the meanwhile, internal events kept occurring which complicated life for potential Romanian ministries. One of these events was the first meetings of the "Academic Society," the precursor of the Romanian Academy. This society was initiated in 1866 by the then-minister of education, C. A. Rosetti. True to liberal nationalist ideology, the Society was an attempt to foster the cultural and political unity of all Romanians, including those in Transilvania, Bucovina, and Russian-held portions of Moldova, under the pretense of compiling a Romanian grammar and dictionary.[2] The proceedings were feted by leading political figures and by Prince Carol. The British consul reported that the banquet held on the 6th of August featured as decorations pictures of Romulus and Remus and a map of Romania "as God made it," including all territories inhabited by Romanians.[3] Such a manifestation was hardly designed to appease Austria[4] and it brought Carol another rebuke from that erstwhile champion of national self-determination, Napoléon III, "They are disquieted in Vienna over the moves of a certain party that wants to form ties with their co-religionaries of Transilvania; I believe your government has nothing to gain in aiding their dangerous propaganda."5

At last on 17 August, Ştefan Golescu was able to constitute a new cabinet. The second phase of liberal rule began. Despite the fact that Ion Brătianu was no longer part of the ministry, it was clearly recognized that "the ministerial change was a feint which fooled no one; at bottom it is still Brătianu who reigns."6 The new cabinet, with the exception of Ludovic Steege, as finance minister, was undistinguished. The minister of justice, Anton Arion, who had as his chief claim to fame a reputation as one of the most violent liberal street agitators in Bucureşti, was typical.7

The principal objective of the new cabinet was to allow Brătianu time to make a pilgrimage to Paris and Germany in order to explain himself and to mend fences.8 In Paris he conferred with Crémioux, on the Jewish problem,9 but it is uncertain whether he got to see the French Emperor as he had hoped.10 Though he seems to have allayed the hostility of certain French circles, the mission did relatively little to mollify the French government.11 In November, the French minister Moustier spoke unfavorably of Brătianu as "representing revolution, agitation and a future cataclysm," while his colleague Rouher denounced "the revolutionary despotism of the Brătianus."12 It is also unknown what Brătianu was able to find out about the recent meeting Napoléon III had had with the Austrian emperor; this meeting, too, was a matter of concern to the Romanians.

Elsewhere, Brătianu had more success. He made once again a favorable impression on Carol's father, seeing him in Switzerland on his way back to Bucureşti.13 Though, Brătianu's mission west did not resolve all his difficulties, it was certainly positive enough to allow him to rejoin the government shortly.

On 25 October, the legislature was convened in special session to deal once more with the financial needs that weighed down so much on Romania. At the same time, the chambers were asked to deal with army reform, a rail concession linking Iaşi and Bucureşti, and various other matters.14 The finance minister, Steege, had resigned at the end of September, and the cabinet was already beginning to totter. The special session of the chambers was in fact a test of the liberals' control of the legislature; Carol was, however, determined to dissolve it if the liberals could not control the majority.[15] This was a distinct possibility because Kogălniceanu and Dimitrie Ghica had already begun to work together to overturn what was left of the liberal regime.[16] The prince, concurring with his father's opinion that Brătianu was "the man of the situation,"[17] decided to defy the French emperor. On 27 October, he re-appointed Ion Brătianu to the ministry of finance, the post which he considered to be of the most immediate importance.

The same day, the chamber of deputies responded with an attack on the financial policies of the Golescu ministry; the cabinet immediately dissolved both chamber and senate and called for new elections.[18] A contributing factor to the dissolution was an attempt by Carol to form a new cabinet under Costache Negri that included Kogălniceanu and Ion Brătianu. Negri and Kogălniceanu had refused to cooperate with Brătianu, which probably was a relief to the Muntenians. They were then able to obtain the dissolution of the parliament for the express purpose of conducting the kind of elections which would produce a more workable situation.[19]

The dissolution produced considerable unhappiness among the opposition, even alarm.[20] These fears were multiplied when the ministry of interior, crucial to controlling the elections set for December, was also given to Ion Brătianu. The apprehensions of the opposition were well-founded. The 1867 elections under Brătianu's direction were a marked contrast to the fairness of the first election held in the fall of 1866. The results reflected the payoff of this kind of "management"—the liberal ministry gained control of both the chamber and the senate.[21] In the senate, the majority was slim but workable. In the chamber, the liberals had 59 seats and their Fraction allies had 23 more for a solid base.[22]

Though the liberals had "won" the elections, their use of pressure, violence, and fraud set an enormously bad precedent. It also spurred the opposition, which had been floundering in disunited protests and haphazard intrigues against the liberals, into a new coordination of efforts. A new conservative committee was formed and began to issue a new journal, **Térra**, (which also appeared in French as **Le Pays roumain**).[23] The opposition were not, of course, united into a party, but they now began concerted efforts to undermine the liberals. The actions taken by Brătianu and his colleagues since March of 1867 had thoroughly frightened their former "coalition" partners of 1866. Fearing both their own political suppression at home and the likelihood that the Muntenians would provoke armed foreign intervention,[24] the conservatives believed only an immediate ouster of the liberals would prevent disaster.

Another crucial development occurring during this period was noticed by the British consul. On 12 November 1867, the new Prussian minister, Count Keyserling, arrived in București. By 8 December, it was already clear that Keyserling was exerting considerable influence over Carol. At about the same time began the division of spheres that subsequently characterized Carol's rule in Romania: he more or less gave direction of internal policy, for better or worse, over to his ministers while keeping the direction of foreign policy in his own hands.[25]

Both Carol and the liberal ministry had great hopes for their new parliament, which opened on 3 January 1868. The prince believed that a strong ministry coupled with a supportive legislature would now enable pressing domestic needs to be met. In turn, Romania's precarious international position would be strengthened. He opened the session of 1868 with an appeal to the chambers to begin a work of construction and improvement instead of idle debate and vindictiveness.[26] He particularly emphasized his determination that all abuses toward the Jews would be prevented. Among other disiderata, army reorganization was seen as "an absolute necessity," and speedy approval of a railroad concession was urged.[27] The chamber almost immediately disappointed Carol by electing as president none other than Anastasie Fătu, a notorious anti-Semite and member of the Iași Fraction.[28] What this indicated was soon become all too clear.

Early in 1868, foreign policy again became an important

internal issue. On the urging of Bismarck and Karl Anton, Carol had begun to try and improve relations with Russia.[29] At the same time Serbian ties with Romania were becoming very close and covert encouragement was being given to Bulgarian rebels using Romania as a base of operations. Bismarck's advice was part of his calculations vis-à-vis France. The liberal ministry, for its part, saw Russian favor as a means of facilitating arms shipments from Prussia and a step toward further action in Transilvania.

The conservatives around **Térra**, on the other hand, were strongly hostile to any dealings with Russia both as unnatural and as part of revolutionary adventurism of the most foolhardy sort. Their leaders, P. P. Carp and Nicolae Blaremberg, quickly raised the issue in the press and parliament. Brătianu replied evasively and accused Carp of aiding the enemies of the country.

Despite constant denials of any support for the raids across the Danube that Bulgarian exiles were making, and though Rosetti professed that "our politics are invariable" and that Romania under the liberals could not possibly make overtures to the Russians,[30] the liberal regime was heavily involved with both.[31] Turkey, France, Austria and England were all highly critical of these reported Romanian policies, as well as reasonably well-informed about what was going on. Once again the French took the lead and urged Brătianu's immediate ouster as the only solution.[32] As in 1867, Brătianu had embarked on a dangerous course of action which roused foreign displeasure. And, as in 1867, by so doing, he handed an apparently squelched internal opposition new life and the means whereby to oppose him.[33]

As far as internal matters per se were concerned, the major issue was the railroad project. In the fall of 1867, an Austro-British consortium under Baron Offenheim made through Petre Mavrogheni an offer for the building of a rail line running from Suceava to Iași to Galați to București. The construction of this facility was perceived by Carol and the liberals as an absolutely vital step, despite Romania's continuing poor financial condition. The building of a rail link between Moldova and Muntenia would be a means of making the country more unified and thereby dispelling its separatist specter. Secondly, the development of a transport net was a crucial item in the economic development of Romania. Until roads and railroads were built, Romania's great agricultural wealth could only be marginally exploited. And without a unified transportation system, the distribution of goods and the development of industry were retarded or prevented. The railroads were seen, thus, as an important factor in the overall growth of the country and the strengthening of its position.

On 25 January, just as the chamber was finally ready to begin debate on the Offenheim concession, Carol received word that a group of Prussian capitalists under the direction of Dr. Bethel Henry Strousberg had formed and was prepared to offer the Romanians better terms on the rail project. The Strousberg group came heavily recommended by influential Prussian circles and by Carol's father and trusted advisor, Karl Anton.[34] The Offenheim group responded with a more favorable counter-offer, thus creating a political dilemma of no small magnitude. Worse yet, Brătianu reported that he feared the chamber might not approve any railroad project whatever. Carol responded firmly on that count: "the future of Romania is in the railroads. Only who will construct them is open to question."[35] When the debate began on 23 February, opposition was outspoken but indecisive. As it progressed a new scandal appeared.

The Jewish question had been quiet since Brătianu's mission to France in October 1867. On 5 March, the matter once again burst onto the scene. Thirty-one deputies, mainly Moldovans of the Fraction group led by the president of the chamber, Dr. Fătu, presented a bill "for the regularization of the state of Jews in Romania."[36] The purpose of the bill was allegedly to counter contentions that the circulars issued in 1867 were based on laws which no longer were valid. Among other provisions, Jews were prohibited from settling in rural areas under any circumstances and in other areas only with special permission, were forbidden to own any immobile property, and were barred from renting or conducting most commercial enterprises. While the measure did, indeed, provide a legal basis for further action against the Jews, it was hardly satisfactory from a liberal point of view and was a clear violation of the rights of indigenous Jews. The Bucureşti rabbi, Antoine Lévy, published a detailed rebuttal,[37] but the proposal immediately became the pretext for new outrages against the Jewish population. An avalanche of foreign protest followed.

Ion Brătianu had learned his lesson; this time he took firm and decisive action. Though both he and Carol were reportedly dismayed that the issue had even come up again,[38] the liberal leader broke openly with the Fraction and in the chamber session of 24 March denounced the proposal as simply fatal to Romania's national interests. He urged the bill's defeat, which immediately followed. The irony of it all was that, despite the government's clear action on the issue, foreign opposition tended to ascribe blame for the measure to the liberals.[39] The Fraction proposal defeated, the chamber moved on to pass the budget including an additional 24 million lei supplement for the army. The railroad issue was still undecided.

The Moldovan anti-Semites, however, were not yet finished. In Bacău, and other areas, prefects, acting on their own authority, proceeded to evict Jewish families from areas in spite of the fact that the ministry had not issued any orders. Some 500 families were reported uprooted with the usual excesses. Carol had passed through Bacău on 5 April on his way to Iaşi, but saw and heard nothing unusual or illegal even from a Jewish delegation.[40] However, by 11 April, the situation in Bacău had deteriorated seriously.

Ion Brătianu, himself, now came to Bacău to investigate reports of abuses. He was actually mobbed, knocked down in a muddy street, and given a severe fright by the aroused partisans of anti-Jewish measures. Brătianu finally had to order the national guard in Bacău disarmed, and the city was occupied by regular army troops to prevent further disorder.[41] Despite these obvious signs that the government was not responsible for the abuses being committed, the protests of foreign consuls multiplied and increasingly focused on the cabinet as the villains of the piece. Crémieux and the Alliance Israélite once again played a leading role.

One immediate result was the resignation of the prime

minister, Ștefan Golescu. Golescu's contribution to the discussion was a circular which attributed most of the rumors flourishing on the Jewish problem to the Austrian consul in Iași. Because he had sent the note without Carol's prior approval, Golescu was now forced out of the government on 26 April.[42]

That same day also featured a revealing parliamentary debate on the Jewish issue between Petre P. Carp and Ion Brătianu. Carp's attempts to saddle Brătianu with the blame for the recent Bacău excesses were unsuccessful. On the other hand, the liberal leader's response, though effective, revealed a distressing tendency to demagogic attack on the opposition.[43] It also became clear that Brătianu had not changed his mind about the necessity for orders such as those he had issued in 1867. His primary concern now was obviously tactical, given Europe's adversary stance on the Jewish question. Eventually, Brătianu even went so far as to suggest that in six months or a year, it might be possible to implement the Fraction proposal.[44] Whether this was itself a tactical move to stall off the Fraction or whether it represented Brătianu's own position is hard to tell. However, it does make somewhat unconvincing his claim in May 1868 that he had been prevented by his group from carrying out promised reforms concerning Jews.[45]

On 30 April, General Nicolae Golescu became the new prime minister, but all the other former cabinet officers remained. Since the general was the brother of the ousted prime minister and yet another member of the Muntenian liberal inner circle, the change was again obviously mostly cosmetic.

Brătianu's equivocation on the Jewish question was beginning to alienate the Fraction, for whom this was the primary issue. Their leader Nicolae Ionescu launched a blistering attack on Brătianu during the senate session on 3 May and demanded publication of all relevant documents on the Jewish issue. The minister's plea that publication was inopportune was overridden by a wide margin. The vote was ignored. The liberals' one-time control over the senate had vanished.

Continued foreign agitation over the Jewish question was causing further erosion of the liberals' support elsewhere. Karl

Anton once again wrote to Carol emphasizing the imperative nature of avoiding any conflict with the influential Jewish community in Europe. He believed that because of the issue all of Romania's recent gains were being cancelled out. He concluded, "Personally, I appreciate and esteem Ion Brătianu very much. His remaining in power is, however, a great danger..."[46] However, with the tasks of army reorganization and ratification of the railroad concessions still pending, Carol felt that the external harm caused by Brătianu's continued presence in the cabinet was outweighed by his indispensability in getting these measures accomplished. The future was, obviously, very hazy.

Events began to move more rapidly in May, though not as smoothly as Carol had hoped. Debate on the railroad concessions occupied the deputies most of the month. Finally the liberal-dominated chamber voted to give the Offenheim group the Suceava-Iași-Roman line and Strousberg the Roman-București section and another section from București to Turnu Severin. The Prussian financier thus gained the major portion of the concessions. The bill then went to the senate. Here a motion of no confidence in the ministry was passed on 31 May on a flimsy pretext by a 32 to 8 vote with 14 abstentions. The government immediately resigned.[47] After an opposition refusal to form a ministry and a chamber-passed vote of confidence in the Golescu ministry, Carol dissolved the recalcitrant senate and called new elections for July. The results of these elections were no surprise; D. A. Sturdza compared the new body to the "renowned Senate of Cuza."[48] When it met in September, the Muntenians' Ștefan Golescu was chosen as its presiding officer.

The chamber took one final action before ending its regular term in June. This was to vote a new law on the organization of the army.[49] The changes on the surface were not great, but cleverly evaded provisions of the Romanian agreement with the Porte restricting numbers. Active service was reduced to three years with four years reserve for the standing army. Five additional military bodies (dorobanți, grăniceri, emergency militia, civic guard, and the gloata—the last including everyone not in the first four) comprised virtually every able-bodied man in the country. These measures were carried out in the fall and resulted in a significant strengthening of the Romanian state's military situation.

In June, Prince Jérôme Napoléon, the Emperor's cousin, paid a brief visit to București. He showed particular friendliness to Brătianu, and was warmly received by the populace,[50] but politics were in general avoided.

The Bulgarian issue once again surfaced during the summer. France urged Carol to dismiss Brătianu on this pretext;[51] Turkey wanted a commission to make an investigation. Fortunately for Brătianu, the Bulgarians suffered serious reverses and quiet returned. The expansion of the Romanian army coupled with its support, even if covert, for the Bulgarians was considerably disturbing to Turkey, Austria and France. It was one more particular in their brief against the liberals.

On 2 August, Carol dismissed the minister of war, Col. Adrian. The reason given was actions prejudicial to Carol's authority;[52] the real reason was to place the reorganization of the army in the hands of the prince's most trusted and energetic minister, Ion Brătianu. This Carol did on 12 August when the cabinet was re-shuffled. At that point, because Nicolae Golescu was on vacation, Brătianu held three cabinet posts ad interim (war, foreign affairs, prime minister) in addition to finance. Arion now assumed interior ad interim and justice. The liberal government was fast becoming a one man regime.

Carol's two principal aims at this point were to get on with the building of the army and the railroads. Both of these measures were designed to raise Romania to the point where it could control its own destiny.[53] The "successful" elections which Brătianu had conducted for the senate made passage of the railroad concessions certain. A special session of the legislature opened on 2 September. In the middle of the month the rail bill was voted 39-4. Brătianu, as minister of finance, was government spokesman for the bill, and his speeches on 16 and 18 September were powerful expositions of the need for building such a railroad and of the challenging and prosperous future he envisioned for Romania and its people as a result.[54]

Ion Brătianu's efforts with the army were equally effective. His ministry established firmly Carol's leadership over the military. It also removed the military from politics by and large, one of the last injuries that needed to be repaired from 11 February 1866.[55] Brătianu's organizational talents came into play, and a new spirit and method were introduced into the hitherto motley Romanian army.[56] A definitive chain of command was established, new regiments were formed, and modern arms were procured. Nearly 20,000 new rifles were purchased and new artillery was acquired. The most important step was to place the training of officer corps on a modern, professional basis. Col. Krensky returned in September 1868 to provide the necessary expertise, along with several Prussian colleagues; and promising young officers were sent to study at German and French military academies. Romania's army began to become what the militarily-minded Carol hoped it would be.

With the railroad issue resolved and the army reorganization definitively underway, Carol retired to Brătianu's country estate near Pitești for an extended rest. The stay was exceptionally pleasing to Carol.[57] It would seem that Brătianu was at the height of power and security. However, appearances were deceiving. Externally, Brătianu had lost his last support. Ironically, with the approval of the Strousberg concession, Bismarck no longer had any motive to keep Brătianu in power. Thus, during November, Keyserling repeatedly communicated the Prussian cabinet's desire that Brătianu be replaced.[58] On 11 November, he read to Carol a telegram from Berlin that stated "categorically that a further stay of Brătianu in the government would have as a consequence serious difficulties, and that Prussia could no longer support the policy followed by the ministry up to now."[59] Carol's uncle, Marquis Pepoli, who was Italy's minister to Vienna, wrote on 12 November 1868, to warn Carol ("as uncle") that Brătianu's continued stay in office only posed dangers for Romania ("Do you dream of the fate of Poland for your country?") and retarded normal development. His own recommendation was to seek rapprochement with Hungary.[60]

Internally, Brătianu's support had serious flaws. His

parliamentary majorities had been obtained by abusing the electoral process and meant relatively little. His supporters and collaborators were also beginning to get restive over his autocratic attitudes. Carol Davila repeatedly complained of this "minister who pretends to do everything without consulting anyone."[61] He monopolized cabinet posts and assumed whatever portfolio was most important for the moment. Brătianu had apparently forgotten his words of 1863: "only two forms of government are possible: Constitutional government, where the nation governs intelligently, and Despotism, that is government of a man and his cohort."[62] The liberals' opponents were, of course, even more unhappy. D. A. Sturdza wrote, "I cannot tell you how disgusted I am with this state of affairs."[63] It was apparent that the slightest misstep would be the last for the Brătianu-dominated cabinet.

At the end of October, Carol and Brătianu discussed the possibility of broadening the cabinet to include Dimitrie Ghica and Mihail Kogălniceanu as a means of lessening foreign opposition.[64] Brătianu, surprisingly, agreed to this proposal and negotiations began in București.[65] All parties soon agreed that a such coalition ministry was acceptable; the only remaining problem was the division of portfolios. This plan had to be partially abandoned on 11 November when Carol communicated to Brătianu Prussia's "categoric" opposition to him. The liberal chief insisted on resigning, a decision which Carol accepted only on Brătianu's guarantee that his parliament would cooperate with a new cabinet.

The legislature re-opened on 15 November. Though a change of ministry was eminent and fraught with uncertainties, Carol's opening address was optimistic.[66] Finances had taken a decided turn for the better compared with a year previously; the budget of 1867 had ended with a surplus large enough to cover the deficit of 1866. Prospects were good for 1868. The railroad concessions would not only unify the country, but would prove an enormous economic boon, while highway construction was now in full progress. Significant development of the army had begun. For the future, changes and improvements were indicated for the areas of education, justice, and institutions of credit. The political situation abroad was less promising, owing to constant rumormongering by Romania's enemies, but Carol could report that various conventions with neighboring countries were being discussed or already closed on such matters as postal cooperation and consular jurisdiction. These negotiations were significant because they served to demonstrate Romanian autonomy. The accomplishments of the liberal regime, for these were what Carol was describing, were indeed considerable.

On 16 November, the Nicolae Golescu government resigned. It was one of the most remarkable in Romanian political history since it occurred in the absence of any kind of parliamentary conflict or even a specific foreign grievance. It was, in fact, purely a tactical move brought on by continuing foreign hostility to the liberal regime. Far from renouncing the reins of power, Brătianu and his colleagues planned a brief interim to cool off external opposition; they would then resume office. Obviously, they believed that their internal control was now sufficiently entrenched to allow such a charade to occur.[67] In reality, the scenario led to chaos and conflict more serious than either Carol or the liberals could have imagined and plunged Romania back into a situation remarkably like that which it had faced in the latter days of Prince Cuza's reign.

Reaction to the fall of the government was mixed. Foreign governments, especially France, were generally pleased; Napoléon III expressed his "entire satisfaction" with the new cabinet.[68] The Muntenian liberals were, of course, resentful at being ousted by foreign pressure, however temporarily, though confident of being recalled. Carol, despite the reluctance indicated by his **Memoirs**, in retrospect seems to have been sure that Brătianu had served out his usefulness. As he wrote to his uncle, Marquis Pepoli, later, Brătianu's "liberal effervescence" had permitted the populace to engage in too many excessive activities. It was now time for him to be replaced so that a calmer development could ensue.[69] The promising era of liberal power had come to a somewhat ambiguous conclusion.

Chapter 11

The Fifth Phase: Conflict and Crisis

"O, how full of briars is this working-day world!"
Shakespeare, **As You Like It**, I.iii.12

The resignation of the liberal government in 1868 proved to be the end of the experiment with party government. The new cabinet represented a return by Carol to rule by political coalition.[1] The new combination was led by the moderate Muntenian conservative, Dimitrie Ghica, and the moderate Moldovan liberal Mihail Kogălniceanu; they were united largely by opposition to the former ministry. Though the new cabinet represented various nuances (Al. G. Golescu, Basile Boerescu, Al. Papadopol Calimah were all moderates of various stripes), it did not include a single member of the Muntenian liberal group. This presented serious potential difficulties because the liberals still controlled the parliament. Ion Brătianu's resignation was, in fact, immediately followed by his election as president of the chamber; Nicolae Golescu was chosen to head the senate. The liberals had promised support for the new government; but, as C. A. Rosetti perceived, such a situation was highly untenable.[2]

The new cabinet, composed of diverse elements and interests, and operating in an extremely difficult situation both externally and internally, began very prudently. Their program was of the utmost generality and vagueness.[3] However, by its very vagueness (i.e., refusing to support or justify the policies of its liberal predecessor), the new cabinet soon unleashed a torrent of hostile debate in the chambers. The Muntenian liberals, though accepting the new cabinet as a necessary, but temporary evil, wanted nothing less than for the new ministers to follow their bidding.[4] In turn, the conservative parliamentary minority wanted to dwell on the "tyrannical" record of the now-departed

Brătianu ministries. Debate soon deteriorated into the futile oratorical showmanship which always plagued Romanian politics, demonstrated especially at moments least favorable for such exercises. In the end, nothing was achieved except disorder.[5] More importantly, the relationship between the liberals and the prince began to decline.

One cause was an 8 January 1869 Rosetti-orchestrated banquet allegedly given by the citizens of București in honor of Ion Brătianu.[6] This gathering was simply a pretext for the liberals to demonstrate their political popularity and to "encourage" the prince to restore them to office. The tone of the meeting was anti-governmental; more significantly, it eventually became hostile to Prince Carol as well. Brătianu, called on the carpet by the prince to explain, gave assurances of his loyalty but admitted that not all members of his party shared his view.[7] As a result, relations between Carol and the liberals cooled considerably. It is not beyond the realm of the likely that this supposed "internal dissention" among the liberals was a purely manufactured product designed to hasten Brătianu's return to power.

The D. Ghica government, after this, began to pursue a more active policy against the liberals. It became plain that the new cabinet had no intention of functioning as a mere surrogate for the liberals. Indeed, strong minded men such as Ghica and Kogălniceanu were not likely candidates for manipulation by anyone. Furthermore, both of them had agreed to come to power under the odd circumstances described in the last chapter because they were genuinely alarmed by the developments of 1867-1868 and by Brătianu's tenure in office. Their primary goal was to prevent Brătianu's return to power.

They were also motivated by fears that the illegitimate ways in which the substantial electoral gains of the liberals had been obtained in 1868 were a precursor of further machinations, including an attempt to modify the constitution of 1866.[8] Since this instrument's complicated electoral law was all that lay between the large landholders and political extinction, the restoration of Brătianu to power had to be avoided. It was in light of this that Dimitrie Ghica, serving as both prime minister and foreign minister, directed a large part of his energies toward taking advantage of an international climate hostile toward the liberals.[9]

The main tactic was to emphasize to the powers that Romania's internal order could be preserved and irredentist adventures curtailed only if the Muntenians were kept out of office.[10] With international suspicion of the liberals at a high level, this was an effective strategy.[11] At the same time, various actions were initiated to persuade hitherto hostile foreign powers that a conservative-moderate led Romania was deserving of support and encouragement. Thus, various "radical" or "nationalist" measures proposed or passed through one chamber or another by the liberals were withdrawn or killed by the new cabinet. These activities, while further exciting the opposition of the liberals, demonstrated effectively to the powers that the Ghica ministry was quite different from its predecessors and unlikely to create difficulties.

On the positive side, Ghica was determined to use the occasion to demand concessions and favors from the powers (especially the Ottoman Empire), in exchange for maintaining order in Romania. The Porte was told that if results were not forthcoming on certain matters such as the right to mint money and consular jurisdiction, the new regime of order in București would surely fall.[12] The European agents were to be informed that only Great Power support would "help us give satisfaction to the legitimate needs of the country." If no support were obtained, then the "single possible government" in Europe's interest in Romania would be replaced by the liberals—with dire results.[13] This was to be the constant theme of the prime minister's policy throughout his tenure.[14]

For Ghica's major collaborator, Mihail Kogălniceanu, the new cabinet presented a two-fold opportunity. First of all, it was an occasion to revive his personal political fortunes which had fallen to a low with the coup of 1866. Secondly, he was anxious to gain a measure of satisfaction for the failure of the liberals to honor the Concordia agreement of 1866-1867.[15] As minister of interior he was in an excellent position to achieve these aims. At the same time, Kogălniceanu and Ghica hoped that in coalition they would be able to take a page from the liberals' book and establish a powerful political base on the strength of governmental action and royal favor.

The intransigence of the liberals played into the hands of the ministry. Continued obstruction on the part of the liberal majorities in the assembly led Ghica to offer his resignation to Carol in January of 1869. When the monarch refused it, the way was clear to a showdown with the liberal parliamentarians. A demand by Ghica for a vote of confidence was met reluctantly by the liberals to avoid furnishing a pretext for dissolution. The ministry countered by appointing as head of the Bucureşti garrison General A. D. Macedonski, who was the author of a violent attack on the Brătianu army reorganization, was totally unacceptable to the Muntenians. The resultant reaction[16] was sufficient for the government to dissolve the chamber on 28 January.[17]

The fall of the liberal chamber in January 1869, was an event of considerable significance. First of all it demonstrated that Romanian political development had not yet reached the stage where orderly parliamentary evolution would proceed. The inversion of normal practices continued—a vote of no-confidence or a governmental lack of support did not lead to the formation of a new government. Rather it sounded the death knell of the parliament. Secondly, the dissolution of the chamber meant that the way was now clear for Ghica and Kogălniceanu to establish their own inflated electoral base.

The elections, too represented an inversion of standard practice. Rather than elections in which the voters indicated the direction government should take and providing the representatives to carry out that mandate, the Romanian practice was for the government to indicate the direction electors should follow in order to provide for deputies obedient to the government's program. Kogălniceanu, conducting the elections with his fabled "moral influence," produced a vastly changed and more amenable parliament. The ministry won 157 seats; the opposition 10.[18] This time it was the liberals' turn to complain about electoral violations, but to unavail. In June, the senate was also dissolved and electoral magic worked the desired transformation of that body as well into a pro-ministry appendage.

The liberals became more and more estranged from the prince as these events unfolded. They were increasingly dismayed to find that their strategic withdrawal from office was leading to a gradual disintegration of their power. Their hostility turned ever more on the prince.[19] The prince, in turn, was caught on the horns of a serious dilemma. Preferring to rule with the liberals, he felt constrained by European opinion to maintain the opposing factions in power.[20]

Brătianu and his colleagues, however, showed very little understanding of or sympathy for the problem facing the prince and Romania. When a five-hour interview with Carol failed to persuade the young ruler to alter his course, Brătianu made bold enough to warn him that a political "catastrophe" would result if the liberals were not recalled to power. Carol replied "a Hohenzollern cannot be as easily overthrown as a parvenu prince."[21] Both men were making obvious allusions to Prince Cuza and his fall.

Such exchanges, of course, made it even less likely that the liberals would be returned to office. Resenting what he rightly took to be liberal attempts at political blackmail, Carol continued, with less and less reluctance, to support the opposition coalition. In turn, Brătianu and Rosetti slowly came to realize that events between November 1868 and the spring of 1869, had completely altered the political balance of power against them. They accordingly began to slide into the anti-regime attitudes and subversive tactics that they had employed against Carol's predecessor. It is also obvious that such a tack further alienated Carol from the liberals as he came to feel that their anti-dynastic actions were more than just a political device.

Despite benefiting from the now favorable conjuncture of external and internal factors, the Ghica-Kogălniceanu cabinet was nevertheless unable to do more than react to the liberals. The problem was that the coalition was seriously divided within itself now that the elections were over.[22] These had been a vehicle for Kogălniceanu to try and establish a viable moderate liberal bloc, possibly as a preliminary to the emergence of an organized party.[23] In addition, the temporary elimination of the liberals from the political picture lessened the bond that held the coalition in check and serious divisions now appeared.

In addition to Ghica, the moderate conservative, and Kogălniceanu, the moderate liberal, there was a third strong-willed figure in the government in the person of the minister of justice, Basile Boerescu. Boerescu represented an ambiguous moderate position neither quite liberal nor quite conservative. It gradually became apparent in 1869 that each of these men, apart from a strong commitment against the liberals, was trying to stake out a position for his own political future and trying to establish a power base independent of his current partners.[24] Such scheming was hardly conducive to producing positive coalition actions. Mutual suspicion led to internal dissention and prevented any serious cooperative activity except that directed against the liberals. Coupled with the liberals' growing hostility to the throne, these developments brought Romanian politics once more to sorry times. The hopes of 1866 for a stable, coherent evolution of Romanian affairs had nearly been dissipated.

It may be too pessimistic to say that Romanian politics had become by 1869 solely a contest for power devoid of any idealism or other motives. Obviously there are exceptions to such a generalization. However, the continual rhetoric of Romanian political leaders was beginning to take on a rather threadbare look as seemingly endless groups, factions, coteries, and individuals strove for ascendancy. The dissolution of the liberal chambers and the Kogălniceanu elections were slowly coming to be preludes to the reappearance of the violent conflict and crisis that had characterized Romanian development between 1861-1866. In any case, it was clear that the system of 1866 had no more resolved Romania's problems than those of 1858, 1861, or 1864.

In addition, to the more hard line conservatives, the

re-emergence of Kogălniceanu and his now-open domination of the parliament was only slightly less offensive than the rule of Brătianu had been. To them, Kogălniceanu remained "the man of 2 May," the promoter of agrarian upheaval. The moderate liberals were uncertain of what positive aims they desired, but they were not about to permit the conservatives to reverse reforms hitherto enacted. Their sole point of contact remained opposition to the Brătianu-Rosetti group. The result was endless debate over insignificant issues when the new parliament opened on 29 April 1869.

A detailed recounting of the spring session of 1869 would be only slightly less futile than the session itself. After interminable discussion over election validations had consumed a large portion of time, the session largely degenerated into a forum for attacks on the now long-ousted liberals. A commission was even set up to investigate the liberals' conduct of finances in the 1866-1868 period, a fishing expedition hoping to unavail to land some scandal. Despite Carol's opening call for the settlement of the "questions of great importance" which had necessitated calling the session at an unfavorable time of year,[25] almost nothing was accomplished. By June, the chamber virtually dissolved since an insufficient number of deputies were in attendance.[26] The plain fact was that (leaving aside indifference or other more pressing obligations), the parliament was too fragmented and too intellectually bankrupt to engage in positive actions. By "representing" various factions of a cabinet itself disorganized, the parliament proved one of the most fruitless in Romanian history.[27]

Given the international situation, however, Carol was content to allow coalition cabinet members dispute for power among themselves as long as the powers were kept from resuming their suspicious and negative attitudes toward Romania. The principal threat that now faced the prince was clearly the liberals. As under Cuza, the liberals felt that they were entitled to a share in the government of the country. Finding themselves excluded and apparently dispensable, it was not long before they turned against Carol as they had against Cuza. The prince was, of course, aware of this. While he believed the situation was "not desperate," he felt sufficiently concerned to forbear leaving the country for a planned visit with his parents in March. More specifically, he continued to be cognizant that because Brătianu had "many followers in the country,...one must always take him into account."[28]

The anti-liberal activity of the parliament further intensified the Muntenian liberals' hostility toward Carol since they rightly perceived that he was now the barrier to their return to power. As against Cuza, the first stage of opposition had been conducted in the parliamentary forum. When that avenue was drastically reduced by Kogălniceanu, Rosetti's presses became the mainstay. By August, 1869, the columns of **Românul** were demonstrating a pronounced anti-dynastic attitude.[29] Though it is not likely that the liberals actually wanted to oust Carol, it is clear they believed that Carol could be coerced into restoring them to office as a "parvenu prince" might.

At the same time, steps were taken of a more conspiratorial nature. And as in the days of Cuza, a major effort was devoted to activities abroad. A whole series of reports from Paris and Vienna during 1869 warned the government of extensive liberal negotiations with the French.[30] As in 1865-1866, the intention was to gain the support of France by fostering the impression that the Romanian prince was overly influenced by interests hostile to those of Napoléon III and France. In Carol's case, this was the-not-very-difficult-to-believe accusation that Prussia (and Bismarck) held the upper hand in Bucureşti. Meetings by Dumitru Brătianu with the French foreign minister and by Ion Brătianu with Napoléon III, himself, were reported in September, but with uncertain results.[31] Nevertheless, it was clear that a new campaign abroad was in operation and that it already extended into high circles in France. What French sympathy would mean remained to be seen. And even if official[32] and liberal circles in France were to support the Romanian liberals as a function of anti-Prussianism, it seems unlikely that Napoléon III would have urged Carol to restore a ministry that the French ruler had been so instrumental in ousting.[33]

In August, Carol found a respite from the increasingly discouraging internal situation by taking a trip to the west ostensibly to visit his family in Sigmaringen and perhaps to pay his respects to Paris and Vienna.[34] The real purpose was, however, to provide a princess for Romania.[35] After some negotiations, Carol was married on 3 November, to Princess Elisabeth of Wied. The step was one that had been sought as necessary toward establishing a dynasty in Romania almost from Carol's accession. It was also hoped that the marriage would win the young prince support from his subjects and place him above the political turmoil that was beginning to threaten to engulf Romania once more. The prince was also able to conduct extensive and fruitful negotiations with both Napoléon III and the Habsburgs. Thus, when he returned to Romania on 10 November, he had considerably bolstered his position in a variety of ways. As Carol had hoped, the wedding was well received by the populace, though observers were struck by the lack of real enthusiasm in the welcoming crowds.[36]

On 15 November, the parliament again convened. The final disintegration of the coalition cabinet now occurred. Kogălniceanu clearly controlled the assembly, but within the cabinet his aims were mistrusted and opposed. The divergencies of the ministry were reflected in the chambers; the result was a complete inability of the parliament or government to function.[37] Boerescu and Kogălniceanu finally resigned their posts at the end of January, 1870. Dimitrie Ghica faced with Kogălniceanu's parliament followed on 1 February.

The fall of the Ghica-Kogălniceanu ministry showed that a coalition could not be expected to govern Romania either. Rather than leading to a stabilizing of Romanian political development, such a government only worsened the conflict and provoked crises. On the other hand, the events of 1868-1870 showed that no political group had yet achieved sufficient political support to rule singly. Kogălniceanu had made a strong effort to establish such support, but was not more able to do so than Brătianu and Rosetti earlier. In addition, his use of electoral influence firmly fixed such administrative abuses in the system. As Dimitrie

Bolintineanu caustically noted, after a revolution "against despotism and for liberty" in 1866, despotism now appeared to be "endemic" in Romania.[38]

The era was further important because it deepened the rift between Romanian liberals, especially the Brătianu-Rosetti group and Kogălniceanu.[39] The failure of the liberals to cooperate opened the way for the conservatives to take power completely. The events of 1868-1869 revealed that the liberals had seriously overestimated their position and underestimated the forces arrayed against them. When their imprudent agitation led to the alienation of the prince as well, their position was lost and their carefully gathered gains of 1867-1868 swept away. The responsibility which the liberals bear for the deterioration in the political order in 1869-1870 is heavy. Though they had a parliamentary majority, their insistence on speedy restoration to power and their clumsy, ill-disguised attempts to pressure Carol ignored international realities. Far too much external opposition had been built up for the prince to recall them to power so quickly. The liberals' lack of restraint prolonged their exclusion from power and made their subsequent resort to other methods largely self-imposed.

The prince, too, shares the blame for the course which events took after 1870. His acquiescence in electoral maneuvering by Kogălniceanu (and Brătianu earlier), gave sanction to an illegal activity that cut short the electoral development of Romania. Secondly, by allowing his ministries to control selection of the parliament rather than the other way around, Romanian politics was diverted into the channels of coterie rule and influence-peddling rather than that of real parliamentary growth. The stunting of this growth, in turn, created for Romania the problems of political development which expended so much of her effort during her first twenty years. Avoidance of these difficulties would not, of course, have guaranteed a better development. The point is to see how these events prevented (or made more difficult) such development.

Given the developments discussed above, Prince Carol was obviously the key element in the political equation. No group could rule alone except with his blessing. So far he had not yet been willing to accept an entirely conservative ministry. The events of 1870-1871 were to change his mind decisively.

Chapter 12

The Sixth Phase: Abdication Once More

"Every one fault seeming monstrous till
his fellow fault came to match it."
Shakespeare, **As You Like It**, III.ii.377

The new prime minister, named on 2 February, was Alexandru G. Golescu, sometime partisan of Ion Ghica. Mihail Kogălniceanu, who had hoped to be called in as a replacement for Dimitrie Ghica to rule with the parliament of his making, was passed over. He was so alienated by this action that he was quoted as saying "this dynasty can no longer be sustained."[1] Also passed over was Ion Brătianu, who had a long interview with Prince Carol on 28 January.[2] The Muntenian liberal leader again predicted disaster for Romania if his group was not summoned to power and pleaded that he could no longer hold his followers in check. Carol again resisted liberal intimidation; he replied that he would hold Brătianu fully responsible for any actions his partisans might take. The rift between the once close collaborators was practically complete.[3]

The situation faced by the new Golescu government was unpromising. Both the ministry and Carol had to contend with an ever-growing opposition. The picture drawn by Dimitrie Ghica in a letter to Carol on 1 February gives a good summary.[4] The forces of revolt, he said, were only waiting for an opportune time to act. Neither the police, nor the national guard, nor the army were really trustworthy supports of the regime. Both Moldova and national finances were in a state of disorder and needed attention. Only a unified, energetic ministry could avoid "catastrophe."

The Golescu cabinet, however, earned the dubious distinction of being the weakest of any to date.[5] Though its ministers were sober and well-intentioned, they were to a man very pedestrian in character and nature. The prince had wanted to name Ion Ghica, but had settled for the latter's associate, Golescu, when Ghica refused.[6] Though the new government at once faced and survived a vote of confidence of 67-31, it was unable to make any headway with the chamber. The mass resignation of the liberals in protest against an illegal government (i.e. non-parliamentary) and an illegal parliament (i.e. Kogălniceanu-elected) contributed to further uproar.

The government's weakness was further complicated by increasing rumors concerning the railroad concessions signed, under Carol's influence, with the German financier Strousberg. Charges of speculation and other malfeasance were made against Strousberg and against Carol's personal representative in Berlin, Ambronn.[7] The issue was grist to the mill of those who were trying to foster the ever-increasing anti-Prussian sentiment. The cabinet, under fire at home, resorted to the avenue of diplomatic endeavor in an attempt to win support. Representation at the Porte concerning money and titles were made in a vain attempt to shore up the prestige of the cabinet. Though the question of issuing a Romanian currency was finally resolved,[8] the Golescu government's days were numbered.

There were other serious manifestations against Carol. On 17 February, the former prince, Cuza, was actually validated by the chamber as the winner of a special election for a chamber seat.[9] Though Carol professed to be pleased with this unexpected event (in a letter to Cuza),[10] it was an obvious insult directed toward the throne. Meanwhile, Golescu complained, "unlimited freedom of the press allows them [the opposition] a free field which they abuse to the point of impudence and defamation without limits. Their pages are pamphlets not journals. At their head marches **Românul** distributing from day to day to its satellites words of calumny."[11]

The Muntenian liberals, indeed, were becoming more heavily involved in conspiratorial activities than ever. From Paris it was reported that the liberals were being actively supported by certain mysterious French circles and were making effective strides toward winning greater public support. The growth of their influence was seen as "alarming."[12] Even more alarming were events which took place at Ploeşti.

On 26 March, an actual armed rising seemed underway in Ploeşti, a long-time center of liberal strength. The details of the matter are obscure. The government stressed that a disorderly crowd under the influence of "the Ploeşti demagogues and 2 or 3 journalists" was easily dispersed.[13] The incident was apparently spontaneous, though the culmination of several weeks of restlessness.[14] It had disturbing implications. A similar disturbance took place in April in Piteşti, another liberal stronghold. This incident seems to have resulted from a governmental provocation designed to embarrass the opposition.[15] Though a conspiracy was not yet a concrete reality; it was apparent that some kind of revolutionary situation was brewing.

In addition, not only were the Brătianu-Rosetti liberals and the Kogălniceanu forces actively opposing Carol, but there was also serious hostility on the conservative side as well. Nicolae Blaremberg, an influential member of the conspiracy against Cuza, was now the publisher of *Térra*, a newspaper of pronounced anti-dynastic views. The conservatives, while not actually desirous of ousting Carol, were becoming impatient with Carol's minority, coalition, and factional ministries, expecially as these always seemed to exclude them.

Carol was not without response to these events. Realizing that the army would be a key factor in any renewed struggle for power,[16] he began to make even more assiduous efforts to cultivate the military. February and March 1870, for example, saw extensive inspections of various units, and dinners held to promote good relations between the prince and the army.[17] The second step was an attempt to strengthen the cabinet.

The weaknesses of the Golescu ministry increasingly became a liability to Carol. The chambers' refusal to cooperate with the government over even the most unimportant matters led to a crisis at the end of March. As Golescu tried unsuccessfully to establish a new stronger cabinet, the country was virtually without government. Significantly, the lack of government was hardly discernable. In April the Golescu cabinet resigned.

New factions and groups joined the fray. Aside from the Muntenian liberals, Dimitrie Ghica, Kogălniceanu, other personalities and coteries were actively seeking a larger voice in government. The Iași Fraction, redoubled its efforts in Moldova. Ion Ghica, as always, waited in the wings. Possibly, from Carol's point of view, the only hopeful development was the appearance of a new faction, the so-called "young conservatives" of the Junimea Group, under the political leadership of the outspoken P. P. Carp. The Junimists were centered around a literary society in Iași led by a brilliant young professor, Titu Maiorescu. Well-educated, cosmopolitan, they were heavily influenced by conservative German political evolutionism which was expressed in Maiorescu's famous critique of "forms without foundations."[18] The Junimists thus had an intellectual program for their politics, something with possibilities of developing into a coherent political platform. The Maiorescu (Junimea) attack on political and cultural forms which they believed had no "natural" foundations in the Romanian past led them to oppose almost all of the constitutional devices favored by the liberals. They viewed these measures as simply inappropriate to Romanian development and in fact harmful. Junimea as a political force was not yet a large factor since even its cultural domination of Romania was yet in the future. It was however, a promising programatic addition to a Romanian body politic accustomed to focusing on personalities not ideas.[19]

Though the Junimists had not yet decided to participate in politics as a group, several of their members now formed the nucleus for yet another cabinet. On 20 April, the veteran conservative Manolache Costache Epureanu was named prime minister. His cabinet, the eighth in the less than four years since Carol's installation, was composed of young conservatives in their late 20's and early 30's. Two of the Junimist leaders, P. P. Carp and Vasile Pogor, were included. Carp, as foreign minister, and Epureanu were the dominant figures. Epureanu had always been a stalwart supporter of Carol, but Carp had been recently associated with the anti-dynastic conservatives led by N.

Blaremberg. His cooptation into the cabinet was perhaps a move to disarm the conservative opposition.[20] The principle problems of the new government were to remedy an increasingly poor financial situation, "conciliate" the opposition, and show decisive energy.[21]

The first concrete action of the Epureanu cabinet was to hold new elections since it was clear that nothing could be accomplished with chambers under Kogălniceanu's influence. The vote took place in May and June. Despite the government's "direction" of the polling, the results were very disappointing. Since the cabinet obtained only a very slim majority;[22] it would be very restricted in its actions. Energetic measures internally were precluded.

The inability of the government to "elect" a suitable assembly was a further barometer of the precarious political situation in Romania. At the same time, external poltical developments were beginning once more to impinge on the internal of Romania. The outbreak of war in July between France and Prussia placed Carol and the ministry in an especially poor situation. Romanian opinion on all sides (conservative, liberal, whatever) was nearly unanimous in favor of their French "brothers". Carp, the foreign minister, declared: "Where the Latin race is, there will be the Romanian soul too."[23] He spoke for most Romanians.

Carol, not unnaturally, was supportive of Prussia. The currents hostile to the prince intensified, as the opposition now had a rallying point around which anti-dynasts of all colors could unite.[24] Manifestations in favor of France became both a cover and pretext for anti-dynastic action. As in the plot against Cuza, the foes of the prince had little more than seeking the ouster of the ruler in common. Unlike the plotting against Cuza, the disparate forces hostile to Carol never coalesced into a coalition of any kind. Nevertheless, the opposition, especially the liberals, believing a French victory could provide the occasion for Carol's ouster,[25] began to work more actively toward that end.[26] The cabinet was now hamstrung both externally and internally.

Carol's situation was indeed seriously jeopardized by the Franco-Prussian war. As a German, as a Hohenzollern and as the brother of Leopold of Hohenzollern whose candidacy for the Spanish throne had been the immediate precipitant of the war, his relationship with France was tenuous. In fact, Gramont, the French foreign minister, declared to Strat in Paris that, "Because your sovereign conspires against French interest," France would not hesitate to overthrow him and "give satisfaction to a public opinion which many times has reproached the Emperor for having put a Hohenzollern on the Danube."[27] A more encouraging dispatch followed, however. Strat reported that Napoléon III wanted it communicated to Carol that he could depend on the Emperor's backing and that the French government had "broken off all relations with Romanian adversaries of the prince."[28] It became clear that Carol did not have to worry about losing French support as long as he did not openly align with Prussia. That this was the case is born out by the lack of evident success for missions by Dumitru Brătianu to Vienna and Paris in July.[29] Frustrated on the diplomatic front, the liberals looked to internal approaches.

On 8 August 1870, a new uprising took place in Ploeşti. In comparison to the March events, this incident was of a much more extensive and serious nature. As Prussian troops moved further into the heart of France, and as it became obvious that French victory was a fantasy, the anti-dynastic schemes of the liberals were deepening into a conspiracy to oust Prince Carol. The man that they had installed just four years earlier was now accused of being a tool of Prussia and an enemy of the Latin race. Under the leadership of C. A. Rosetti, Ion Brătianu, and Eugeniu Carada, a network of of conspirators was formed across the country. This time Rosetti was sent abroad to conduct the propaganda wars (Brătianu's reputation was still tarnished because of 1867 and 1868), while Ion Brătianu pulled the strings at home and Carada serverd as direct spokesman and traveling organizer.

Based on their strength in the cities, the Muntenian liberals hoped to dethrone the prince, establish a regency[30] under General N. Golescu, and proclaim Prince Jérôme Napoléon as prince.[31] The date chosen was 8 August, but for unknown reasons was postponed. Word of the delay, however, apparently never reached Ploeşti. On the night of 7 August, last minute preparations continued to be made under the leadership of Al. Candiano Popescu, yet another 1866 activist.

At the appointed hour on 8 August, the rebels, numbering some thousands quickly occupied key governmental and military installations in Ploeşti. Candiano proclaimed himself prefect and read dispatches purporting to be from Ion Brătianu in Bucureşti announcing the "definitive success of liberty on all Romanian territory."[32] The takeover of Ploeşti was well-organized, swift, and successful. Unfortunately for the rebels, none of the other planned revolts occurred, which left the government free to focus immediate action on Ploeşti. Troops were dispatched from Bucureşti, mass arrests of liberal leaders were made and government control quickly restored.[33] Candiano, fleeing in the face of the loyalist troops, was apprehended shortly thereafter.

The cabinet tended to treat the affair lightly. Carp's dispatches acknowledge the scope of the plot, but betray no real alarm.[34] The importance of the event, Carp believed, was "to give us a serious motive to arrest" their Muntenian rivals.[35] Carol, too, had taken the matter to be insignificant at first. Though he refused to believe that Brătianu and Nicolae Golescu had anything to do with the rebels, the prince soon came to see that the implications were much deeper than at first sight. The result was to turn his thoughts into a more pessimistic vein.[36]

Indeed, the incident, far from providing the government with an opportunity to silence the liberal opposition as Carp had hoped, became just one more platform for anti-dynastic manifestations. The liberals had covered their tracks well and most of the leaders, including Brătianu, were released for lack of evidence.[37] The trial of those who remained, led by Carada and Candiano, was turned into a forum for attacks on the throne and government.[38] As the trial proceeded, the government became more and more alarmed.[39] On 17 October, the verdict was returned—acquittal for all the accused[40] who were promptly acclaimed as heroes![41]

As with the abortive revolt against Cuza in 1865, the defeat of the rebels was transformed into a victory. The Brătianu-Rosetti group was exhilarated by the whole affair. Maria Rosetti, C. A.'s wife, writing to Pia Brătianu, the wife of Ion, expressed the liberals' sentiment well with the wish that she were young again so that these "adventures" would be easier.[42] Their enthusiasm was heightened by the proclamation of the French Republic in September. Rosetti, having escaped "the Prussian of Bucureşti" to France, was certain that the new French government would be a support for him and his allies in Romania.[43]

Carol now began to think seriously of abdication. Like his predecessor, Prince Cuza, he reached the conclusion that Romania was ungovernable. The fact that the Ploeşti rebels were acquitted without exception in the face of obvious treasonous activities strengthened that conviction.[44]

The chambers which opened on 15 November proved to be as unruly as ever.[45] Carol was continually attacked, directly and indirectly.[46] Astonishingly, the committee of twenty chosen to respond to Carol's message to the assembly included three of the Ploeşti rebels including Candiano Popescu. Disheartened by the events of 1869-1870, the prince was convinced that he no longer wanted to preside over the destinies of Romania under the existing circumstances.

Carol now resolved to pressure the powers for a revision of Romania's constitution so as to give the prince more authority and control. This, he believed, was the only way Romania could find order amidst her chaotic and bitter political factions. The establishing of order in Romania, in turn, was of vital concern to the powers—to prevent a re-opening of the Eastern Question. These measures would prepare the way for a more stable development; Carol could then abdicate his thankless position. At the end of November, he discussed the problem with Epureanu and dispatched letters outlining his thoughts to the powers.[47] The prince was immediately rebuked by Bismarck, but it was too late to retreat from his intention.[48]

Depressed and discouraged, December 1870 brought Carol yet another crushing blow. The Prussian fiancier Strousberg announced that he was unable to repay the loans made on his railroad concession. Investigation revealed not only financial misconduct on the part of Strousberg, but also by two of Carol's own Prussian associates who had been charged with supervising the Romanian interest in the matter. To make matters worse, the Prussian government made it plain that the Romanians were going to be forced to make good on the losses.[49] Carol was the target of further innuendo and attack. He now wrote to his father that he had definitely decided to leave the Romanian throne. He would do so as soon as he could get the powers to approve modification of the 1866 constitution. "It is not in my power to decide the moment, only that it will not be very far off."[50] On 12 December, a vote of no confidence brought an end to the Epureanu government.

Epureanu had urged Carol to consult the chambers for the new ministry, hoping that some governmental-parliamentary cooperation might result. Their choice was the enigmatic Ion Ghica, who became Carol's prime minister for the third time on 18 December.[51] The move once more antagonized the conservatives, but Carol by this point, according to his own testimony, was now only interested in preparing to leave the country without endangering its interests.[52] Rumors were circulating concerning Carol's appeal to the powers; unfavorable publicity made it appear as if Carol were either ready to push for Romanian independence[53] or was appealling to the powers over the assembly. And he had already dispatched a soon-to-be famous letter indicting Romanian political life in terms of disgust and discouragement. The parallels with Cuza in December of 1865 are striking.

The new Ghica government seemed content to speed the disintegration of Carol's position. His cabinet included several Brătianu-Rosetti partisans. The București council was dissolved, and elections placed control in the hands of the Muntenian liberals. "Success" was assured by appointing a Rosetti confidant, Simion Mihăilescu, as prefect of București police.[54] Lastly, the entire Strousberg dossier was placed before the chambers, thus providing the ammunition for a massive attack on Carol and the throne.[55]

Because of all this, it appeared that Ghica was somehow acting in collaboration with the liberals instead of defending Carol against them. The degree of cooperation between Ghica and the Brătianu-Rosetti group is rather difficult to ascertain. Certainly they had been stridently opposed as late as May, 1870.[56] However, by September, there appears to have been some reconciliation, mainly because they shared common hostilities to the conservatives.[57] While it is doubtful that Ghica wished to see the liberals restored to power,[58] it is possible that Carol's intention of modifying the constitution was leading Ghica to hinder in what ever ways available. The other possibility was that Ghica's actions were part of one more effort to win the throne for himself.[59] Whatever the case, Carol now stood virtrually alone as public attention focused on opposition to the throne and the railroad scandal.

The deposition of the Strousberg dossiers led to the election of a commission to study the matter. With a single exception, the committee was composed of anti-dynasts.[60] They began work on 12 January; their task was to formulate an indictment against Carol. The credibility of the prince fell correspondingly as new revelations of financial machinations were made public.

Then, yet another bombshell burst. On 15/27 January 1871, the bitter letter written by Carol and designed to be leaked to the press appeared in the **Augsburger Allegemeine Zeitung**.[61] It was a harsh, but not entirely unfair,[62] indictment of Romanian political life and of her leaders as men who "refuse to be led, but who do not know how to lead." Carol placed the blame for Romania's disorderly development on her "quasi-republican" constitution. Publication of the letter caused an immense sensation. Coupled with the Strousberg issue and continually growing anti-Prussian sentiment as Bismarck's armies bombarded Paris, this letter very nearly produced Carol's end. Even Carol's Romanian friends felt insulted by the criticsm and parliamentary furor reached new excesses. The ouster of the "foreigner" was no longer merely the aim of a selfish minority.

On 11 February 1871, **Românul** celebrated rather pointedly the anniversary of that "holy day" in 1866 when Romania had ousted a constitution-violating prince and his corrupt henchmen. The proclaiming of the Paris commune was the occasion for similarly exaggerated and veiled pronouncements by **Românul** obviously addressed to Carol. France was congratulated for ridding itself of a "false" ruler and for instituting a "true" government.[63]

Events reached what proved to be their culminating point on 10-11 March 1871.[64] The precipitant was an ill-advised celebration of the birthday of the "new" German Emperor held by the German residents of the Romanian capital. Given the circumstances of pro-French sentiment, the Strousberg issue, and anti-dynastic feeling, the dinner was considered by many a provocation. The banquet drew, in addition to its invited guests, a howling mob of Francophiles, liberals, students and street rabble. The hall was bombarded with stones. Carol, notified of the disorder just a few blocks from the palace, summoned Ion Ghica and the prefect of police Simion Mihăilescu. They were nowhere to be found.

The mob, now flushed with its first success, began to march toward the palace shouting, "Long live the republic," and "Down with the Prince." The situation looked grave. At this juncture, General Solomon (ironically one of the few officers who had refused to aid in Cuza's ouster) apppeared, and his troops soon dispersed the crowd. Ion Ghica, finally appearing at the palace at 1 a.m., was dismissed as prime minister (what he had been doing has never been explained). Carol announced that he was convening the regency of 1866 in order to resign.

On the morning of 11 March, Ion Ghica issued the following circular: "The ministry has given its resignation. General Golescu and Lascăr Catargiu are at this moment at the palace."[65] At 11:30 a.m., Catargiu, Golescu, and D. A. Sturdza (representing the absent third regent Haralambie) met with Carol who announced his abdication. Considerable argument ensued as the three argued that such an action would be disastrous for Romania. In the end, Carol agreed to remain if a strong ministry could be formed.

The next move was to consult the parliament. Five hours of

debate proved inconclusive. As evening drew near again, the streets Bucureşti again filled with restless crowds. At midnight, Catargiu announced to Carol the formation of a new cabinet under his direction. With the swearing-in of the new ministry at 11 a.m. on 12 March, the revolutionary situation began to recede. The ministry "with a firm hand" promised by Catargiu soon was able to restore order, dissolve the hostile assembly, and begin a reign of nearly five years. The throne was preserved.

Had a new internal war broken out? In terms of the analysis developed earlier, the answer is obviously yes. The political process had broken down and an increasing number of its participants were resorting to violence in an attempt to bring about political change.

On the other hand, this violence did not rise to the level of a revolutionary outbreak for a number of reasons. First of all, several of the most important pre-conditions for revolution had not yet been reached. The most important of these lay in the area of support for the regime. Though the liberals had passed over to a bitterly hostile attitude toward Carol, motivated by some of the same desires for power that had led them to oppose Cuza, another major section of the anti-Cuza coalition, the conservatives, remained loyal to the prince. This is because, although they were unhappy with Carol's failure to call on them instead of Brătianu and others, the prince did not constitute a threat to their property or social position. Thus, when the March events pushed Carol toward voluntary abdication, the conservatives stepped in and stabilized the situation.

This was facilitated by a second support for the regime, the military. Both in Ploeşti in 1870 and in March of 1871, Carol retained the active backing of the army--and his position as well. As studies of revolutionary situations demonstrate, competent, loyal military support is a very important pillar of the ruling elite.

When we consider the area of conditions conducive to internal war, a critical factor in 1870-1871 was the failure of any consistent conspiracy to organize against Carol as it had against Cuza five years earlier. Despite scattered incidents, the liberals never really managed to coordinate even their own activities, as the abortive Ploesti revolt showed. Thus, though Carol's position had deteriorated seriously, much of the decline was circumstantial. Lacking a well-planned, conscious effort as a catalyst, the situation never reached sufficient development to present a full-scale internal war or revolution. Though there was a considerable amount of fiscal distress in 1870-1871, this does not seem to have reached the crisis level. It is possible that had the railroad defaults continued on to their expensive conclusion, the financial situation might have become critical, but this occurred later. Finally, when we consider the factor of the relative gap between anticipated and actual need satisfaction (the "J" Curve), the 1870-1871 abdication crisis presents an ambiguous situation. People were clearly unhappy with Carol, from whom they had expected great things. On the other hand, how deep and how far this dissatisfaction ran is difficult to ascertain.

With end of the abdication crisis and the accession of the Catargiu government, a new thread of political development begins in Romanian history. A number of trends that would be important in later Romanian political life still remained to be established. However, it was in this decade of conflict and crisis that most of the basic patterns in modern Romanian political culture took initial shape. It is a summary of these trends as well as a summary of the work of Prince Cuza and Prince Carol that forms our concluding chapter.

Part IV: Conclusion

"There are occasions and causes why and wherefore in all things."
Shakespeare, **King Henry V**, V.i.3

Chapter 13

Romania in the 1870's

"Men at some time are masters of their fates: the fault,
dear Brutus, is not in our stars, but in ourselves..."
Shakespeare, *Julius Caesar*, I.ii.134

Study of Romanian politics between 1861 and 1871 bears out well the theme of conflict and crisis, thereby making one of the most interesting periods in Romanian history one of its most confusing as well. The first decade of its unified, independent internal political activity also offers a good deal of insight into Romanian development as a whole and into Romanian culture and civilization as it rapidly unfolded in the 19th century.

The legacies of the reign of Alexandru Ioan Cuza are difficult to assess because of the vibrant activity of the period and the astonishing number of significant events which the Romanians crammed into a mere decade following the Crimean War. It was as if the Romanian people were determined to give an equal account of themselves, however foreshortened their opportunities were compared to more fortunately situated peoples. What is remarkable is how well, by and large, the Romanians succeeded.

Given the problems of ruling his newly-created and backward realm with less than whole-hearted support, Prince Cuza did remarkably well. His most important achievement was precisely the goal at which his election in 1859 had been aimed: the creation of a Romanian national state through union of the two previously separate Principalities. The accomplishment of definitive union in 1861 and the re-affirmation of autonomy in 1864 through Cuza's persistent efforts were successes that had not been expected so quickly by the nationalist leaders of 1859. Cuza truly established the unity of Romania as a diplomatic fact and deserves his reputation as the "Prince of Union." His successful resolution of the difficult monasteries issue was a further triumph.

In internal affairs, Cuza's record was considerably less sparkling. The handicaps imposed by the Paris-created system of 1859-1864 and the generally intransigent behavior of the conservative parliamentary majorities were mitigating factors. Nevertheless, after 1864, when he was operating under his own governmental scheme, Cuza fared little better except to achieve the agrarian reform he and his associates had long sought. The execution and failure of the reform (hindered, it is true, to an extent by factors outside of Cuza's control) were typical of the administrative shortcomings he and his advisors possessed.

The intangible effects of the agrarian law were, however, significant. Coupled with the broadening of the electoral base of the country, a measure of democratization and equalization was introduced by Prince Cuza and Mihail Kogălniceanu that would not be erased. The land reform of 1864 was, therefore, an important step in altering the status of the Romanian peasantry and in the development of a more open political system.

The changes attempted by Cuza in the army, the legal system, and the schools, while remaining untested, inadequate, or poorly administered, all established important precedents. The effect of these reforms, as well, was to liberalize and modernize all levels and groups in Romanian society, even the conservatives (as was shown by the acceptance by the latter of the new constitution of 1866).[1]

Unable to work with the conservatives or to trust the liberals, Cuza was led eventually to the coup of 2 May. The event made possible most of the reforms Cuza had wanted to achieve. It also made possible Cuza's ouster as the bitter opposition created by the act of 2 May and the very real mistakes of the government led directly to a state of internal war.[2] Cuza's forced abdication, thus, is best explained not as the result of regrettable personal habits, malaise, or the perversity of the opposition, but rather as the product of the almost permanent state of conflict and crisis that existed between the prince and the political majority of the time, a contradiction that Cuza was never able to overcome.

With the failure of the ruling elite and the accumulation of other factors conducive to internal war, the opposition was able to coalesce, conspire, and successfully oust the Cuza government. In the context of this conflict and crisis, Cuza had also failed to resolve important questions of internal development, particularly in the realms of administration and finance; how his successors would fare remained to be seen. In the apt summary of E. Lovinescu:

> Seen up close, the reign of Cuza impresses one with the bitter character of the political struggles, confused by the immixture of personal elements. Seen farther away, and en bloc, it represents the unification of the power of the state, the strengthening through indirect means of sovereign authority under the form of democratizing public life and, in reality, through the relative weakening of the agrarian oligarchy.[3]

It was by these achievements that Cuza set the stage for the meeting of the serious problems of development on their own terms by his successors.

The forced abdication of Prince Cuza in 1866 made possible a fresh start of sorts on the problems of political development. The interim and coalition governments of 1866 registered significant successes in winning acceptance of the legitimacy of the act of 11 February, in bringing Carol to the Romanian throne, and in establishing a new constitutional order. In the areas of finance and administration, where Cuza had left chaos, considerable advances were also made. The imposition by the conservatives of a restrictive electoral system on Romania in this constitution, however, was to prove unfortunate for political development. Nevertheless, the fact remains that the Romanian constitution of 1866 was a remarkably liberal document, and its internal arrangements were at least the equal of any in Europe.[4]

The record of the Ion Ghica government that succeeded the coalition of 1866 was mixed. The recognition of Carol by the Sultan made final the legal status of the new regime. The elections carried out under Ghica's direction were fairly contested—and unsatisfying to nearly everyone. The result was a growing contempt for Ghica's "English" constitutionalism, and a desire by both Carol and the Muntenian liberals for a firmer governmental hand. Though normal development continued, the roots of the eventual deterioration of 1870-1871 were to be found in these reactions to Ghica's ministry.

The accession to power of the Brătianu-Rosetti liberal group marked a significant development in Romanian politics. For the first time, a political group with a coherent program took the reins of power. They made an enthusiastic start by instilling a new liveliness and order in the bureaucracy and by achieving a series of legislative successes. This promising beginning was soon obscured by the unwise actions of Ion Brătianu in regard to the Jewish question and by a failure to be alert to the reactions of foreign governments. Disturbed by the encouragement given by the liberals to irredentist and national movements, as well as by the supposed radical character of the ministry, foreign regimes hostile to such policies were able to use the uproar over the Jewish question to bring the ouster of the cabinet.

Brătianu's lack of attention to public and governmental opinion abroad was a serious shortcoming and one surprising in such a practiced manipulator of foreign opinion. True, internal necessities, such as the need for the cooperation of the Moldovan Fraction, caused him difficulties. However, he never seemed to take these external forces seriously until too late. The national issues that damaged him abroad were another matter. In the end, they were probably unavoidable. Certainly the liberal regime could hardly be expected to take concrete steps to harass nationalist groups, whether Romanian, Serbian, or Bulgarian. In some of their activities, they could have been more cautious; viz., the encouragement of Transilvanian Romanian irredentism was both indiscreet and unlikely to succeed. It is probable, however, that had the Jewish issue not arisen, these matters would not have been serious enough to cause the fall of the government.

In connection with Brătianu's handling of the Jewish problem, the conclusion of Ernest Desjardins is fair and concise: the problem was a real one for the Romanians, but other means than those pursued by the liberal government should have been taken.[5] Jewish fears that "Brătianu has planned the destruction of our race in this country,"[6] were exaggerated and misleading. Nevertheless, the conduct of the government and especially its subalterns was deplorable. The eventual refusal of the Romanians to accept a joint Turkish-Romanian investigation of the Galaţi drownings in 1867 casts more than a little suspicion on their performance.

The second liberal era was more productive. Carol's speech opening the parliament in November of 1868 gave a reasonable summary of their successes in the areas of finance, the army, and the railroads. The measures taken, largely under the personal direction of Ion Brătianu, made important contributions toward the emergence of a stable economy and the raising of Romania from its subservient economic and military status. Brătianu's activities in 1868 demonstrated that he now realized the importance of foreign sensibilities. Unfortunately, he had by then lost his non-Romanian supporters. It was because he lacked the backing of a single foreign power and had won the active hostility of several that Brătianu was ousted in the fall of 1868, despite being at the peak of domestic political success.

From the standpoint of political development, the very length of the liberal tenure was a factor of considerable importance. It was the first period of significant administrative continuity since the birth of modern Romania. The country's chaotic bureaucracy finally had a chance to develop more stability under energetic leadership.

On the other hand, constitutional political growth was dealt a serious blow by the liberal government's disregard for constitutional niceties, especially electoral. It is perhaps arguable that Ion Brătianu's forceful style of administration was more suited to nineteenth century Romania than Ion Ghica's. However, the introduction of electoral fraud and violence as a method of ruling is not justifiable. It permitted the perversion of the infant Romanian constitutional system before it had a change to develop at all, and it set an infinitely bad precedent. Carol's acquiescence in this practice was an important error. After the elections of the fall of 1866, Romania did not have another "fair" election until 1928. These failures of 1867-1868 were decisive in preventing the formation of a fully functioning system of political parties in Romania.

Uncontestably, the ouster of the liberal regime in 1868 had owed mainly to the hostility of foreign governments and their pressure on Carol. The fall of the Brătianu-Rosetti group, however, also owed to the short-sighted desire for domination that caused Brătianu to alienate Mihail Kogălniceanu and his supporters. Their accession to power in 1867 had been facilitated by the so-called "Concordia" agreement, a pact that had recognized the need for the liberals of all stripes to cooperate if they did not want to leave the conservatives an open field. Once in power, Brătianu and Rosetti proceeded to ignore this agreement almost immediately. When Kogălniceanu managed to reappear on the political scene, it was in alliance with the conservative Dimitrie Ghica.

The return to a coalition ministry under Ghica and Kogălniceanu in 1868-1870 resulted in a rapid degeneration of the political order. "The absence of organized, coherent political parties contributed in great measure to the maintenance of a continual struggle...the result was an acute governmental instability."[7] By 1870, the situation verged on internal war. In that year and the next, politically-motivated violence did brake out. And in 1871, only five years after the hopeful installation of Carol, the prince felt constrained to hand in his abdication. Cuza had failed to discover how change or development could be made peacefully in the relationship of political domination. Carol, by 1871, had not been able to do so either. Neither prince, then, was really able to solve one of the principal problems of political development, the establishing of a political system capable of peaceful change and evolution.

Prince Carol's initial five years on the Romanian throne were more productive in some ways than those of Cuza, though internal development failed to continue along the peaceful path that had apparently opened in May of 1866. Only the lack of an organized opposition and the conservatives' reluctance to participate in another internal war had kept Carol from the fate of Cuza, while hopes that the prince would serve as a rallying point to end or moderate political conflict did not materialize.

In the long run, the years 1866-1871 can be seen as the young prince's baptism by fire, even though he nearly perished in the process. It is plain throughout that, while Carol was a disciplined man of certain firm ideas, he was desirous of making the system of 1866 work, not merely trying to concentrate power in his own hands. The unfortunate result was to blunt his youthful optimism and to convince him that more autocratic government (in partnership with various elements of the Romanian elite) was the only alternative.

The developments of 1866-1871 also showed that the coup of 11 February was not truly as "national" as it had claimed. By ostracizing certain segments of the political spectrum and by constant infighting, the coalition ensured a return to struggle and petty conflict if a stable, honest regime were not established. The liberals undermined political honesty; foreign pressure ended attempts at stable government. Though the constitution of 1866 was a significant, liberal document, the gap between its ideals and its practice seriously compromised it.

In fairness it should be observed that despite the disappointing record of its early political development, Romania was certainly no worse than what we can read of in England at the beginning of the nineteenth century where rotten boroughs, political censorship, and other outrages were common. Romania, from an economic and cultural point of view, was surely more than half-a-century behind England, yet many of her institutions were as advanced. If the discrepancy between theory and practice loomed large in Romania, it is still noteworthy that the theory was so developed.

As a matter of fact, from a political standpoint, Romania was never again to know an era with as much parliamentary freedom and richness, especially as 1866-1871. It is unfortunate that more was not done with it. As one observer notes, "the dominant characteristic [of 1866-1871] was parliamentary debate as a form of oratorical sport."[8] No time was left for dealing with the real problems and needs of the country. This habit of useless debate persisted well into the twentieth century.

What other implications did the developments of 1861-1871 have for the future of Romania? The frequency with which conflicts led to crises which resulted in internal war-like situations was not positive. The use of the coup or the attempted coup to seize power was probably a factor in the non-appearance of political parties. Why build an organization and a structure if a coup could wipe them out in an instant? Conflicts and crises are a healthy and normal part of political life; attempting to resolve them through internal war is quite often neither.

The survival of Carol in 1871 ended the instability of the Romanian throne, which had been a problem for centuries. The establishment of a foreign prince in 1866 had proven successful, though not quite as originally assumed. With this, the basis was laid for the future development of the Romanian political system. Carol's position became firm, and he went on to serve a tenure equaled by only one previous Romanian ruler.

A less promising development was that the parliamentary experiences of 1861-1871 caused Carol and most Romanian leaders to regard honest parliamentary government as impossible or even undesirable in Romania. The problem, however, was not that constitutional government had been tried and shown wanting; but rather that the application of and adherence to these principles were at fault. The central problem for the Romanian politician was to discover how one could rule within a constitutional framework without loosening hold on the levers of power. The result of these developments was that while violence as a political tactic eventually lessened, fraud became an accepted mode of operation for all participants in the system.

The establishment of a narrow electorate had the effect of retarding the appearance in Romania of real political parties. There were no real parties as such and as long as so few people could actually participate in Romanian politics, it was to remain a matter of personalities, clubs, factions, and the like. It was also the unfortunate case that electoral operations in Romania generally revealed more about who was conducting them than about public opinion. In addition, there remained the curious phenomenon in Romania that a vote of no confidence in the government generally meant the fall of the parliament rather than the ministry.

Because of these factors, Romania never really developed a parliamentary system on the Western model, nor did it ever completely resolve the problem of peaceful governmental change. A significant result was tremendous ministerial instability with all of its attendant problems: political, administrative, and financial. All of these problems were the direct result of the failures of development in the pre-1871 era.

Despite these shortcomings, the political struggles that kept Romania continually in turmoil between 1861 and 1871 were critical to the pattern of politics that eventually emerged. It had begun to be clear that conflict and crisis were essential elements of Romanian political culture. 1864 had tried to solve one crisis through unilateral action of the prince; it failed. 1866 had tried to resolve another crisis through the ouster of that prince and the creation of a new system with a foreign prince; it failed, though to a lesser extent. People often try to avoid conflict; in politics, to do so is to delude oneself about the political process. The problem is to avoid futile crises or to learn how to cope with them. It was only after 1871, that the Romanians were able to adapt to the life of conflict and crisis that had become a principal characteristic of their modern political life. In so doing, they were confirming Dahrendorf's thesis stated above: "conflict between antagonistic interests gives lasting expression to the fundamental uncertainty of human existence, by ever giving rise to new solutions and ever casting doubt on them..."[9]

Both of the eras which comprise our study, thus, had their successes and failures. Prince Cuza was the more successful in the realm of diplomacy, solidifying Romania's international status. He was also more successful in the democratization of public life through a widened electoral system and the agrarian reform. Cuza, in the end, became a symbol for the first great step toward the Romanian national state, the Union of 1859; he also became a symbol of the Romanian national dream. "The dead don't always die completely, some of them live through what they leave behind, their deeds and accomplishments...," N. Iorga wrote of Cuza.[10] This image is Alexandru Ioan Cuza's true memorial.

Cuza's successors had the greater achievement in the problems of finance and development. Monetary reform was important; so was the rationalization of the budget. The efforts made to end the wide-spread corruption of Cuza's day, were at least in part successful. The measures taken with regard to the army and transportation, under Prince Carol's urging, were also significant advances toward making Romania less subject to external pressures. Finally, separatism as a political option came to an end. After 1871, the union of the principalities never came into serious question, though regionalism continued. If Carol never really elicited the warmth of response that Cuza did, he came to be respected and recognized for being the one whose independent Romanian Kingdom (1878-1881) eventually paved the way for the appearance of "România Mare" in 1918. This was Carol of Hohenzollern's memorial.[11]

Political development in Romania after 1871 proceeded along different and perhaps less fluid routes. New factors would emerge; new forces would make themselves felt. On the other hand, the influences of the events and developments of 1861-1871 would prove to be crucial and formative in Romanian life until World War I. Even thereafter, when the face of Europe and of the newly-emerged Romanian national state were such an apparently dramatic contrast to what had come before, basic patterns and trends begun in the initial decade of modern Romanian political life would still remain significant. Conflict and crisis would continue to typify Romanian politics, producing change and advance as well as pettiness and regress.

The Romanians' game between 1856 and 1871 was a very risky one and their hand was relatively poor; they played it superbly. "The Past is Prologue," we are told. For Romania in the 19th and 20th centuries, this has been a blessing, a bane...and an inspiration.

Part V:

Notes and Appendices

"My Library was dukedom large enough."
Shakespeare, **The Tempest**, I.ii.109

NOTES

● CHAPTER ONE: pp. 15-25

[1] On the basic diplomatic questions involving Romania, see Barbara Jelavich, **Russia and the Formation of the Romanian National State, 1821-1878** [Cambridge: Cambridge University Press, 1984]; R. V. Bossy, **Agenţia diplomatică a României în Paris şi legăturile politice franco-române sub Cuza Vodă** [Bucureşti: Cartea Românească, 1931], **L'Autriche et les Principautés-Unies** [Bucureşti: Naţionala, 1938], and "Politica externă," in: Al. Lăpedatu, et al., **Alexandru Ioan Cuza 1859-1866** [Bucureşti: Cartea Românească, 1932], pp. 33-54; two works by Leonid Boicu: **Geneza chestiunii române ca problemă internaţională** [Iaşi: Editura Junimea, 1975] and **Diplomaţia europeană şi triumful cauzei române (1856-1859)** [Iaşi: Editura Junimea, 1978]; Nicolae Corivan, **Relaţiile diplomatice ale României de la 1859 la 1877** [Bucureşti: Editura Ştiinţifică şi Enciclopedică, 1984], and "Politica externă a lui Alexandru I. Cuza," **Danubius**, Nr. 6-7 (1972-1973), pp. 139-161; G. G. Florescu, "Aspecte privind dezvoltarea relaţiilor internaţionale ale Principatelor Unite, 1859-1866," **Studii**, Vol. 17 (1964), pp. 67-86; Gh. Cristea, "Coordonnées de la politique extérieure de la Roumanie sous le règne d'Alexandru Ioan Cuza (1859-1866)," **Revue Roumaine d'Histoire**, Vol. 18 (1979), pp. 3-20; and Leonid Boicu, V. Cristian, and Gh. Platon, eds., **România în relaţiile internaţionale, 1699-1939** [Iaşi: Editura Junimea, 1980], which has an excellent bibliography, pp. 529-548; and the works given in notes 2 and 3 below. On the Eastern Question, M. S. Anderson, **The Eastern Question** [London: Macmillan, 1966] provides a competent survey. For the European diplomatic scene generally in this era, the standard work is W. E. Mosse, **The Rise and Fall of the Crimean System, 1855-1871** [London: Macmillan, 1963].

²Such as W. G. East, **The Union of Moldavia and Wallachia, 1859** [Cambridge:Cambridge University Press, 1929]; T. W. Riker, **The Making of Roumania** [Oxford: Clarendon Press, 1931]; and Barbara Jelavich, **Russian and the Rumanian National Cause, 1858-1859** [Bloomington: Indiana University Publications, 1959, reprinted with bibliographical additions, Hamden:Archon Press, 1974]; and a veritable avalanche of works by Romanian scholars. These are illustrative: Andrei Oţetea, et al., eds., **Studii privind Unirea Principatelor** [Bucureşti: Editura Academiei, 1960], a collection of articles on virtually every aspect related to this great event; Dan Berindei's article, "L'Historiographie roumaine et le problème de l'unité étatique," **Revue Roumaine d'Histoire**, Vol. 9 (1970), pp. 745-765, which provides a good review, and his book, **Epoca Unirii** [Bucureşti: Editura Academiei, 1979], which gives a useful synthesis of the era; Dumitru Vitcu, **Diplomaţii Unirii** [Bucureşti: Editura Academiei, 1979], on the leading diplomats; Beatrice Marinescu, **Romanian-British Political Relations, 1848-1877** [Bucureşti: Editura Academiei, 1983]; Stela Măries,"Die preussische Diplomatie und die Vereinigung de rumänischen Fürstenturmer. Bemerkungen aufgrund unveröffentlichter deutscher Unterlangen," **Anuarul Institutului de Istorie şi Arheologie A. D. Xenopol**, Vol. 18 (1981), pp. 35-67, on the Prussian connection; and the recent collective volume, **Unirea Principatelor şi puterile europene** [Bucureşti:Editura Academiei, 1984]. Additional materials are given in my review essays "Unity and Continuity in Romanian History," **Canadian Review of Studies in Nationalism**, Vol. 8 (1981), Bibliography, pp. 29-69, and "Romania," in: Gale Stokes, ed., **Nationalism in the Balkans** [New York: Garland Press, 1984], pp. 31-67.

³On Cuza and the Cuza era, the standard works are Gerald J. Bobango, **The Emergence of the Romanian National State** [Boulder and New York: East European Quarterly, 1979], C. C. Giurescu, **Viaţa şi opera lui Cuza Vodă**, second revised edition [Bucureşti: Editura Ştiinţifică, 1970], and Berindei's **Epoca Unirii**, 1979. Bobango's study focuses on the Union of 1859 and

the consolidation of the Romanian nation state which followed under Cuza. It is a story told with grace, wit, and penetrating scholarship. His article, "Recent Historiography on the Cuza Era, 1859-1866," **Balkanistica**, Vol. 7 (1981-1982), pp. 121-132, provides additional bibliographical information. Giurescu was the first to really organize and explore the extensive Cuza archives held by the Romanian Academy; his study brought to light many previously obscure points. Berindei's book provides a review of the premises, achievement, and consequences of union, with Cuza as a pivotal figure. Leonid Boicu, Gh. Platon, and Al. Zub, eds., **Cuza Vodă in memoriam** [Iaşi: Editura Junimea, 1973], is a very comprehensive, high-quality collection dealing with the entire scope of Cuza's life and activity and should be consulted for nearly every aspect of the study that follows. Other works on Cuza include: Marin Mihalache, **Cuza Vodă** [Bucureşti: Editura Tineretului, 1967]; Vasile Curticăpeanu, **Epoca lui Cuza Vodă** [Bucureşti: Editura Enciclopedică, 1973]; Irina Rădulescu-Valasoglu, **Alexandru Ioan Cuza şi politica europeană** [Bucureşti: Editura Academiei, 1974]; Valeriu Stan, **Alexandru Ioan Cuza, 1820-1873** [Bucureşti: Editura Ştiinţifică şi Enciclopedică, 1984]; Matei Vlad, "Rolul lui Alexandru Ioan Cuza la făurirea României moderne," **Studii şi Articole de Istorie**, Volume 6 (1964), pp. 93-114; and the sympathetic biography of Cuza's wife by Lucia Borş, **Doamna Elena Cuza**, second revised edition, [Bucureşti: Naţionala-Ciornei, n.d.].

Additional bibliography can be found in Cornelia Bodea and Grigore Chiriţă, "Formarea statului naţional," **Studii**, Vol. 15 (1962), pp. 1597-1611; V. Cristian, "L'Union des Principautés Roumaines dans l'historiographie etrangère. Bref aperçu," **Anuarul Institutului de Istorie şi Arheologie A. D. Xenopol**, Vol. 17 (1980), pp. 21-55; and the **Bibliografia istorică a României** series described in Appendix Four.

For the Carol period, however, there is no really satisfactory study; M. Polihroniade and Alexandru-Christian Tell, **Domnia lui Carol**, Volume I: 1866-1877 [Bucureşti: Vremea, 1937] is primarily useful on general matters. The most complete biography of Carol is Paul Lindenberg's **König Karl von**

Rumänien, two volumes, [Berlin: Hafen-Verlag, 1923]. It is similar to several other works by Lindenberg in French, German, and Romanian and rather pedestrian. The essays in C. Kirițescu, et al., **Domnia Regelui Carol I** [București: Independența, 1941] are uneven, but useful. The same is true of the collection edited by Al. Tzigara-Samurcaș, **Din viața Regelui Carol I** [Bucuresti: Naționala, 1939]. For Carol's father, K. Th. Zingeler, **Karl Anton Fürst von Hohenzollern** [Stuttgart: Deutsche Verlags-Anstalt, 1911] is dull, but adequate. Though the work, **Domnii regulamentari și historia celor trei ani de la 11 februariu pînă astâdi** [București: Naționala, 1869], by D. Bolintineanu is primarily a polemic against Dimitrie Ghica, it is very useful for the period 1866-1869. Titu Maiorescu, **Istoria contimporană a României (1866-1900)** [București: Socec, 1925] is not really a history at all, but rather the introductions for Maiorescu's published parliamentary discourses issued separately. They are lucid and suggestive.

[4]On these issues and on Romanian historiography per se, see Lucian Boia, **Evoluția istoriografiei române** [București: Universitatea din București, 1976]; Al. Zub, **De la istoria critică la criticism** [București: Editura Academiei, 1985]; and my series of articles, "The Birth of Critical Historiography in Romania: The Contributions of Ioan Bogdan, Dimitrie Onciul, and Constantin Giurescu," **Analele Universității București. Istorie**, Vol. 32 (1983), pp. 59-76, "Inter-War Romanian Historiography in Transition: The Debut of Gh. I. Brătianu, C. C. Giurescu, P. P. Panaitescu, and the Școala Nouă, 1919-1931," in Lucian Boia, ed., **Études d'historiographie** [București: Universitatea din București, 1985], pp. 227-239, and "The Master of Synthesis: Constantin C. Giurescu and the Coming of Age of Romanian Historiography, 1919-1947," in Steven Fischer-Galati, Radu R. Florescu, and George R. Ursul, eds., **Romania Between East and West** [Boulder and New York: East European Quarterly, 1982], pp. 23-108.

[5]These included the following: Apostol Stan, **Grupări și curente politice în România între unire și independență (1859-1877)** [București: Editura Științifică și Enciclopedică,

1979]; P. Cîncea, **Viaţa politică din România în primul deceniu al independenţei de stat** [Bucureşti:Editura Ştiinţifică, 1974], covering 1878-1888; Traian Lungu, **Viaţa politică în România la sfîrşitul secolului al XIX-lea (1888-1899)** [Bucureşti: Editura Ştiinţifică, 1967]; Mircea Iosa and Traian Lungu, **Viaţa politică în România 1899-1910** [Bucureşti: Editura Politică, 1977]; Anastasie Iordache, **Viaţa politică în România 1910-1914** [Bucureşti: Editura Ştiinţifică, 1972]; and Constantin Nuţu, **România în anii neutralităţii 1914-1916** [Bucureşti: Editura Ştiinţifică, 1972]. Among the principal drawbacks presented by some of these books are a resort to a topical approach when certain periods involve "awkward" personalities, an overemphasis on nearly non-existent workers groups, and the frequent use of so-called class analysis to "explain" certain problems and issues rather than actually elucidate them.

[6]Paraschiva Cáncea, Mircea Iosa, and Apostol Stan, eds., **Istoria parlamentului şi a vieţii parlamentare din România pînă la 1918** [Bucureşti:Editura Academiei, 1983], an impressive though uneven work.

[7]Julien Freund, **The Sociology of Max Weber** [New York: Vintage Books, 1969], p. 221.

[8]Maurice Duverger, **Political Parties** [New York: Wiley, 1963], p. xv.

[9]Raymond C. Grew, ed., **Crises of Political Development in Europe and the United States** [Princeton: Princeton University Press], 1978, passim.

[10]Grew, **Crises**, 1978, p. 11.

[11]Cf. Grew, **Crises**, 1978, pp. 16-18.

[12]See, inter alia, Harry Eckstein, ed., **Internal War** [New York: The Free Press, 1964], and his "On the Etiology of Internal Wars," **History and Theory**, Vol. 4, pp. 133-163; and Ralf Dahrendorf, **Essays in the Theory of Society** [Stanford: Stanford University Press, 1968], for the theory, and his **Class and Class Conflict in Industrial Society** [Stanford: Stanford University Press, 1959], for an application. Important collateral contributions on the relationship of uncertainty to such analyses

may be found in the work of F. A. Hayek, such as "The Use of Knowledge in Society," **The American Economic Review**, Vol. 35 (1945), pp. 519-530; G. L. S. Shackle, such as **Expectation in Economics** [Cambridge: Cambridge University Press, 1949]; and Thomas Sowell, such as **Knowledge and Decisions** [New York: Basic Books, 1980].

[13]The quotations are from Dahrendorf, **Essays**, 1968, pp. 128, 227.

[14]Eckstein, **Internal War**, 1964, p. 1.

[15]Eckstein, "Etiology," (1965), pp. 137-140.

[16]See especially Eckstein, **Internal War**, 1964, pp. 25-29.

●CHAPTER TWO: pp. 26-33

[1]Gh. Platon's "Romania la sfîrşitul secolului al XIX-lea. Observaţii privind specificul dezvoltării," in: Nicolae Edroiu, Aurel Răduţiu, and Pompiliu Teodor, eds., **Stat. Societate. Naţiune. Interpretări istorice** [Cluj-Napoca: Editura Dacia, 1982], pp. 128-139, is an excellent presentation of many of the key issues in Romanian development. Also helpful, focusing on the European context, is Damian Hurezeanu, "L'Histoire moderne de la Roumanie dans la perspective du processus historique européen," **Nouvelles Études d'Histoire**, Vol. 5 (1975), pp. 141-157. See also the works cited in Chapter Three, note 19.

[2]For reasons of convenience, "Romania" will be used throughout.

[3]Texts are reprinted in Gh. Petrescu, et al, eds., **Acte şi documente relative la istoria renascerei României**, ten volumes in eleven [Bucureşti: Göbl, 1889-1909], Volume VII, pp. 266-316.

[4]See D. P. Marţian, "Privire generală asupra situaţiunii ţării în 1861," reprinted from **Anale Economice** (1861), in: Victor Slăvescu, ed., **Vieaţa şi opera economistului Dionisie Pop Marţian 1829-1865**, two volumes [Bucureşti: Naţionala, 1944], Volume II, p. 158.

[5]In the words of N. Iorga, writing in 1905, "The peasants, who formed the overwhelming majority of the population, played

no political role whatever." See N. Iorga, **Istoria poporului Românesc** [București: Casa Școalelor, 1928], Volume IV, Part II, pp. 183-184. The agrarian issue was one that plagued Romanian politics until after World War I. The literature is extensive, but not wholly satisfactory. The best works are: Radu Rosetti, **Pentru ce s'au răsculat țaranii** [București: Socec, 1907], still in many ways the most helpful; David Mitrany, **The Land and the Peasant in Rumania** [London: Oxford, 1930]; I. C. Filitti, **Proprietatea solului în Principatele Române pînă 1864** [București: Bucovina, 1935]; Marcel Emerit, **Les paysans roumains depuis le traité d'Adrianople jusqu'à la libération des terres (1829-1864)** [Paris: Sirey, 1937]; Ilie Corfus, **Agricultura în Țările Române 1848-1864** [București: Editura Științifică și Enciclopedică, 1982]; I. Adam and N. Marcu, **Studii despre dezvoltarea capitalism în agricultura Rominiei**, two volumes, [București: Editura de Stat and Editura Științifică, 1956-1959]; N. Adăniloaie and Dan Berindei, **Reforma agrară din 1864** [București: Editura Academiei, 1967]; Constantin Corbu, **Țărănimea din România în perioada 1848-1864** [București: Editura Științifică, 1973], **Țărănimea din România între 1864 și 1888** [București: Editura Științifică, 1970], and **Rolul țărănimii în istoria României. (sec. XIX)** [București: Editura Științifică și Enciclopedică, 1982]; Vladimir Diculescu, "Aspects of Romanian Agriculture Modernization from the Adrianople Treaty to Early 20th Century," **Revue Roumaine des Sciences Sociales. Sciences Économiques**, Vol.22, pp. 215-221; Philip G. Eidelberg, **The Great Rumanian Peasant Revolt of 1907** [Leiden: E. J. Brill, 1974]; and Gheorghe Cristea's comprehensive **Contribuții la istoria problemei agrare în România. Învoielile agricole (1866-1882). Legislații și aplicare** [București: Editura Academiei, 1977], and "Probleme ale modernizării agriculturii României (1864-1877)," **Studii și Materiale de Istorie Modernă**, Vol. 7 (1983), pp. 147-203.

[6]The main sources for this information are: Heinrich Filek von Wittinghausen, **Das Fürstenthum Romanien. Geographisch -militärisch dargestellt** [Wien:Gerold, 1869], based on military

sources; M. G. Obédénare [M. G. Obedenaru], **La Roumanie économique** [Paris: Ernest Leroux, 1876]; George D. Cioriceanu, **La Roumanie économique et ses rapports avec l'étranger de 1860 à 1915** [Paris: Marcel Giard, 1928]; and Polihroniade and Tell, **Carol I**, 1937, pp. 49-148. Statistics for 1849-1865 were used as representative for the period and have been rounded. Statistical information for this era is not very reliable. For recent studies of Muntenia and Moldova, see Louis Roman, "Démographie et société aux pays roumains (XVIe-XIXe siècles)," **Nouvelles Études d'Histoire**, Vol. 6 (1980), pp. 283-295; and Ecaterina Negruți, "Cercetări privind evoluția demografică a Moldovei în secolul al XIX-lea," **Anuarul Institutului de Istorie și Arheologie A. D. Xenopol**, Vol. 19 (1982), pp. 35-41. In "Situația demografică a Moldovei în secolul al XIX-lea," **Revista de Istorie**, Vol. 34 (1981), p. 244, Negruți opts for a Moldovan population figure of less than 1.4 million. This is based taking only 3.5 persons per family rather than the usual five. If we use the latter, the result is 1.9 million, which is close to the estimates used above.

[7]The figure is uncertain. Cf. N. A. Bogdan, **Orașul Iași**, second revised edition [Iași: Naționala, 1913-1915], pp. 74-76; and Gh. Platon, "Populația orașului Iași de la jumătatea secolului al XVIII-lea pînă la 1859," in: Ștefan Pascu, ed., **Populație și societate** [Cluj: Editura Dacia, 1972], pp. 259-343, who estimates 66,000.

[8]The Milcov River is a stream of no significance except as the boundary between Moldova and Muntenia.

[9]An approximation based mainly on Nicolae Suțu, **Notions statistiques sur la Moldavie** [Iași: A. Hennig, 1849], reprinted in Victor Slăvescu, **Vieața și opera economistului Nicolae Suțu, 1798-1871** [București: Naționala, 1941], pp. 267-280. The discrepancy owes to a large unclassified group excluded from the tax rolls.

[10]A contemporary estimate by Ion Ghica, cited in Constantin C. Giurescu, **Contribuțiuni la studiul originilor și dezvoltării burgheziei române pînă la 1848** [București: Editura Științifică, 1972], p. 7.

[11]Cited and discussed in Polihroniade and Tell, **Carol I**, 1937, pp.56-58. These estimates coincide with Nicolae Suțu's **Quelques observations sur la statistique de la Roumanie** [Focșani: Goldner, 1867], reprinted in Slăvescu, **Vieața Suțu**, 1941, pp. 361-419. Again, there is a large "unclassified" group forming 13% of the total.

[12]There is information for the pre-1848 situation in Giurescu, **Contribuțiuni**, 1972, but none for thereafter. Compare this with D. P. Marțian's 1863 comments on the non-existence of a native Romanian middle class and the role played by non-ethnic Romanians in commerce, "Revista economică a anului 1863," in: Slăvescu, **Marțian**, 1944, Volume II, pp. 384-385.

[13]On the Romanian economy generally for this period, see the following: Cioriceanu, **La Roumanie**, 1928; several studies by Gh. Zane, collected in his **Studii**, Elena Zane, ed. [București: Editura Eminescu, 1980]: "Problemele economice ale Unirii în lumina mesajului din 6 decembrie 1859 al lui Alexandru Ioan Cuza," pp. 152-162, "Politica economică a Principatelor în epoca Unirii și capitalul străin," pp. 163-203, and "Probleme de economie financiară în timpul domniei lui Alexandru Ioan Cuza," pp. 204-256; John R. Lampe and Marvin R. Jackson, **Balkan Economic History, 1550-1950** [Bloomington:Indiana University Press, 1982], pp. 80-108, 159-328; Dan Berindei,"Industria în perioada 1859-1864," **Studii și Materiale de Istorie Modernă**, Vol. 7 (1983), pp. 115-145; and Marin Lupu, "Studii privind dezvoltarea economiei României în perioada capitalismului," **Studii și Cercetări Economice** [București: Academia de Studii Economice, 1967], pp. 245-371;

Several other works on Romanian economic history used frequently for this study were: Th. C. Aslan, **Finanțele României dela Regulamentul Organic până astăzi, 1831-1905** [București:Göbl, 1905], and **Studiu asupra monopolurilor în România** [București: Göbl, 1906]; the numerous studies of C. I. Băicoianu, especially **Istoria politicei noastre monetare și a băncii naționale**, three volumes in five, [București: Cartea Românească, 1932-1933], **Istoria politicei nóstre vamale și comerciale de la Regulamentul Organic și până în present**

[București: n.p., 1904], and **Studii economice, politice și sociale 1898-1940** [București: Tiparul Românesc, 1941]; Gh. M. Dobrovici, **Istoricul datoriei publice a României** [București: Albert Baer, 1913], a good source of statistical and other information, along with his **Istoricul desvoltării economice și financiare a României și imprumuturile contractate 1823-1933** [București: Universul, 1934]; and Costin C. Kirițescu's **Sistemul bănesc al leului și precursorii lui**, three volumes, [București: Editura Academiei, 1964-1971], which go well with the similar Băicoianu work above.

Other studies on Romanian economic development include: N. I. Păiănu, **Industria mare în România 1866-1906** [București: Albert Baer, 1906], which appeared also in French and German; V. Popovici, ed., **Dezvoltarea economiei Moldovei între anii 1848 și 1864** [București: Editura Academiei, 1963]; N. Razmiritza, **Essai d'économie Roumaine moderne 1831-1931** [Paris: Librairie Général de Droit et de Jurisprudence, 1932] a topical treatment; Gh. Zane, **Industria din România în a doua jumătate a secolului al XIX-lea** [București: Editura Academiei, 1970], an excellent introductory work with a good bibliography; N. N. Constantinescu, **Aspecte ale dezvoltării capitalismului premonopolist în Romînia** [București: Editura de Stat, 1957], his "The Problem of Industrial Revolution in Romania," **Revue Roumaine des Sciences Sociales. Sciences Économiques**, Vol.20 (1976), pp. 67-92, and Olga and N. N. Constantinescu, **Cu privire la problema revoluției industriale în Romînia** [București: Editura Științifică, 1957]; Constanța Bogdan, "Les finances publiques pendant la période 1859-1916," **Revue Roumaine des Sciences Sociales. Sciences Économiques**, Vol.22 (1978), pp. 197-213; Constantin Bușe, "Unele considerații privind viața economică a României între 1862 și 1876," **Analele Universității din București. Istorie**, Vol. 22 (1973), pp. 49-61, which deals primarily with trade; and Victor Jinga, **Principii și orientări ale comerțului exterior al României (1859-1916)** [Cluj-Napoca: Editura Dacia, 1975].

[14]D. P. Marțian, "Privire generală asupra situațiunii țării,

Bugetul pe anul 1860," in: Slăvescu, **Marțian**, 1944, Volume II, pp. 98-101.

[15]D. P. Marțian, "Revista economico-politică a anului 1864," in: Slăvescu, **Marțian**, 1944, Volume II, pp.437.

[16]Marțian, "Revista 1864," in: Slăvescu, **Marțian**, 1944, Volume II, pp. 435-436.

[17]See especially G. Ibrăileanu, **Spiritul critic în cultura Romînească** [Iași: Viața Romînească, 1909]; and E. Lovinescu, **Istoria civilizației Române moderne**, three volumes [București: Ancora, 1924-1925]. The existence of this regionalism, it needs to be stressed, in no way leads to or supports the bizarre and untenable contention by some (e.g., A. Lazarev and other Soviet "authorities") that the Moldovans and Muntenians are or ever were separate ethnic groups.

[18]See P. P. Panaitescu's instructive "De ce au fost Țara Românească și Moldova țări separate?" in his **Interpretări Românești** [București: Universul, 1947], pp. 131-148.

[19]See Ion C. Brătianu, "Bilanțul situațiune," **Românul**, 18 August-1 September 1858, reprinted in: G. Marinescu and C. Grecescu, eds., **Ion C. Brătianu. Acte și cuvântări. Volume I, Part I (Iunie 1848-Decembrie 1859)** [București: Cartea Românească, 1938], pp. 208-227, for an excellent review of what the Romanians had achieved between 1848-1858.

●CHAPTER THREE: pp. 37-50

[1][București: Albert Baer, 1910], pp. ii-iii. The study, unfortunately for our purposes, ends with 1866.

[2]Duverger, **Parties**, 1963, p. 228.

[3]Xenopol, **Partidelor politice**, 1910, pp. 393-395.

[4]Duverger, **Parties**, 1963, p. xxiii.

[5]This has been confirmed for the period under consideration by the researches of Apostol Stan, **Grupări**, 1979, passim. Apart from the pathbreaking work of Xenopol (up to 1866) and Stan, there is very little monographic literature of substance on Romanian politics seen as a whole. V. Russu has made a number of significant and thoughtful contributions to the study of

Romanian politics, particularly for the period 1866-1871; a general synthesis of his work will shed considerable light on these matters. An excellent example is his essay "Considerații privind teoria alianței burghezo-moșierești," **Anuarul Institutului de Istorie și Arheologie A.D. Xenopol**, Vol. 15 (1978), pp. 455-463, which simply destroys a theory that has been a staple of Romanian so-called Marxist analysis.

On very general lines, there are D. Gusti, et al., **Doctrinele partidelor politice** [București: Institutul Social Român, n.d.], mostly for a later period; and Gr. Peucescu, "Despre partidele politice," **Convorbiri Literare**, Volume 11 (1877-1878), pp. 354-364, 389-401, 435-446, a thoughtful discussion of Romanian political development and its deficiencies. Vasile Maciu's "Formarea regimului politic în România (1810 1881), **A.R. MSI**, new series, Vol. 5 (1980), pp. 9-28, is a survey of state arrangements. Gh. Platon, "Statul—cadru politic de dezvoltare a națiunii române," **Analele Științifice ale Universității Al. I. Cuza. Istorie**, Vol. 28 (1982), pp. 11-30, and Dan Berindei, "Statul modern în viziunea făuritorilor Unirii Principatelor," in Edroiu, **Stat**, 1982, pp. 118-127, both stress the role of the state in Romanian political development, as a vehicle and as an inspiration. Ilie Smultea's **Political Development and Bureaucracy in Romania Prior to World War II** [Berkeley: Unpublished Ph.D. dissertation, 1968] is of some help, but based on secondary works.

On the functioning of the Romanian parliament, in addition to the solid study of Câncea, **Parlamentul**, 1983, the work of George. D. Nicolescu, **Parlamentul Romîn** [București: Socec, 1903], contains much of value, and G. A. Alexianu and I. C. Filitti, "Regimul parlamentar în România," in D. Gusti, ed., **Enciclopedia României** [București: Naționala, 1938], Volume I, pp. 245-264, is a good sketch. G. E. Lahovary, **Histoire d'une fiction. Le government des partis** [București: L'Independance Roumain, 1897] has some valuable and valid points, but is too general and too polemical. George D. Nicolescu and Albert Hermely's **Deputății noștri. 1895-1899** [București: Müller, 1896] provides some biographical information for persons active in this earlier period. There has been only one attempt to make any kind of statistical analysis of the Romanian parliament, Matei Dogan's **Analiza statistică a democrației parlamentare din România** [București: Editura Partidului Social-Democrat, 1946]. While its tables show graphically the instability of the system, its partisan intent prevents it from being as useful as it might have been.

[6]Based on the lists of voters for Moldova and Muntenia given in Petrescu, **Acte și documente**, 1892, Volume VII, pp. 981-1006 (for Moldova) and 1900, Volume VIII, pp. 49-85 (for Muntenia).

[7]See P. Rîșcanu, "Cuza Vodă," in E. Lovinescu, ed., **Antologia scriitorilor ocazionali** [București: Casa Școalelor, 1943], pp. 218-219.

[8]The quotation is from Lovinescu, **Istoria**, 1925, Volume II, p. 30.

[9]Bobango, **Emergence**, 1979, p. 91.

[10]Lovinescu, **Istoria**, 1925, Volume II, p. 35.

[11]According to Duverger (**Parties**, 1963, pp. xxiii-xxx), the extension of the franchise is the key to the development of parties. This proposition both bears out and explains Romanian developments.

[12]Stan, **Grupări**, 1979, p. 10.

[13]On the precariousness of the terms "revolutionary," "counter-revolutionary," "progressive," and "reactionary," as synonyms for "conservative" and "liberal," see Roberto Michels, **First Lectures in Political Sociology** [New York: Harper Torchbooks, 1965], pp. 148-151.

[14]On the other hand, this should not be taken to imply that there were no Romanian liberals in the classical European sense or that there were no linkages between Romanian liberalism and West European liberalism. For what is meant by classical liberalism, cf. F. A. Hayek, "Liberalism," in his:**New Studies in Philosophy, Politics, Economics, and the History of Ideas** [Chicago: University of Chicago Press, 1978], pp. 119-151, which stresses British influences, and Irene Collins, "Liberalism in Nineteenth-Century Europe," in:Eugene C. Black, ed., **European**

Political History, 1815-1870: Aspects of Liberalism [New York:Harper Torchbooks, 1967], pp. 103-127, which leans toward the French. For Romanian liberalism, cf. Eugen Demetrescu, **Liberalismul economic în desvoltarea României moderne** [București:Cartea Românească, 1940]; Stan, **Grupări**, 1979, pp. 15ff; Victoria Brown, "The Adaptation of a Western Political Theory in a Peripheral State: The Case of Romanian Liberalism," in: Fischer-Galati, **Romania Between East and West**, 1982, pp. 269-301; and Gh. Platon, "Le libéralisme roumain au XIXe siècle: émergence, étapes, formes d'expression," in: Al. Zub, ed., **Culture and Society** [Iași:Editura Academiei, 1985], pp. 63-86. As for conservatism, it is interesting that it seems to almost be assumed a priori that it will be indigenous and not transnational. This doubtless deserves further investigation. Robert Nisbet's **Conservatism: Dream and Reality** [Minneapolis: University of Minnesota Press, 1986], and F. A. Hayek's essay "Why I Am Not A Conservative," in his **The Constitution of Liberty** [London: Routledge and Kegan Paul, 1960], pp. 397-411, suggest some potential directions and definitions. Since it is argued here that there were no political parties in the standard sense, the doctrinal question is possibly moot. In any case, it does not seem to impinge on our study apart from the obvious need to identify people and the groups or factions they worked with or represented.

[15]See Stan, **Grupări**, 1979, pp. 123-127.

[16]Cf. P. V. Haneș' preface to Barbu Katargiu, **Discursuri parlamentare (1859-1862 Iunie 8)**, P. V. Haneș, ed., [București: Minerva, 1914], p. XIIff.

[17]Stan, **Grupări**, 1979, pp. 53-55.

[18]Stan, **Grupări**, 1979, pp. 62-64.

[19]This alleged correlation is based on the widely-circulated and completely unsupported assertions of Ștefan Zeletin's **Burghezia română**. Origina și rolul ei istoric [București:Cultura Națională, 1925]. Despite Gh. Zane's early and complete demolition of Zeletin as historian in "Burghezia romînă și marxismul," **Viața Romînească**, Vol. 19 (1927), pp. 244-260, 323-334, Zeletin's fantasies have subsequently achieved the status

of historical commonplace. Further discussion and bibliography on this question can be found in my "Romanian Perspectives on Romanian National Development," **Balkanistica**, Vol. 7 (1981-1982), pp. 92-120, "Procesul dezvoltării naționale române. Contribuția lui Ștefan Zeletin," forthcoming, and "Myth and Reality in Romanian National Development," also forthcoming. Because of his dependence on Xenopol and Zeletin, the sections of Andrew Janos' original and stimulating essay "Modernization and Decay in Historical Perspective:The Case of Romania," in: Kenneth Jowitt, ed., **Social Change in Romania, 1860-1940** [Berkeley: Institute of International Studies, 1978], pp. 72-116, which deal with this problem and era are seriously flawed. The usually sound study of Apostol Stan (**Grupări**, 1979, pp. 37-50) makes a valiant but vain effort to show a correlation between class and group. Even less convincing is D. Drăghicescu's earlier **Partide politice și clase sociale** [București: n.p., 1922]. Such "class analysis" really fails, generally, because of its anecdotal foundations and because of the numerous "exceptions" to alleged rules, e.g., so-called "big boiars" who are liberals (Ion Ghica, the Golescus) and conservative leaders with no property or social standing (Titu Maiorescu, Basile Boerescu). And, it should be noted, even if there were a correlation betwen Romanian social status and political inclination [which has yet to be shown], that would not in itself demonstrate that there is any causal relationship. To make such an assumption is to commit a fallacy of generalization. Cf. David Hackett Fischer, **Historians' Fallacies** [New York: Harper, 1970], pp. 103ff.

[20]Cf. for example the testimony of Nicolae Suțu, **Memoires du Prince Nicolas Soutzo** [Wein: Gerold, 1899], p. 365.

[21]Biographical materials for Cuza's collaborators are reasonably available. The complex career of Mihail Kogălniceanu has attracted the most attention. Fortunately for this literature there is the exhaustive compilation by Al. Zub, **Mihail Kogălniceanu 1817-1891. Biobibliografie** [București: Editura Enciclopedică Română, 1971], which contains 8,149 entries and an extensive chronology. Zub is also the author of the two best books on Kogălniceanu: **Mihail Kogălniceanu istoric** [Iași: Editura

Junimea, 1974], and **Mihail Kogălniceanu. Un fondateur de la Roumanie moderne** [București: Editura Științifică și Enciclopedică, 1978]. Other biographies of Kogălniceanu include: Virgil Ionescu, **Mihail Kogălniceanu** [București: Editura Științifică, 1963], and **Opera lui Mihail Kogălniceanu sub raportul faptei și gîndirii social-economice** [Craiova: Scrisul Românesc, 1979]; Augustin Z. N. Pop, **Pe urmele lui Mihail Kogălniceanu** [București: Editura Sport-Turism, 1979]; and Radu Dragnea, **Mihail Kogălniceanu**, second edition, [București: Române Unite, 1926], a traditionalist interpretation. For Costache Negri, there are: Dumitru Vitcu, "Costache Negri," in his **Diplomații**, 1979, pp. 84-124; Al. Lăpedatu, "Între Cuza-Vodă și Costache Negri," in: **Omagiu lui Ioan Lupaș** [București: n.p, 1943], pp. 450-462; Gh. N. Munteanu-Bârlad, **Costache Negri. Viața și vrodnicia sa** [București: Minerva, 1911]; the short introductions by Emil Boldan to his editions of C. Negri, **Scrieri** [București: Editura pentru Literatură, 1966], Volume I, pp. ii-lxxxi, Costache Negri, **Scrieri social-politice**, E. Boldan, ed. [București: Editura Politică, 1979), pp. 5-59; and Alexandru Ioan Cuza and Costache Negri, **Corespondență**, E. Boldan, ed.[București: Editura Minerva, 1980], pp. v-xlv; Paul Păltănea, "Noi contribuții la biografia lui Costache Negri," **Danubius**, Nr. 2-3, (1969), pp. 137-147, and "Costache Negri. Alte contribuții biografice," **Revista de Istorie**, Vol. 29 (1976), pp. 1325-1343; Apostol Stan, "Costache Negri, candidat al Partidei Naționale la tronul Moldovei în ianuarie 1859," **Danubius**, Nr. 8-9, (1979), pp. 183-192; Pericle Martinescu's **Costache Negri** [București: Editura Tineretului, 1966]; and Andrei Pippidi, "Noi manuscrise ale lui C. Negri," **Anuarul Intitutului de Istorie și Arheologie A. D. Xenopol**, Vol. 18 (1981), pp. 583-596, which is critical of Boldan.

For Vasile Alecsandri there are numerous biographies, mainly concerning his literary career. The best of these is G. Bogdan-Duică, **Vasile Alecsandri. Povestirea unei vieți** [București: Cultura Românească, 1926]; Elena Rădulescu-Pogoneanu, **Vieața lui Alecsandri** [Craiova: Scrisul Românesc, 1940], and G. C. Nicolescu, **Viața lui Vasile Alecsandri** [București: Editura pentru Literatură, 1962]. Dumitru Vitcu covers his diplomatic career in "Vasile Alecsandri," in Vitcu, **Diplomații**, 1979, pp. 40-83. For Nicolae Kretzulescu, there are two reasonably useful studies: A. D. Xenopol's **Nicolae Kretzulescu** [București: Socec, 1915] and G. Barbu's work of the same name [București: Editura Științifică, 1964]. Radu R. Rosetti's "Un uitat, Generalui Ion Em. Florescu," **A. R. MSI**, Series III, Volume 19 (1937), pp. 1-31, is helpful. Bolintineanu and Bolliac have also been treated from a primarily literary point of view. The most useful of these are Teodor Vârgolici, **Dimitrie Bolintineanu și epoca sa** [București: Editura Academiei, 1966], and O. Papadima, **Cezar Boliac** [București: Editura Academiei, 1966]. Ion Strat is the subject of an excellent monograph by Victor Slăvescu, **Ion Strat**, two volumes, [București: Naționala, 1946]. Other collaborators of Cuza's that ought to be mentioned are three Frenchmen: his secretary Arthur Baligot de Beyne, the consul at Iași, Victor Place, and the medical doctor, Carol Davila For the former, there is no existing study. Place is the subject of two fine studies, Marcel Emerit, **Victor Place et la politique française en Roumanie à l'époque de l'Union** [București: Marvan, 1931]; and Victor Slăvescu, **Domnitorul Cuza și Victor Place** [București: Cartea Românească, 1942]; while for Davila there is the thorough G. Barbu, **Carol Davila și timpul său** [Bucuresti: Editura Științifică, 1958]. There are no studies of Cuza's "camarilla."

[22]Preface to **Letopisițile Țării Moldovii** [Iași: 1852], reprinted in Mihail Kogălniceanu, **Opere**, Volume II: Scrieri istorice, Al. Zub, ed. [București: Editura Academiei, 1976], pp. 448 ff.

[23]See Kogălniceanu's autobiographical "Prolegomena" to **Dezrobirea țiganiloru** [București: Göbl, 1891], reprinted in Kogălniceanu, **Opere**, Volume II, pp. 603 ff.. See also N. Cartojan, "M. Kogălniceanu la Berlin," **Arhiva Românească**, Vol. 3 (1939), pp. 29-41; D. C. Amzăr, "Kogălniceanu la Berlin," **Cercetări Literare**, Vol. 3 (1939), pp. 195-318; Ioan Lupaș, "Leopold von Ranke und Mihail Kogălniceanu," in his **Zur Geschichte der Rumänen** [Sibiu: Krafft and Drotleff, 1943],

pp. 490-501; and Al. Zub, **Kogălniceanu istoric**, 1974, pp. 82-131.

[24]"Profesie de credință", in Mihail Kogălniceanu, **Scrieri**, Geo Șerban, ed., [București:Editura Tineretului, 1967], pp. 236-238. The original text is dated 14 February 1860. This priority of the national is apparent in Kogălniceanu's call for free trade and a free economy, with the proviso that protectionism elsewhere meant Romania would have to protect its own industry just as a gardener protects and waters his young trees and flowers. National desiderata were also foremost in his support for funding of credit institutions, public works to promote trade and commerce, and public education (p. 237). Cf. Stan, **Grupări**, 1979, pp. 68-69.

[25]"Profesie de credința," in Kogălniceanu, **Scrieri**, 1967, p. 237-238.

[26]Cf. Kogălniceanu, **Opere**, Volume II, pp. 007-8.

[27]Stan, **Grupări**, 1979, pp. 55-57. Their forte was skillful exploitation of urban crowds to intimidate their rivals.

[28]I. C. Brătianu, "Bilanțul anului 1859," a series of articles published in **Românul**, January 1860, reprinted in: [Vintilă Brătianu, C. Banu, and G. D. Creanga, eds.], **Din scrierile și cuvîntarile lui Ion C. Brătianu, 1821-1891**, Part I: **1848-1868** [București: Göbl, 1903], pp. 206-230.

[29]Resumés are given in **Istoricul partidului Național-Liberal de la 1848 și până astazi** [București: Independența, 1923], pp. 52-54. See also Vintilă C. A. Rosetti's useful **Amintiri istorice. Scrieri adunate și anotate și Programele Liberale de la 1848 pêne astă-di** [București: Românul, 1889], pp. 151-153. Cp. Stan, **Grupări**, 1979, pp. 60-61.

[30]Ion C. Brătianu and C. A. Rosetti to Edgar Quinet, 26 June 1848, published in **Din scrierile Brătianu**, 1903, Part I, pp. 12-14. Everett Garrison Walters' **Ion C. Brătianu: The Making of a Nationalist Politician 1821-1866** [Unpublished Ph. D. dissertation, The Ohio State University, 1972], has an excellent discussion of the pre-1848 French experiences of Brătianu and his friends. The Muntenian liberals are the only group that has had much historical work done on it. The book by

N. N. Hêrjeu, **Istoria partidului naţional-liberal** [Bucureşti: Speranţa, 1915] is a useful work, but only volume I to 1866 appeared. A hostile commentary by a contemporary is E. Quinezu, **Adeveru-lu asupra caderei ministerului Brătianu sau Liberalismu-lu si istori'a lui in Romani'a** [Bucureşti: Nationala, 1871]. The works cited above in notes #14 and #29 should also be consulted. For Ion Brătianu, there is as yet no good biography. The most useful of what has been written are: N. Iorga, "Activitatea politică şi literară a lui Ioan C. Brătianu," in his **Portrete şi comemorări** [Bucureşti: Alcalay, n. d.], pp. 51-82; and Constant Răutu, **Ion C. Brătianu** [Turnu Severin: Datina, 1940], which is rather uncritical and often wrong. C. A. Rosetti fairs the best of any figure under consideration; there are two very good and complimentary biographies of him: Vasile Netea's **C. A. Rosetti** [Bucureşti: Editura Ştiinţifică, 1970] is a careful work that focuses favorably on Rosetti's political career; Marin Bucur's **C. A. Rosetti** [Bucureşti: Minerva, 1970] discusses Rosetti as a publicist from a very critical stance. In addition, there is the commemorative volume, A. Stefănescu-Galaţi, ed., **Lui C. A. Rosetti (1816-1916)**, second edition [Bucureşti: Democraţia, 1916]; Alexandru Cebuc, "C. A. Rosetti—tipograf, editor şi librar," **Bucureşti**, Vol. 7 (1969), pp. 67-80, on Rosetti's business enterprises; Dana Dumitriu, **Introducere în opere lui C. A. Rosetti** [Bucureşti: Editura Minerva, 1984], a literary treatment; and Elisabeta Ioniţă, **Maria Rosetti** [Bucureşti: Editura Militară, 1979], on his wife and family. An extended treatment of Rosetti's close collaborator Winterhalder is given in Gh. Zane, "Enric Winterhalder," **Studii de Istorie a Gîndirii Economice**, Nr. 15 (1971), pp. 1-42. For Dumitru Brătianu, see the preface by Al. Cretzianu to Dumitru Brătianu, **Din arhiva lui Dumitru Brătianu**, two volumes [Bucureşti: Independenţa, 1933], pp. 3-96; Dumitru Vitcu, "Dumitru Brătianu," in his **Diplomaţii**, 1979, pp. 154-186; and Anastasie Iordache, **Pe urmele lui Dumitru Brătianu** [Bucureşti: Editura Sport-Turism, 1984]. Also useful is N. Bănescu, "Dumitru and Ion Brătianu," in: N. Iorga, et al., **Figuri revoluţionare Române** [Bucureşti: Cartea Românească,

1937], pp. 104-125.

For the Golescus there are a number of useful works: G. Bengesco, **Les Golesco** [Paris: Plon-Nourrit, 1921]; Anastasie Iordache, **Goleștii. Locul și rolul lor în istoria României** [București: Editura Științifică și Enciclopedică, 1979], and **Pe urmele Goleștilor** [București: Editura Sport-Turism, 1982]; and George Fotino's monumental **Din vremea renașterii naționale a Țării Românești. Boierii Golești**, four volumes, [București: Naționala, 1939], the first volume being a study of the family based on documents published in the other three. Nicolae Golescu's military role is touched on in Maria Totu, "Generalul Nicolae Golescu, Inspector general al gărzii civice din România (1866-1868)," **Studii și Comunicări de Istorie și Etnografie** (Golești), Vol.2 (1978), pp. 185-199. The same publication, Vol. 3 (1980), pp. 79-88, carries Vasile Novac's "România în concepția lui Ștefan Golescu." For Eugeniu Carada, two pedestrian biographies give him an acceptable coverage: M. Gr. Romașcanu, **Eugeniu Carada (1836-1910)** [București: Cartea Românească, 1937], and Constant Răutu, **Eugeniu Carada** [Craiova: Ramuri, 1940]. Constantin Corbu's "Alexandru Candiano-Popescu— participant și cronicar al vieții politice din a doua jumătate a veacului trecut," **Revista de Istorie**, Vol. 33 (1980), pp. 1737-1763, reviews the career of a younger liberal.

[31]In his article, "Naționalitatea," published in 1853 and reprinted in **Din scrierile Brătianu**, 1903, Part I, p. 43.

[32]See Rosetti in **Românul**, 16 November 1863: "We want the republic. But because to want the republic when all Europe is in constitutional monarchy is to be deranged...we were, we are, and we will be for constitutional government until France, Germany, Austria will be republics," quoted in C. A. Rosetti, **Gînditorul-Omul**, Radu Pantazi, ed. [București:Editura Politică, 1969], p. 32. Compare this with Ion Brătianu's recollection in 1884 that "we abandoned our theories and our convictions and, acting as true politicians, we became monarchists... in the true interests of our country." Cited by G. Bengesco, **Bibiographie Franco-Roumaine**, second edition, [Paris: Leroux, 1907], pp. xxiv-xxv.

³³Ion Hudiţa, "Franţa şi Cuza Vodă. Lovitura de stat proiectată în 1863, după documente inedite," **Hrisovul**, Vol. 1 (1941), p. 280.

³⁴See C. A. Rosetti to Ion Ghica, 20 April 1849, reprinted in Ion Ghica, **Amintiri din pribegia după 1848**, Olimpiu Boitoş, ed., three volumes, [Craiova: Scrisul Românesc, n.d.], Volume I, pp. 69-75.

³⁵Compare Stan, **Grupări**, 1979, pp. 144 ff..

³⁶For a discussion, see Gelu Neamţu, "Mihail Kogălniceanu şi Transilvania," **Studii**, Vol. 20 (1967), pp. 915-932. Cf. Bobango, **Emergence**, 1979, pp. 104 ff.; and Stan, **Grupări**, 1979, pp. 149 ff..

³⁷Walters, **Brătianu**, 1972, sees nationalism as their one consistent idea. It will be observed how easily "nationalism" becomes a means by which all principles are jettisoned as needed.

³⁸See especially Brătianu's speech of 11 February 1863, reprinted in **Din scrierile Brătianu**, 1903, Part I, pp. 275-314; and Walters' sympathetic discussion (**Brătianu**, 1972, pp. 82-87, 169-205). Anti-Brătianu critics have been less considerate of the nuances, e.g., the Marxist analysis of Lucreţiu Pătrăşcanu, **Un veac de frământări sociale. 1821-1907** [Bucureşti: Cartea Rusă, 1945], passim; and the conservative view of I. C. Filitti, "Retuşări la un portret al lui Ion C. Brătianu," in his **Pagini de istoria României moderne** [Bucureşti:Lupta, 1935], pp. 12-14. Particularly telling is Filitti's criticism of a Brătianu attempt to minimize the misery of the peasant situation in an 1859 memoir to Cuza (published in **Din scrierile Brătianu**, 1903, Part I, pp. 182-191) by describing it as both character building and comparable to the lot of "any peasant class in civilized society." Compare also the acid remarks of Bobango, **Emergence**, 1979, pp. 125-127, and the support for the liberals given by Stan, **Grupări**, 1979, pp. 121-123.

³⁹Suspicions of Cuza's authoritarianism were not entirely unfounded. In 1859, barely after taking office, the prince wrote Napoléon III that he personally favored dictatorship, a taste bolstered by having "to choose between traitors and fools" for

ministers (as he remarked to the British consul in 1860). See Riker, **Making of Roumania**, 1931, pp. 242-256.

[40]Cuza, quoted in Henry, **Cuza**, 1930, p. 6.

[41]Bobango, **Emergence**, 1979, pp. 92, 95. Cf. Stan, **Grupări**, 1979, p. 64, on Cuza's ally Nicolae Kretzulescu.

[42]See Ion Brătianu's articles on "Burghezia," published in **Românul** in 1858, and reprinted in: **Acte Brătianu**, 1938, Volume I, Part I, pp. 183-198.

[43]Cf. Stan, **Grupări**, 1979, pp. 65-66, who quotes a contemporary to the effect that other political leaders "fled from him [Ion Ghica] by instinct." Ghica has been the subject of several creditable biographical efforts. The best of these are N. Georgescu-Tistu, **Ion Ghica Scriitorul** [București: Naționala, 1935] and D. Păcurariu, **Ion Ghica** [București: Editura pentru Literatură, 1965]. Also useful is Vasile Netea, "Ion Ghica, 1816-1897," in Val. Georgescu, et al., **Diplomați iluștri** [București: Editura Politică, 1973], Volume III, pp. 219-288. Finally, there is an interesting contemporary study of Ghica by C. D. Aricescu, **Politica d-lui Ioan Ghica, ex-bey de Samosu** [București: Weiss, 1870], who was a political enemy of Ghica's. There is not much worth mentioning on D. A. Sturdza, despite the vast quantity of documents available on his career. The commemorative volume **Dimitrie A. Sturdza. Serbare la împlinirea vîrstei de 70 de ani** [București: Carol Göbl, 1903], pp. 9-13, has a convenient chronology of Sturdza's life. For Al. G. Golescu, Anastasie Iordache's sketch **Al. G. Golescu** [București: Editura Științifică, 1974] does an acceptable job. On Ion Bălăceanu, who was the illegitmate son of Prince A. D. Ghica, see the study by Vasile Maciu, "Memorialistul Ion Bălăceanu (1825-1914)," in: E. Condurachi, ed., **Omagiu lui P. Constantinescu-Iași** [București:Editura Academiei, 1965], pp. 447-454; Vitcu, "Ion Bălăceanu," in his **Diplomații**, 1979, pp. 187-210.

For the Iași Independent Liberal Fraction, there is nothing on them as a group, but a great deal on the thought of their ideological guru, Simion Bărnuțiu. Adequate coverage is given by Petre Pandrea, **Filosofia politico-juridică a lui Simion**

Bărnuţiu [Bucureşti: Fundaţia Pentru Literatură şi Artă Regele Carol II, 1935], and Radu Pantazi, Simion Bărnuţiu. **Opera şi gîndirea** [Bucureşti: Editura Ştiinţifică, 1967].
[44]See my "Romanian Perspectives," (1981-1982), pp. 96-99.
[45] Published materials on the Romanian conservatives are relatively scarce. One exploratory piece is V. Russu's "Consideraţii privind constituirea partidului conservator din România," **Analele Ştiinţifice ale Universităţii Al. I. Cuza. Istorie**. Vol. 18 (1872), Nr. 2, p. 117-146. For Barbu Catargiu, there are only brief sketches; this situation is the case for most conservative leaders. See I. C. Filitti's "Un liberal clasic, Barbu Catargiu," in Filitti, **Pagini**, 1935, pp. 1-7; Victor Slăvescu's introduction (pp. 263-273) to "Scrisori inedite ale lui Barbu Catargiu, ianuarie-octombrie 1861," **Arhiva Românească**, Vol. 7 (1941), pp. 263-290; the prefaces by P. P. Haneş and Anghel Demetrescu to Katargiu, **Discursuri**, 1914, which also compare and contrast Catargiu and Kogălniceanu. Ştefan Antim's "Barbu Catargi," in his **Studii şi portrete** [Craiova: Ramuri, n.d. (1937)], pp. 14-20, is helpful. Cp. Stan, **Grupări**, 1979, pp. 84-87. The two major biographies which do exist for conservative leaders, however, are excellent: C. Gane, **P. P. Carp**, two volumes, [Bucureşti: Universul, 1936]; and E. Lovinescu, **T. Maiorescu**, two volumes, [Bucureşti: Fundaţia pentru literatură şi artă Regele Carol II, 1940]. Shorter treatments include: V. Slăvescu, "Vieaţa şi opera lui Petre Mavrogheni," **A. R. MSI**, Series III, Volume 21 (1939), pp. 569-652, and his prefaces to **Vieaţa Suţu**, 1941, and **Vieaţa şi opera economistului Alexandru D. Moruzi, 1815-1878** [Bucureşti: Naţionala, 1941]; G. Dobre, "Nicolae Suţu: intre iluzii şi realităţi," **Studii de Istorie a Gîndirii Economice**, Nr. 16 (1971), pp. 33-41; M. Theodorian-Carada, **Beizadea Mitica**. Patriotism—ordine—progres [Bucureşti: Informaţia Zilei, n.d.], dealing with Dimitrie Ghica; Emil Ioachimovici's **O pagină din istoria politică a României. Manolache Kostache Epureanu** [Bucureşti: D. C. Ionescu, 1913]; and Nicolae Vătămanu, "Doctorul Apostol Arsache (1789-1874), **Studia et Acta Musei Nicolae Bălcescu**, Vol. 1 (1969), pp. 365-376;

[46]Typical of the Filitti view is his "Barbu Catargiu," in Filitti, **Pagini**, 1935, pp. 1-7.

[47]26 April 1868, reprinted in P. P. Carp, **Discursuri**, Volume I: **1868-1888** [Bucureşti: Socec, 1907], p. 10.

[48]A key factor in Cuza's election. See Jelavich, **Rumanian National Cause**, 1959, p. 54. The conservatives had too many chiefs and not enough followers.

[49]Cf. A. C. Moruzi to C. N. Brăiloiu, 23 January 1862, cited in Stan, **Grupări**, 1979, p. 90.

[50]Consult Stan, **Grupări**, pp. 86-93 for these matters.

[51]On conservatism generally, cp. Stan, **Grupări**, 1979, pp. 79-94, which reflects the weaknesses of existing scholarship on Romanian conservatism.

[52]Cf. Barbu Catargiu on Ion C. Brătianu as "an inexhaustible fountain of aberrations, a receptacle of all extravangances and insanities...," quoted in Stan, **Grupări**, 1979, p. 62.

[53]See Basile Boerescu, **Discursuri politice 1859-1883**, two volumes [Bucureşti: Socec, 1910], Volume I, p. 15, in a speech to the Assembly, 12 February 1859, in which he chides Dimitrie Ghica and Gh. Ştirbey for their "go-slow" conservatism.

[54]For an opposing view, see Stan, **Grupări**, 1979, pp. 62-64. For treatment of the more moderate conservatives: Apostol Stan, **Vasile Boerescu** [Bucureşti: Editura Ştiinţifică, 1974] provides a brief survey; and **Christian Tell, 1808-1884** [Craiova: Scrisul Românesc, 1976], is the title of a biography by Anastasie Iordache and Constantin Vlăduţ. Vlăduţ earlier published "Christian Tell (1807-1884)," **Revue Roumaine d'Histoire**, pp. 855-871.

[55]C. D. Severeanu, **Din amintirile mele (1853-1929)** [Bucureşti: Voinţa, 1929], Volume II, p. 201, voices this view.

[56]A free translation from Mihai Eminescu, **Scrieri politice şi literare**. Volume I: **1870-1877**, Ion Scurtu, ed., [Bucureşti: Minerva, 1905], p. 100.

[57]Bolintineanu, **Domnii regulamentari**, 1869, p. 100: "Romanian political leaders lack principles."

[58]This scorning of "Politicianism" is given its fullest expression in C. Rădulescu-Motru's **Cultura Română şi politicianismul**,

third edition [București: Socec, 1904].

[59]P. P. Carp in a speech of 15 March 1871 to the chamber, quoted in Nicolescu, **Parlamentul Român**, 1903, Volume I, p. xi.

[60]For a discussion of "interior" groups, see D. Brogan's foreward to Duverger, **Parties**, 1963, pp. vii-viii and Duverger's analysis in Book I.

[61]Pp. 37ff. above.

•CHAPTER FOUR: pp. 51-70

[1]Some thought that this was not entirely an accident. Even those who were not this cynical saw that the Convention really ignored Romanian disiderata. Cf. D. P. Marțian: the Convention is "a compromise which had balancing the opposing views of the Powers more in mind than the needs of the Romanians." in Slăvescu, **Marțian**, 1944, Volume II, p. 154.

[2]On this problem, and on the development of constitutional life generally, see Andrei Rădulescu, "Organizarea Statului," in Lăpedatu, **Cuza**, 1932, pp. 55-98; Constantin C. Angelescu, "Unificarea legislației Principatelor-Unite Române sub domnia lui Alexandru Ioan Cuza," in: Boicu, **Cuza Vodă**, 1973, pp. 364-373, and "Dezvoltarea constituțională a Principatelor-Unite de la 1859 la 1862," **Studii și Cercetări Științifică. Iași. Istorie**. Vol. 10 (1959), pp. 151-174; Anicuță Popescu, "Unificarea și modernizarea legislației în timpul domniei lui Alexandru I. Cuza," **Studii și Materiale de Istorie Modernă**, Vol. 7 (1983), pp. 61-114; Valeriu Stan, "Desăvîrșirea Unirii Principatelor Române pe plan administrative (1859-1864)," **Studii și Materiale de Istorie Modernă**, Vol. 7 (1983), pp. 7-60; I. Tanoviceanu, "Pagini din istoria Domniei lui Cuza Vodă," **Revista pentru Istorie, Archeologie, și Filologie**, Volume 12 (1911), pp. 249-267, Volume 13 (1912), pp. 1-23; and Câncea, **Istoria parlamentului**, 1983. The basic documents are in I. Vîntu and G. G. Florescu, **Unirea Princpatelor în lumina actelor fundamentale și constituționale** [București: Editura Academiei, 1965].

[3] Romanians generally consider 24 January 1862, the opening of the unified parliament, as the date of "Union."

[4] Cuza's official proclamation of 11 December 1861 declared, "Union is achieved; the Romanian nationality is founded."

[5] Angelescu, "Unificarea legislaţiei," in Boicu, **Cuza Vodă**, 1973, pp. 389-392.

[6] Stan, **Grupări**, 1979, p. 51.

[7] Ion C. Brătianu to Alexandru I. Cuza, February 1859, published in: **Acte Brătianu**, 1938, Volume I, Part I, pp. 267-276.

[8] See Barbu Catargiu, Assembly speech of 24 June 1859, reprinted in: Katargiu, **Discursuri**, pp. 143-151; and Barbu Catargiu to Apostol Arsachi and C. N. Brăiloiu, 6 June 1861, cited in Stan, **Grupări**, 1979, p. 120.

[9] Brătianu to Cuza, February 1859, **Acte Brătianu**, 1938, Volume I, Part I, p. 275.

[10] See Radu Rosetti, **Amintiri**, Volume II: **Din copilărie** [Bucureşti: Fundaţia Culturale Principele Carol, 1925], pp. 190-191.

[11] See Bobango, **Emergence**, 1979, pp. 93-94.

[12] Hudiţa, "Franţa şi Cuza Vodă," (1941), p. 275.

[13] See Al. Lăpedatu, "Viaţa politică internă," in Lăpedatu, **Cuza**, 1932, passim.

[14] Quoted in Stan, **Grupări**, 1979, p. 131.

[15] **Românul**, cited in Stan, **Grupări**, 1979, p.133.

[16] Cp. Stan, **Grupări**, 1979, pp. 130-138.

[17] See Xenopol, **Partidelor politice**, 1910, pp. 391-392 for Kogălniceanu's frank statement in this regard and Riker, **Making of Roumania**, 1931, pp. 202-208, for Cuza's affirmation in 1859.

[18] See Bobango, **Emergence**, 1979, pp. 41ff., for a definitive refutation. This does not alter the fact that some people resented Cuza's governing rather than just ruling.

[19] A fact recognized by the press of the day. See Xenopol, **Partidelor politice**, 1910, p. 405n. On Cuza and the groups, see Stan, **Grupări**, pp. 158-164.

[20] Cp. Al. Lăpedatu, in Lăpedatu, **Cuza**, 1932, p. 27: "The

peasantry did not have and could not have as yet a predominent role in public life."

[21] Stan, **Grupări**, 1979, p. 100.

[22] D. P. Marțian identified this as the key economic issue. See Slăvescu, **Marțian**, 1944, Volume II, p. 368.

[23] On the not inconsiderable unrest, street activity, and violence of these years, see Bobango, **Emergence**, 1979, pp. 98-100; the documents published by N. Iorga, "Mișcarea țărănească din 1862," **Revista Istorică**, Vol. 23 (1937), pp. 210-216; and a series of articles by Dan Berindei: "Mișcarea țărănească condusă de Mircea Mălăeru (ianuarie 1862)," **Buletin Științific al Academiei RPR**, Vol. 3 (1951), pp. 37-63; "Știri noi cu privire la Mircea Mălăeru și la mișcarea țărănească din 1862," **Studii**, Vol. 8 (1955), pp. 95-101; "Frămîntări social-politice Bucureștene în anii 1859-1862," **Materiale de Istorie și Muzeografie**, Vol. 1 (1955), pp. 81-100; "Frămîntări orășenești din noiembrie 1860 în Țara Romînească," **Studii și Articole de Istorie**, Vol. 1 (1956), pp. 264-313; and "Frămîntări politice în Țara Românească în primăvară și vara 1861. Petiția de la 11 Iunie 1861," **Revista de Istorie**, Vol. 34 (1981), pp. 75-109.

[24] These events are well described in Bobango, **Emergence**, 1979, pp. 124-129. The documents are found in D. C. Sturdza-Șcheeanu, ed., **Acte și legiuiri privitoare la chestia țărănească. Seria I: Dela Vasile Lupu până la 1866**, Volume II: **1856-1866** [București: Socec, 1907], pp. 404-723. See also Demetrescu's preface to Katargiu, **Discursuri**, 1914, p. 38.

[25] Barbu Catargiu, Assembly speech of 8 June 1862, reprinted in Katargiu, **Discursuri**, 1914, p. 368.

[26] Among curious factors are the apparent knowledge which Brătianu, Rosetti, and others had about the affair (e.g. a statement by Brătianu in 1886) and the dismissal of the prosecutor just as the investigation began to move forward. Cf. Demetrescu's preface to Katargiu, **Discursuri**, 1914, pp. 42-44; Tr. Ionescu-Nișcov, "În legătură cu asasinarea lui Barbu Catargiu," **Revista Istorică**, Vol. 26 (1940), pp. 21-30; and Al. Lăpedatu: "În jurul asasinării lui Barbu Catargiu," **A. R.**

MSI, Seria III, Vol. 14 (1933), pp. 185-226; "Un aventurier ungur în Principatele Române în epoca unirii lor (Gh. Bogáthy)," A.R. MSI, Seria III, Vol. 22 (1939-1940), pp. 43-147; and "Mărturii și precizări nouă cu privire la sfîrșitul lui Barbu Catargiu (8 Iunie, 1862)," A. R. MSI, Seria III, Vol. 21 (1939), pp. 111-140.

[27]Xenopol, **Partidelor politice**, 1910, p. 434.

[28]Quoted in Riker, **Making of Roumania**, 1931, pp. 403-404.

[29]The claim that the liberals opposed Cuza merely to get credit for all reforms (as asserted in P. Constantinescu-Iași, et al., **Istoria Romîniei** [București: Editura Academiei, 1964], Volume IV, p. 349), is dubious. That they wanted power is more plausible, but not necessarily perverse politically.

[30]Cf. the Rosetti Kogălniceanu correspondence cited in Stan, **Grupări**, 1979, pp. 70-73. Stan notes that Cuza was also very uneasy about potential liberal coalitions.

[31]Stan, **Grupări**, 1979, p. 76.

[32]Giurescu, **Cuza Vodă**, 1970, p. 166, credits Gh. Știrbey, of the conservatives, with seeking a modus vivendi with the Muntenian liberals as early as 1861.

[33]A useful contemporary statement on the difficulties facing Cuza in November 1862, may be found in "Mémoir sur les Principautés-unies présenté a Mr. Drouin de Lhuys, Novembre 1862," reprinted in Gh. Duzinchevici, "Chestiuni din vremea lui Cuza-Vodă," **Cercetări Istorice**, Vol. 10-12 (1934-1936), nr. 1, pp. 97-101.

[34]On the diplomatic issues, consult Riker, **Making of Roumania**, 1931, pp. 362, 404-405; Jelavich, **Rumanian National Cause**, 1959, pp. 103-114; and Jelavich, **Russia**, 1984.

[35]He had been specifically exempted from such responsibility by the Convention of Paris. See Basile Boerescu, **Codicile Romane**, second edition, [București: Laboratoriloru Români, 1873], p. 18.

[36]The text of the resolution is found in **Din scrierile**, **Brătianu**, 1903, Part I, pp. 270-274.

[37]Din scrierile Brătianu, 1903, Part I, p. 291-292. Cf. also p. 312: "only two forms of government are possible: Constitutional government, where the nation governs intelligently, and Despotism, that is, government of a man and his cohorts."
[38]The phrase "Monstrous Coalition" was coined by Cezar Bolliac, a Cuzist. Cf. Papadima, **Boliac**, 1966, p. 253.
[39]Din scrierile Brătianu, 1903, Part I, p. 311.
[40]Din scrierile Brătianu, 1903, Part I, p. 313.
[41]Cuza's defenders pointed out the interesting fact that since the signers of the amendment had formed the ministries for 38 of the 48 months of Cuza's rule they were indicting, they were indirectly attacking their own performances.
[42]Quoted in Păcurariu, **Ion Ghica**, 1965, p. 207.
[43]Cf. Bobango, **Emergence**, 1979, pp. 138-142. Milkowski's [T. T. Jez] memoirs make no mention of any contact with Rosetti. On Cuza's relationships with the Poles, Serbs, and Magyars, see Leonid Boicu, "Cuza Vodă față de lupta popoarelor pentru emancipare națională," in: Boicu, **Cuza Vodă**, 1973, pp. 235-260. Also relevant are: C. C. Giurescu, "Tranzitul armelor sîrbești prin România sub Cuza-Vodă (1862)," **Romanoslavica**, Vol. 11 (1965), pp. 33-65; P. P. Panaitescu, "Principatelor Romîne, Cuza Vodă și polonii," **Romanoslavica**, Vol. 5 (1962), pp. 71-84; Miodrag Milin,"Relațiile româno-sîrbe în timpul domniei lui Alexandru Ioan Cuza," **Revista de Istorie**, Vol. 37 (1984), pp. 63-76; Gh. Duzinchevici, "Chestiuni," (1934-1936), pp. 90-104, on both Polish and Serbian questions; and Béla Borsi-Kálmán, **Együtt vagy külön: a Kossuth-emigráció és a román nemzeti mozgalom kapcsolatának történetéhez** [Budapest: Magvető Kiadó, 1984], on the Magyars. On Romanian contacts generally with foreign revolutionaries and nationalists, a useful work is Al. Marcu, **Conspiratori și conspirații în epoca renașterii politice a României, 1848-1877** [București: Cartea Românească, 1930].
[44]See Eder [București] to Rechberg [Vienna], 22 June/4 July 1862, reprinted in Lăpedatu, "Mărturii," (1939), pp. 26-28. Cuza had by this time made clear to the foreign consuls that a dictatorship was inevitable. See especially Riker, **Making of**

Roumania, 1931, pp. 418-421; Constantin C. Angelescu, **Proectul de Constituţie al lui Cuza Vodă dela 1863** [Bucureşti: Libertatea, 1935], and "Unificarea legislaţiei," in: Boicu, **Cuza Vodă**, 1973, pp. 382-387; and I. C. Filitti, "Un proect de constituţie inedit al lui Cuza Vodă dela 1863," **Anuarul Institutului de Istorie Naţională**, Vol. 5 (1928-1930), pp. 354-401.

[45]Netea, **C. A. Rosetti**, 1970, p. 270 for this and the subsequent quote.

[46]See also Ion Brătianu to Pia Brătianu, 10 September 1863, reprinted in Ion Nistor, ed., **Din Corespondenţa familiei Ion C. Brătianu**, Volume I: **1859-1883** [Bucureşti: Independenţa, 1933], pp. 20-21.

[47]On this see Al. C. Golescu's long letter to Ştefan Golescu in July, 1863, reprinted in George Fotino, **Boierii Goleşti**, 1939, Volume IV, pp. 380-404.

[48]There were also at this time some anti-governmental efforts in Iaşi, but there is no evidence to connect these with the coalition.

[49]Panu's trip had been originally set in August of 1863.

[50]See Panu's letter to D. Ghica that the coup of 2 May "has changed everything," cited in A. D. Xenopol, **Istoria Românilor din Dacia Traiană**, third edition, fourteen volumes, [Bucureşti: Cartea Românească, 1925-1930], Volume XIV, p. 19.

[51]Some desultory negotiations between Cuza and the opposition in June proved fruitless except to perhaps further alienate Cuza and Ion Brătianu.

[52]Text of the memorandum is published in Gh. Duzinchevici, "Din vremea lui Cuza Vodă," **Cercetări Istorice**, Vols. 8-9 (1932-1933), nr. 2, pp. 67-69.

[53]See note 44 above.

[54]Hudiţa publishes in an annex ["Franţa şi Cuza Vodă," (1941), pp. 419-421] a draft letter (obviously never sent!) prepared by Cuza for the French ambassador in Constantinople, Moustier, "dated" 1/13 December 1863 explaining the "coup" and giving its "justification." Cuza assures Moustier that "anarchy" has been averted and that he has had "the satisfaction of noting

the excellent effects of this act of vigor," applauded by "the mass of the population." Cuza later apparently "lost" the uncanny powers that allowed him to preview the future here.

[55] Documents in Sturdza-Şcheeanu, **Acte şi legiuiri**, 1907, Ser. I, Volume II, pp. 724-835.

[56] These letters are printed, along with the Rosetti-Panu letters, in the annex to A. D. Xenopol, **Domnia lui Cuza Vodă** [Iaşi: Dacia, 1903], Volume II, pp. 367-413. See also Ion Brătianu's letters to his wife in April-May, 1864, in Nistor, **Corespondenţa Brătianu**, 1933, Volume I, pp. 22-26; and C. A. Rosetti, **Corespondenţa**, Marin Bucur, ed. [Bucureşti: Editur Minerva, 1980], pp. 373-383.

[57] Netea, **Rosetti**, 1970, p. 273.

[58] C. A. Rosetti to A. Panu, 6/18 June 1864, reprinted in Rosetti, **Corespondenţa**, 1980, pp. 374-377. Cf. Ion Brătianu in Nistor, **Corespondenţa Brătianu**, 1933, Volume I, p. 25.

[59] Relevant documents are in Vasile M. Kogălniceanu, ed., **Acte relative la 2 maiu 1864** [Bucureşti: Göbl, 1894]. In April, 1864, according to Bolintineanu, the ministry was within an ace of ordering the arrest and incarceration of the whole opposition. Kogălniceanu and cooler heads prevailed, and it was left for 2 May to be the decisive day. See N. Blaremberg, **Essai comparé sur les institutions et les lois de la Roumanie** [Bucureşti: Peuple Roumain, 1885], p. 723.

[60] Xenopol, **Partidelor politice**, 1910, p. 456.

●CHAPTER FIVE: pp. 71-101

[1] Cited in Netea, **Rosetti**, 1970, pp. 278-279.

[2] Bobango, **Emergence**, 1979, pp. 167-169.

[3] See particularly Xenopol, **Partidelor Politice**, 1910, pp. 460-466; Lăpedatu, in Lăpedatu, **Cuza**, 1932, pp. 22-23; and Bobango, **Emergence**, 1979, pp. 169-172.

[4] Netea, **Rosetti**, 1970, pp. 274-275. Cf. C. A. Rosetti to A. Panu, 10/22 July 1864, reprinted in Rosetti, **Corespondenţa**, 1980, p. 382, for a pathetic letter written a day after **Românul** was shut down (9 July 1864).

[5]Sabina Cantacuzino, **Din viața familiei I. C. Brătianu 1821-1891**, second edition, [București:Universul, 1934], pp. 41-47. To make matters worse, Rosetti hated country life.
[6]Mihalache, **Cuza Vodă**, 1967, p. 199.
[7]Romașcanu, **Carada**, 1937, p. 66
[8]Bucur, **C. A. Rosetti**, 1970, pp. 231-232, notes that Rosetti felt persecuted anyway; events subsequent to 2 May encouraged such a feeling. On the error of closing Rosetti down, see Grigore Chiriță, "Preludiile și cauzele detronării lui Cuza Vodă," **Revista de Istorie**, Vol. 29 (1976), pp. 360-361.
[9]E. Carada to A. Panu, 3 June 1864, reprinted in Romașcanu, **Carada**, 1937, pp. 88-90. In another bitter letter to Panu (pp. 91-93), Carada described the events of May as an act of lèse nationalité.
[10]C. A. Rosetti to A. Panu, 6/18 June 1864, in Rosetti, **Corespondența**, 1980, pp. 374-377. Dimitrie Ghica is alleged to have said, "Better a dictatorship by Pisoski [a Cuza crony] than of Brătianu and Rosetti."
[11]Cf. Nicolae Suțu, **Memoirs**, 1899, p. 393.
[12]Michelet included a laudatory sketch about C. A. Rosetti's wife, Maria, in his **Legendes démocratiques du nord** [Paris: Garnier Frères, 1854], while his close collaborator Quinet was married to a Romanian. Both had been mentors of the Brătianu's and their friends. Dumesnil was a close personal friend of Ion Brătianu. See Netea, **Rosetti**, 1970, pp. 278-280; Xenopol, **Istoria**, 1930, Volume XIV, pp. 18-19; and various notes in Marin Bucur, ed., **Documente inedite din arhivele franceza privitoare la Români în secolul al XIX-lea** [București: Editura Academiei, 1969], passim.
[13][Paris: Renou and Meaulde, n.d.]; [Paris: Dentu, 1864]; and [Paris: Dentu, 1864]. The last was published anonymously but written by Rosetti.
[14]Text of the powers' resolution is in D. A. Sturdza, **Insemnătatea europeană a realizarea definitive a dorințelor rostite de divanurile ad-hoc in 7/19 și 9/21 octomvrie 1857 și autoritatea faptului indeplinit executat in 1866 de cei indreptățiți** [București: Göbl, 1912], pp.

129-131. For a discussion of constitutional change in the 1864-1866 era, see Angelescu, "Unificarea legislaţiei," in : Boicu, **Cuza Vodă**, 1973, pp. 392-404.

[15]See V. Russu, "Monstruoasa coaliţie şi detronarea lui Al. I. Cuza," in: Boicu, **Cuza Vodă**, 1973, pp. 507 and 510.

[16]Dan Berindei, "Les antécédents de l'abdication du Prince Cuza," **Revue Roumaine d'Histoire**, Vol. 18(1979), p. 785, clears up some of the confusion on this count.

[17]Apart from the excellent pieces mentioned in the preceding two notes, consult Bobango, **Emergence**, 1979, Stan, **Grupări**, 1979, and Chiriţă, "Preludiile," (1976), pp. 347-371.

[18]Russu, "Detronarea," in: Boicu, **Cuza Vodă**, 1973, pp. 523-525; Chiriţă, "Preludiile," (1976), p. 357-360

[19]Berindei, "Antécédents,"(1979), pp. 785-788.

[20]Russu, "Detronarea," in: Boicu, **Cuza Vodă**, 1973, pp. 526-533; Berindei, "Antécédents," (1979), pp. 789-791; Chiriţă, "Preludiile," (1976), p. 358. The liberal Ion Ghica group also was an active participant in these discussions and basically shared the Muntenians' antipathy toward Cuza.

[21]Cf. Ion C. Brătianu, Assembly debate of 28 January 1869, reprinted in **Acte Brătianu**, 1935, Volume I, Part 2, pp. 79-80, which recounts a meeting at Ion Ghica's house in 1863 with Panu, Brâncoveanu, and others present, at which the matter of Cuza's ouster came up. Brătianu ended the discussion with the question: "Who will we put in his place?" Once the country's autonomy was secure, then a change would be possible. In this same account, incidentally, Brătianu dates his doubts about Cuza to 1863 and his abandonment of support for Cuza at 1864.

[22]Russu,"Detronarea," in: Boicu, **Cuza Vodă**, 1973, pp. 523-533.

[23]Chiriţă, "Preludiile," (1976), pp. 357-357; Russu, "Detronarea," in: Boicu, **Cuza Vodă**, 1973, p. 535.

[24]See the account by Nicolae Blaremberg, one of the founders, in his **Essai**, 1885, pp. 724-726.

[25]Berindei, "Antécédents,"(1979), pp. 794-796. On Masonry and Romanian politics, see also Mihai D. Sturdza, "Junimea

societate secretă," **Ethos**, Vol. 1(1973), pp. 81-110. Several of the military men involved in Cuza's ouster were lodge members. Berindei wisely concludes that there are ties here, but their precise nature is unclear.

[26]Documents in Sturdza-Şcheeanu, **Acte şi legiuiri**, 1907, Ser. I. Volume II, pp. 836-1037.

[27]Article 6 of the agrarian law of 1864 provided technically for the state to provide land for those newly married (and other special cases), but it remained a dead letter until 1876. See N. Adăniloaie, "Improprietărirea însurăţeilor," **Studii**, Vol. 22 (1969), pp. 887-903.

[28]Texts in Boerescu, **Codicile Române**, 1873.

[29]When Cuza was ousted, the British consul reported that Librecht's safe contained £50,243 in specie and securities, he owned a new £15,000 house (the most elaborate in Bucureşti, and a small estate. "Singular savings on a salary of about £700 a year for 6 years." See J. Green to Clarendon, 15/27 Feb. 1866, nr. 27, PRO London, FO/78/1920.

[30]Bobango, **Emergence**, 1979, pp. 179-182; Giurescu, **Cuza**, 1970, p. 337; Chiriţă, "Preludiile," (1976), pp. 361-363; Berindei, "Antécédents," (1979), pp. 797-798.

[31]It should be emphasized that while a revolution is a form of internal war, all internal wars are not revolutions. In fact, very few internal wars are revolutions. On the criteria employed here, the events of 1865-1866 in Romania did not constitute a revolution.

[32]R. Rosetti, **Amintiri**, 1925, Volume II, pp. 209, 191-192.

[33]For details on these matters see especially Th. C. Aslan, **Finanţele României dela Regulamentul Organic până astăzi, 1831-1905** [Bucureşti: Carol Göbl, 1905], pp. 85-120; Gh. M. Dobrovici, **Istoricul desvoltării economice şi financiare a României şi imprumuturile contractate 1823-1933** [Bucureşti: Universul, 1934], pp. 66-80; Apostol Stan, "Fiscalitatea în ultimii ani ai domniei lui Cuza Vodă în lumina unor documente inedite," **Studii**, Vol. 23 (1970), pp. 81-86. and Xenopol, **Istoria**, 1930, Volume XIV, pp. 139-185.

[34]Bobango, **Emergence**, 1979, pp. 179-179.

[35]See James C. Davies, "Toward a Theory of Revolution," **The American Sociological Review**, Vol. 27 (1962), p. 6, for the "J-Curve;" C. Dalyell to E. Hammond, private letter, 26 January/7 February 1866, PRO London, FO/78/1920, folios 21-23,, on the starvation and deplorable conditions in Romanian which he believed made a jacquerie likely; and Russu, "Detronarea," in: Boicu, **Cuza Vodă**, 1973, pp. 511-512, on discontent.

[36]Quoted in Bobango, **Emergence**, 1979, pp. 194-195.

[37]See Al. Papadopol Calimah, **Amintiri și istorie 1853-1888**, BAR București, Mss. Rom. 846, folio 438, on Cuza's alarming health condition.

[38]Cuza's reputation as a womanizer was well-known and offensive, even to the not very upright citizens of București. See Giurescu, **Cuza**, 1970, pp. 379-380; Severeanu, **Amintiri**, 1929, Volume II, pp. 24-25, 31-32; and Borș, **Elena Cuza**, n.d., passim.

[39]Bobango, **Emergence**, 1979, pp. 192-193.

[40] C. C. Giurescu, **Alexandru Ioan Cuza** [București: Editura Militară, 1973], is on Cuza's military career. The volume **The Crucial Decade: East Central European Society and National Defense, 1859-1870**, edited by Béla K. Király [New York: Brooklyn College Press, 1984], pp. 361-426, has an entire series of articles on the military during Cuza's reign, which is also the subject of Ilie Ceaușescu,"Armata Unirii. Politica militară a domnitorului Alexandru Ioan Cuza (1859-1866)," **File din Istoria Militară a Poporului Român**, Vol. 7 (1980), pp. 60-95; Șerban Constantinescu and Elena Pălănceanu, "Despre organizarea armatei romāne în anii 1862-1866," **Cercetări Istorice**, Vol. 1 (1979), pp. 117-135; Constantin Căzănișteanu, "Le développement de l'armée roumaine pendant le règne d'Alexandru Ioan Cuza (1859-1866)," **Revue Internationale d'Histoire Militaire**, Vol. 9 (1975), pp. 22-30; Teodor Popescu, "Modernizarea forțelor armate românești în timpul domniei lui Alexandru Ion Cuza," **Revista de Istorie**, Vol. 32 (1979), pp. 79-102; and Constantin Olteanu, **The Romanian Armed Power Concept**: A historical approach [București: Military Publishing

House, 1982], pp. 123-144.

[41]A. S. București's MAI files contain massive quantities of documents on this unexplored subject. On the agricultural crisis, see Gh. Cristea, "Criza agrară din 1865-1866 și consecințele sale social-economice," **Studii și Materiale de Istorie Modernă**, Vol. 5 (1975), pp. 101-135.

[42]One of two sons by Maria Obrenovici (Cuza's wife was childless). The absurd attempt by Cuza to present the lad as orphaned by a flood did little to appease public sensibilities.

[43]Berindei ["Antécédents," (1979), p. 798] agrees; Russu ["Detronarea," in:Boicu, **Cuza Vodă**, 1973, pp. 542-543] doesn't because the declaration was narrowly focused on the foreign prince issue. But, as has been shown above, this was the whole raison d'être of the coalition.

[44]The original document is found in BAR București, Mss. Rom. 5314, folio 1. It is in Rosetti's hand; Ion Ghica's signature appears to have been added later.

[45]A point not lost on contemporaries; see N. Gane, **Amintiri, (1848-1891)** [Craiova: Scrisul Românesc, n.d.], pp. 100-101.

[46]**Din scrierile Brătianu**, 1903, Part I, p. 295.

[47]With no thanks to the opposition, it might be added.

[48]For differing motives, of course: the conservatives for protection of their property "rights;" moderates and liberals for dealing with nationalist aims such as independence and irredenta.

[49]Blaremberg, **Essai**, 1885, pp. 687-688.

[50]See Rosetti to Paul Bataillard, 5 May 1865, reprinted in Răutu, **Brătianu**, 1940, p. 76.

[51]Xenopol, **Partidelor politice**, 1910, p. 469.

[52]Rumored to be printed in Austria, Switzerland, and various places all over Romania, **Clopotul** probably was being done right in București. See Netea, **Rosetti**, 1970, pp. 280-281.

[53]Gane, **Amintiri**, n.d., pp. 99-100.

[54]R. Metternich (Paris) to Foreign Minister [Mensdorff], (Wein), 25 April/7 May, 1865, reprinted in Bossy, **L'Autriche**, 1938, p. 393, reporting on a conversation with Drouyn de Lhuys, the French Foreign Minister. Drouyn is said to feel it will be difficult to find a prince for such a situation. Metternich

concludes: "If this affair comes to pass, I foresee a very delicate situation for us, for which it would be good to prepare in advance."

[55] The letter is reprinted in **Din scrierile Brătianu**, 1903, Part I, pp. 399-402.

[56] Quoted in Romașcanu, **Carada**, 1937, p. 102.

[57] See especially Bobango, **Emergence**, 1979, pp. 185-191.

[58] See the significant letter to Cuza in late August by his foreign minister, N. Rosetti-Bălănescu, published and discussed in Radu R. Rosetti, "Un document inedit asupra mișcării dela 3 August 1865," **A.R. MSI**, Seria III, Vol. 15 (1934), pp. 93-106. The writer can hardly be accused of a bias for the opposition. Ion Brătianu's jocular attitude in his letters from prison also suggests non-complicity. See Nistor, **Corespondența Brătianu**, 1934, Volume I, pp. 31-52. The Rosetti-Bălănescu letter flatly contradicts the version of events given by other cabinet officers.

[59] Bobango, **Emergence**, 1979, pp. 187-189.

[60] Reprint in Rosetti, "Un document," (1934), of a letter to Cuza late in August, 1865.

[61] Bolintineanu, **Domnii regulamentari**, 1869, pp. 48-50.

[62] Rosetti, "Un document," (1934), p. 104.

[63] See Eckstein, "Internal War," (1965), p. 154: "The worst situation of all seems to arise when a regime, having driven its opponents underground, inflamed their enmity, heightened their contempt, and cemented their organization, suddenly relaxes its repression...."

[64] The prospectus for the review in found in BAR București, Mss. Rom. 5314, folio 9.

[65] The text of this letter is printed in Ioan Hudița, "Contribuțiuni la istoria lui Cuza-Vodă," **Arhiva** (Iași), Vol. 38 (1931), nrs. 2-4, pp. 155-160.

[66] The relevant portion of the speech is quoted in Titu Maiorescu, **Istoria**, 1925, p. 7.

[67] See Papadopol Calimah, **Amintiri**, Mss. Rom. 846, folios 436-437.

[68] Rosetti, **Amintiri**, 1925, Volume II, pp. 204-205.

[69] Maiorescu, **Istoria**, 1925, p. 7.

[70]Green to Clarendon, 24 December 1865/5 January 1866, nr. 2, PRO London FO/78/1920.
[71]Green to Clarendon, 20 February/4 March 1866, nr. 3, PRO London, FO/78/1920.
[72]See especially Bobango, **Emergence**, 1979, pp. 194-200.
[73]Borş, **E. Cuza**, n.d., pp. 172-173.
[74]Reprinted in E. Perticari-Davila, **Din viaţa şi corspondenţa lui Carol Davila** [Bucureşti: Fundaţia pentru Literatură şi Artă Regele Carol II, 1935], pp. 743-744.
[75]Giurescu, **Cuza, 1970, p. 363.**
[76][Paris: Dentu, 1866]; [Paris: Chez tous les Libraires, 1866]; and [Paris: Luxembourg, 1866].
[77]Brătianu's correspondence mentions specific contacts with Paul Bataillard and Armand Lévy. See Nistor, **Corespondenţa Brătianu**, 1934, Volume I, p. 58.
[78]The quotation is from a Cuza letter in 1863, reprinted in Henry, **Cuza**, 1930, as document 11.
[79]Tillos to Drouyn, 20 Jan./1 Feb. 1866, published in Henry, **Cuza**, 1930, as document 41. Consult Henry for similar dispatches of Tillos.
[80]Al. Candiano-Popescu, **Amintiri din viaţa-mi** [Bucureşti: Universul, 1944], Volume I, pp. 83-84.
[81]Bolintineanu, **Domnii regulamentari**, 1869, pp. 51-57.
[82]Ion Bălăceanu, **Souvenirs intimes**, BAR Bucureşti, Arhiva Ion Bălăceanu, I.Mss.3, folios 25, 30.
[83]Ion Bălăceanu, **Souvenirs politiques et diplomatiques 1848-1903**, BAR Bucureşti, Arhiva Ion Bălăceanu, I.Mss.1, pp. 99-100. This is a typed copy of Bălăceanu's memoirs, including an expanded, slightly different version of the **Souvenirs** cited in note 64 above. This mss. was used through the permission of Prof. Vasile Maciu of the University of Bucureşti and is hereafter cited as Bălăceanu, **Memoirs**. The reader should be cautioned that Bălăceanu's account was written long after these events and is obviously embroidered or inaccurate in various places, e.g., some matters of fact are clearly contradicted by contemporary documents (now found in BCS, Fond. St. Georges) produced by Bălăceanu himself. Cf. Vasile Maciu, "Ion Bălăceanu," in:

Condurachi, ed., **Constantinescu-Iași**, 1965, pp. 447-454.

[84] This reconstruction of the events is based largely on three sets of memoirs: Candiano's **Amintiri**, 1944, pp. 89-98; Bălăceanu, **Memoirs**, pp. 99-100; and Th. Văcărescu, "Venirea în țară a Regelui Carol," **Convorbiri Literare**, Volume 48 (1914), pp. 963-972. It might be noted that Eugeniu Carada later denied that Sultana Crețianu had any role in these events (see Theodorian-Carada, **Efimeridele**, 1930, Volume I, p. 60.)

[85] Candiano, **Amintiri**, 1944, pp. 82, 91; Th. Văcărescu, "Memorii," **Convorbiri Literare**, Volume 49 (1915), p. 667; Green to Clarendon, 21 January/2 February 1866, nr. 12, PRO London, FO/78/1920.

[86] See Candiano, **Amintiri**, 1944, p. 101.

[87] Severeanu, **Amintiri**, 1929, Volume II, pp. 32-34. Coincidentally, seven years was both the normal term of military service and the usual tenure of elected Romanian princes.

[88] F. Damé, **Historie de la Roumanie contemporaine** [Paris: F. Alcan, 1900], p. 144.

[89] Green to Clarendon, 26 January/7 February 1866, nr. 14, PRO London, FO/78/1920.

[90] Hêrjeu, **Istoria partidului național-liberal**, 1915, pp. 242-243. This is more or less hearsay for which we have no other evidence.

[91] Bălăceanu, **Memoirs**, pp. 100-102; Blaremberg, **Essai**, 1885, p. 728; Al. Beldiman, "Februarie 1866: Complotul împotriva țarii," **Magazin Istoric**, Vol. 6 (1972), nr. 10, pp. 23-30 (a reprinting, with some omissions, of Beldiman's memories from his newspaper, **Adevărul**, in 1891).

[92] Bălăceanu, **Memoirs**, pp. 100-101. Reports that Beldiman was decoyed by a poker game or booze are probably false.

[93] See Nicolae Golescu quoted in G. Bezviconi, "Principatele dunarene în 1866," **Revista Istorică**, Vol. 26 (1940), pp. 248-249 (these are the memoirs of a traveler in Romania in 1866).

[94] The exclusion was not actually the military's wish but rather part of a scheme by Ion Ghica to cut Rosetti out of the cabinet and strengthen his own hand. Later claims by Bălăceanu

(Souvenirs, folios 43-50) and Bălăceanu and D. A. Sturdza (an open letter to Rosetti and Brătianu, 15 March 1869, BAR Bucureşti, Mss. Rom. 5320, folios 221-222 verso) that Rosetti's exclusion was at his own request are false. This is shown by contradictions in their two accounts. A third Bălăceanu account (in his **Memoirs**, pp. 102-103) does not mention the episode, but portrays Bălăceanu as modestly refusing all proferred posts.
[95]The original is in A. S. Bucureşti, mss. 1367, f. 7.

●**CHAPTER SIX: pp. 102-126**

[1]Texts of the major proclamations of 11 February may be found in A. S. Bucureşti, MAI/Ad/76/1866, folios 3-4; 266. Most official documents may also be found reprinted in **Monitorul Oficial**, the Romanian official record. For a brief, but very careful review of the Romanian situation in 1866, see Grigore Chiriţă, "România în 1866. Coordonate ale politicii interne şi internaţionale," **Revista de Istorie**, Vol. 31 (1978), pp. 2197-2220. Also suggestive in Gh. Platon, "1866—începutul revoluţiei române pentru independenţă. Ecouri în presa europeană (I)," **Anuarul Institutului de Istorie şi Arheologie A. D. Xenopol**, Vol. 21 (1984), pp. 439-452. Stan, **Grupări**, 1979, pp. 220-336, provides an analysis of the major issues facing the post-1866 regime; as does V. Russu in "Din frămîntările politice ale perioadei de instabilitate guvernamentală şi parlamentară (1866-1871). Încercări de revizuire a Constitutiei," **Analele Ştiinţifice al Universităţii Al. I. Cuza. Istorie**, Vol. 18 (1972), pp. 67-84, and "Cauzele luptelor politice dintre grupările liberale şi conservatoare în anii instabilităţii guvernamentale şi parlamentare (1866-1871)," **Cercetări Istorice**, Vol. 9-10 (1978-1979), pp. 411-437. On the period of Carol's election, see also P. Cîncea, "Opoziţia parlamentară faţă de alegera lui Carol de Hohenzollern ca domnitor al României," **Studii şi Articole de Istorie**, Volume 10 (1967), pp. 173-181; and V. Russu, "Frămîntări în perioada instaurării regimului burghezo-moşieresc (martie-iunie 1866)," **Analele Ştiinţifice ale Universităţii Al. I. Cuza. Istorie**, Volume 13 (1967), pp. 119-130;

[2] "Regent" is used here as a translation for "locotenant domnesc," which is not strictly speaking a regent, but a temporary "placeholder."

[3] Cabinet lists are given in: Mioara Tudorică and Ioana Burlacu, "Guvernele României între anii 1866-1945. Liste de miniştri," **Revista Arhivelor**, Vol. 32 (1970), nr. 2, pp. 429-476; Costescu, **Fazele ministeriale**, 1930; and a compilation for the years 1866-1888 found in A. S. Bucureşti, Casa Regală, 7/1866. See Appendix Three below.

[4] Candiano-Popescu, **Amintiri**, 1944, pp. 129-131 gives a graphic account.

[5] Bolintineanu, **Domnii regulamentari**, 1869, p. 67.

[6] Green to Clarendon, 12/24 February 1866, nr. 20 and 16/28 February 1866, nr. 29, PRO London, FO/78/1920.

[7] Green to Clarendon, 15/27 February 1866, nr. 27, PRO London, FO/78/1920.

[8] Th. Văcărescu, "Doue episode din viaţa mea," **Convorbiri Literare**, Vol. 26 (1892), pp. 63-66.

[9] The text of Cuza's statement was given prominent display in the **Monitorul**.

[10] Green to Clarendon, 23 February/7 March 1866, nr. 34, PRO London, FO/78/1920. An intemperate, and unconvincing, opposing view is given by N. Iorga's **Cuza Vodă şi duşmanii săi a doua zi după detronare** [Vălenii-de-Munte: Neamul Românesc, 1909].

[11] See Vrintz to Buol, 21 March/2 April 1857, nr. 29, printed as document 54 in Henry, **Cuza**, 1930.

[12] See Henry, **Cuza**, 1930, pp. 44-47, for details on Philip. Some notes of Eugeniu Carada on the foreign prince question, mss. in BCS Bucureşti, Fond. St. Georges, Pach.LI/D.3, shed interesting light on the probable motivation for Flanders' election.

[13] These events and quotations are recounted in Văcărescu, "Venirea," (1914), pp. 974-976.

[14] Green to E. Hammond, 16/28 February 1866, private, PRO London, FO/78/1920.

[15] See the comment of Gh. Ştirbey: "Ion Gh--- conserves his Byzantine language and manner;...but he has his place in

foreign affairs." Gh. Ştirbey to Barbu Ştirbey, 13/25 March 1866, reprinted in Gh. Ştirbey, **Feuilles d'Automne et Feuilles d'Hiver**, two volumes, [Paris: Calmann-Lévy, 1916], Volume I, pp. 181-183.

[16]For a more thorough treatment of the diplomatic side of 1866, see W. E. Mosse, "England, Russia, and the Roumanian Revolution of 1866," in his **Crimean System**, 1963, pp. 131-157; the relevant parts of the Henry and Riker works already cited; Frederick Kellogg, **Rumanian Nationalism: From Autonomy to Independence, 1866-1878** [Unpublished doctoral dissertation, Indiana University, 1969], which provides the diplomatic compliment to the internal development that is the focus of the present study; and Jelavich, **Russia**, 1984, pp.153 ff.. Napoléon III's policies are conveniently summarized in William E. Echard, **Napoléon III and the Concert of Europe** [Baton Rouge: Louisiana State University Press, 1983].

[17]See for example Green to Clarendon, 7/19 February 1866, nr. 18, PRO London, FO/78/1920, and Tillos to Drouyn, 31 January/12 February 1866, nr. 9, printed as document 46 in Henry, **Cuza**, 1930.

[18]Texts are given in **Archives Diplomatiques**, Vol. 6 (1866), nr. 2, pp. 136-137; 166-168. This publication contains most of the relevant official documents for 1866.

[19]See Moustier to Drouyn, 23 February/7 March 1866, in Henry, **Cuza**, 1930, document 115.

[20]Particularly against Russia. Moustier to Drouyn, 20 April/2 May 1866, in Henry, **Cuza**, 1930, document 254.

[21]Prokesch to Mensdorff, 25 March/6 April 1866, nr. 17A, in Henry, Cuza, 1930, document 184.

[22]All of this is spelled out in a long dispatch to Paris: Mensdorff to Metternich, 17 February/1 March 1866, in Henry, **Cuza**, 1930, document 88.

[23]Mosse, **Crimean System**, 1963, pp. 133-135.

[24]Mosse, **Crimean System**, 1963, pp. 151-154.

[25]Henry, **Cuza**, 1930, thoroughly documents the French position. A very general overview of Napoléon III's policy and activity related to Romania is given in my "Rumanian Unity,"

in: William E. Echard, ed., **Historical Dictionary of the French Second Empire, 1852-1870** [Westport: Greenwood Press, 1985], pp. 582-584; see also N. Corivan, "Principatele Unite în combinațiile politice internaționale ale lui Napoleon al III-lea din anul 1866," **Studii și Materiale de Istorie Modernă**, Vol. 3 (1973), pp. 195-215.

[26]E. Carada to A. Panu, 2/14 June 1864, reprinted in Romașcanu, **Carada**, 1937, pp. 91-93.

[27]Eder to Mensdorff, 14/26 February 1866, in Henry, **Cuza**, 1930, document 71.

[28]See Ion Ghica to the powers, 20 February 1866, published in **Archives Diplomatiques**, Vol. 6 (1866), nr. 2, pp. 287-292.

[29]On the broshures, see the lists given in Bengesco, **Bibliographie**, 1907, p. 68, and Al. & G. Rally, **Bibliographie Franco-Roumaine**, two volumes, [Paris:Leroux, 1930], Volume II, pp. 89-90. On the "subscriptions," see BCS București, Fond, St. Georges, Pach. LI/D.8 which has a receipt from **Le Temps** for 90 subscriptions, apparently paid for by Ion Brătianu, as one example. This seems to have been a common practice.

[30]The irony of the problem is stressed by Titu Maiorescu, **Istoria**, 1925, pp. 8-10. On the army in this period, see Maria Totu, "Mișcarea popularea de întărire a forțelor armate din vara anului 1866," **Analele Universității din București. Istorie**, Vol. 20 (1971), pp. 96-113.

[31]Typical of these was Radu D. Rosetti's "Armata Română în Dioa de 11 Februarii," **Românul**, 16 February 1866.

[32]Text in **Monitorul**, 19 February 1866. Strictly speaking, all restrictions were not removed until the new constitution was adopted.

[33]Data from Aslan, **Finanțele**, 1905, p. 106-109.

[34]Some of this is summarized in the report presented to the chamber on 28 April 1866, as a balance sheet of the Cuza years. It is partisan, but basically accurate. A reprint is given in C. I. Băicoianu, **Istoria monetare**, 1932-1933, Volume I, Part 2, pp. 177-228. This report is further discussed below in Chapter Seven.

[35]Some details in Green to Clarendon, 10/22 March 1866, nr.

42, PRO London, FO/78/1920. One of the most questionable of the concessionaires, Godillot, happened to be a close friend of Napoléon III.

[36]It was revealed in **Monitorul** that the thrifty Librecht had managed to misappropriate over one million lei in his brief tenure. See also Chapter Five, note 29 above.

[37]See Appendix Two on money for this question

[38]**Românul**, 1 March 1866, has a favorable article on these efforts by Enric Winterhalder, Rosetti's close associate and financial advisor.

[39]Texts for this debate are given in Sturdza-Şcheeanu, **Acte şi legiuiri**, 1907, Ser. I, Volume II, pp. 1038-1121. The draft law, initiated by Kogălniceanu in 1865, is discussed in Gh. Cristea's "Anteproiecte ale primei legi de tocmeli (învoiele) agricole," **Studii**, Vol. 25 (1972), pp. 511-527. Cristea discusses the implementation of the law in "Prerogativele consiliilor comunale privind executarea tocmelilor agricole (Legea din martie 1866)," **Revista de Istorie**, Vol. 27 (1974), pp. 553-565; as does V. Russu, "Observaţii privind aplicarea legii învoielilor agricole din 1866," **Analele Ştiinţifice ale Universităţii Al. I. Cuza. Istorie**, Vol. 19 (1973), pp. 103-110; and Ion Pătroiu, "Aspecte ale aplicării în Oltenia a legislaţiei privind raporturile dintre ţărani şi proprietari (1866-1872)," **Analele Universităţi din Craiova. Istorie, Geografie, Filologie**, Vol. 2 (1972), pp. 57-72. Cristea's **Contribuţii la istoria problemei agrare**, 1977, is a recent and comprehensive treatment of these matters.

[40]**Monitorul**, 13 March 1866.

[41]See Constantin C. Angelescu, **Izvoarele constituţiei Române dela 1866** [Bucureşti: Fundaţiei Culturale Principele Carol, 1926], and I. C. Filitti, **Izvoarele constituţiei de la 1866** [Bucureşti: Universul, 1934], which thoroughly and effectively refute the usual assertion that the draft was a hastily-concocted document. A recent study of constitutions generally in Romania is Teodor Leon Pop, **Constituţile României (1831-1965)** [Bucureşti: Editura Ştiinţifică şi Enciclopedică, 1984], which I have not seen.

[42]Details on these matters, including reference to Council of

State documents subsequently destroyed during World War II, may be found in Angelescu, **Izvoarele**, 1926.

[43]Documents relating to this crucial dissolution and election are in A. S. București, MAI/Ad/131/1866.

[44]Green to Clarendon, 23 February/7 March 1866, nr. 34, and 26 February/19 March 1866, nr. 35, PRO London, FO/78/1920. This fear was not without substance; cf. the letter of Th. Văcărescu, prefect of Ploești, to D. Ghica, 2 May 1866, BCS București, Fond. St. Georges, Pach. LI/D.26. A recent study of this issue is Maria Totu's **Garda civică din România. 1848-1884** [București: Editură Militară, 1976], pp. 87ff..

[45]C. A. Rosetti to Ion Brătianu, 18 March 1866, telegraphic, BCS București, Fond. St. Georges, Pach. LI/D.8.

[46]A revealing synopsis of these events and conflicts is given in a letter to Ion Alecsandri from an unidentified București friend, 15/27 March 1866, BAR București, Arhiva Ion Alecsandri, Mss. Rom. 5741, folios 5-7.

[47]Gh. Știrbey to Barbu Știrbey, 13/25 March 1866, reprinted in Știrbey, **Feuilles**, 1916, Volume I, pp. 281-283.

[48]Ion Ghica to Ion Bălăceanu, 12 March 1866, reprinted in Sturdza, **Insemnătatea**, 1912, p. 183.

[49]Text in Sturdza, **Insemnătatea**, 1912, pp. 183-184.

[50]His German name was Karl Ludwig von Hohenzollern Sigmaringen; I have used his Romanian "Carol" throughout.

[51]Texts of these telegrams are in Sturdza, **Insemnătatea**, 1912, p. 184.

[52]Henry, **Cuza**, 1930, p. 60.

[53]See especially Émile Ollivier, **L'Empire libéral** [Paris: Garnier Frères, 1903], Volume VIII, pp. 63-96.

[54]Ollivier, **L'Empire**, 1903, Volume VIII, p. 71, citing Mme. Cornu. Bălăceanu's claim (**Memoirs**, pp. 110-112) that Cornu suggested Carol to him, rather than Brătianu must be discounted in light of both his frequent contradictions and misstatements and his persistent efforts to magnify his own role and to diminish Brătianu's. On Bălăceanu, see Chapter Five, note 83 above. The Napoléon-Cornu correspondence is, unfortunately, of no help in resolving this whole issue. Cf. Marcel Emerit, ed., **Lettres**

de Napoléon III à Madame Cornu, two volumes [Paris: Presses Modernes, 1938].

[55]Ollivier, L'Empire, 1903, Volume VIII, p. 72.

[56]See Mosse, Crimean System, 1963, pp. 142-143.

[57]Ollivier, L'Empire, 1903, Volume VIII, p. 74 gives Napoleon's denial.

[58]See Carol I, Aus dem Leben König Karls von Rumänien, four volumes, [Stuttgart: J. G. Cotta, 1894-1900], Volume I, 1894, entry for 19/31 March 1866. Because various editions are used, this work is cited hereafter as Carol, Memoirs, with the appropriate date. See Appendix Four below for a discussion of the various editions; there are slight additions and deletions in the later Romanian editions as compared to the German first edition.

[59]Ion Brătianu (Berlin) to Ion Bălăceanu (Paris), 20 March/1 April 1866, telegraphic, BAR București, Arhiva Ion Bălăceanu, coresp.30208. Bălăceanu also telegraphed to București the same day with the news that Carol "accepts the Crown without any condition." Bălăceanu to Ion Ghica, 20 March/1 April 1866, nr. 49, copy, BAR București, Arhiva Ion Ghica, VIII.varia.12.

[60]Ion Brătianu to Ion Ghica, 20 March/1 April 1866, telegraphic. Text in Sturdza, Insemnatatea, 1912, p. 190.

[61]See Ion Brătianu to Ion Ghica, 27 March/8 April 1866, nr. 63, telegraphic, copy, BAR București, Arhiva Ion Ghica, VIII.varia.12, which also reiterates Carol's acceptance.

[62]Text of session and message in Archives Diplomatiques, Vol. 7 (1867), nr. 2, pp. 637-646.

[63]Texts of all the protocols of these meetings are given in Archives Diplomatiques, Vol. 7 (1867).

[64]Cowley to Clarendon, 8/20 March 1866, private, cited in Mosse, Crimean System, 1963, p. 141.

[65]Mosse, Crimean System, 1963, pp. 135-136.

[66]Text in A. S. București, MAI/Ad/136/1866, folio 1 and verso.

[67]D. Ghica to all prefects, circa 1 April 1866, A. S. București, MAI/Ad/136/1866, folios 3-5 verso.

[68]Text in Sturdza, Insemnătatea, 1912, p. 210.

⁶⁹Karl Anton to Ion Brătianu, 3/15 April 1866, telegraphic, BCS București, Fond. St. Georges, Pach. LI/D.31.

⁷⁰See **Românul**, 27 February 1866 and 3 April 1866.

⁷¹Modern implications that a republic was possible or desired in 1866 are simply fantasies.

⁷²A special commission had been set up as early as 11 February to oversee Moldova as a special precaution. Consult A. S. București, MAI/Ad/143/1866.

⁷³Documents in A. S. București, MAI/Ad/143/1866. On this episode, see the following: Gh. Bezviconi, "Prințul Constantin Moruzi," **Revista Istorică**, Vol. 26 (1940), pp. 154-170, and "Prințul Constantin Moruzi," **Cetatea Moldovei**, Vol. 6 (1942), pp. 29-49; Gerhard Hilke, "Russlands Haltung zur rumänischen Frage 1864-1866," **Wissenschaftliche Zeitschrift der Martin-Luther-Universität**, Vol. 14 (1965), Nr. 4, pp. 193-209; Gh. Cristea, "Manifestări antidinastice în perioada venirii lui Carol I în România," **Studii**, Vol. 20 (1967), pp. 1073-1091; Mihai Dimitri Sturdza, "La Russie et la désunion des Principautés Roumaines, 1864-1866," **Cahiers du Monde Russe et Soviétique**, Vol. 12 (1971), pp. 247-285; and Barbara Jelavich, "Russia and Moldavian Separatism: The Demonstrations of April, 1866," in: Alexander Fischer, Günter Moltmann, and Klaus Schwabe, eds., **Rußland—Deutschland—Amerika**: Festschrift für Fritz T. Epstein [Weisbaden: Franz Steiner Verlag, 1978], pp. 73-87.

⁷⁴See St. Clair (Iași) to Green, 23 April/4 May 1866, nr. 6, copy in Green to Clarendon, 3/14 May 1866, PRO London, FO/78/1921.

⁷⁵Such as Titu Maiorescu, Vasile Pogor, and B. P. Hasdeu. See Xenopol, **Partidelor politice**, 1910, pp. 503-504.

⁷⁶See Xenopol, **Partidelor politice**, 1910, pp. 504-506, for a short summary; and Stan, **Grupări**, 1979, pp. 178-181.

⁷⁷See Văcărescu, "Venirea," (1914), pp. 992-994.

⁷⁸Green to Clarendon, 29 March/10 April 1866, nr. 53, PRO London, FO/78/1920.

⁷⁹See especially Green to Clarendon, 24 March/5 April 1866, nr. 50, PRO London, FO/78/1920.

⁸⁰On this, see a letter to Ion Alecsandri, 30 March/11 April

1866, BAR Bucureşti, Arhiva Ion Alecsandri, Mss. Rom. 5747, pp. 11-14 verso.

[81] C. A. Rosetti to Prefect of Ialomiţa, n.d., March/April 1866, copy signed by Rosetti, BCS Bucureşti, Fond. St. Georges, Pach. LI/D.21.

[82] Cf. Th. Văcărescu's illustrative discussion on activities in Ploeşti ["Memorii," (1916), pp. 418-436].

[83] Xenopol, **Partidelor politice**, 1910, p. 476.

[84] Xenopol, **Partidelor politice**, 1910, pp. 539-542.

[85] This report is discussed below in Chapter Seven.

[86] Text of the proceedings is in Sturdza, **Insemnătatea**, 1912, pp. 264-293.

[87] Carol, **Memoirs**, 7/19 April 1866, Bismarck added that he anticipated keeping Austria occupied. On Bismarck and Romania in this era, see Z. R. Dittrich, "Bismarck und Rumänien: Die turbulenten Jahre 1866-1868," in: A. P. van Goudoever, ed., **Romanian History 1848-1918** [Groningen: Wolters-Noordhoff, 1979], pp. 19-45; and Aurel A. Mureşianu, "Când Bismarck avut de gând să trimită dorobanţii românii în Ardeal, " **Ţara Bârsei**, Vol. 3 (1931), pp. 211-222.

[88] Bălăceanu to I. Ghica, 29 April/11 May 1866, nr. 114, telegraphic, copy, BAR Bucureşti, Arhiva Ion Ghica, VIII.varia.12.

[89] The word 'unexpectedly" is used to describe Brătianu's arrival in the Romanian texts of Carol's **Memoirs** for they evidently met only by chance. The astute Brătianu made the best of the opportunity to give the impression that he was actually bringing Carol to Romania.

[90] Carol to the regency, 8 May 1866, original draft signed by Carol, BCS Bucureşti, Fond. St. Georges, Pach. LI/D.4.

[91] Interesting contemporary accounts of these events, apart from Carol's **Memoirs**, may be found in Văcărescu, "Venirea," (1914), pp. 1001-1031; and Papadopol Calimah, **Amintiri**, Mss. Rom. 864, folios 453-459.

[92] Riker, **Making of Roumania**, 1931, p. 554.

[93] Henry, **Cuza**, 1930, p. x.

[94] Riker, **Making of Roumania**, 1931, p. 538.

[95] Mosse, **Crimean System**, 1963, pp. 154-156.

•CHAPTER SEVEN: pp. 129-146

[1] See Carol's **Memoirs**, 10 May 1866, for the prince's own perceptive comments on his new ministers.

[2] Claims that the cabinet was a conservative takeover are an exaggeration.

[3] See Carol, **Memoirs**, 26 May 1866.

[4] Text in **Monitorul** of 29 April, reprinted in Băicoianu, **Istoria**, 1932, Volume I, Part II, pp. 177-228; the statement also gives the provisional government's version of the events subsequent to 11 February. Nicolae Kretzulescu's **Le 11/23 Février 1866 à Bucarest** [București: J. Weiss, 1866] is a sharp rebuttal, with many valid criticisms of the legality of the new regime.

[5] A fact recognized by the government elsewhere than in its 28 April report. See, for example, minister of foreign affairs to I. Bălăceanu, 5 July 1866, nr. 3160, BAR București, Mss. Rom. 5315, folios 168-172 verso.

[6] There is some truth, however, to Green's partly jocular observation that the disorderly situation helped the government: "In a country less accustomed to irregularity it would have been impossible to carry on the government for four months in such circumstances." Green to Clarendon, 1/13 June 1866, nr. 100, PRO London, FO/78/1921.

[7] **Monitorul**, 29 April 1866, p. 407.

[8] This is a largely unexplored subject of great importance. The MAI archives in A. S. Bucarest contain extensive reports and materials concerning this topic, to which I can only allude here.

[9] See **Românul**, 20 July 1866.

[10] Cited in Carol, **Memoirs**, 22 June 1866.

[11] These observations, both political and material, coincide with those of Émile Picot, Carol's French secretary, in a long letter to Mme. Cornu in November of 1866, reprinted in N. Georgescu-Tistu, **Correspondance d'un secrétaire princier en Roumanie: Émile Picot (1866-1868)** [Paris: Gamber, 1927],

pp. 10-25. Picot was another Cornu protégé.

[12]Al. Lăpedatu, "11 Februarie 1866, în perspectiva istorică a trei sferturi de veac," A.R. MSI, Ser. III, Vol. 23 (1940-1941), p. 313, summarizes this faith in nationalist slogans well.

[13]A contemporary statement of this hopefulness may be found in Bolintineanu, Domnii Regulamentari, 1869, p. 63.

[14]Clarendon to Cowley, 1 March 1866, private, cited by Mosse, Crimean System, 1963, p. 138.

[15]No doubt a factor in the refusal of Philip of Flanders.

[16]Carol I, Cuvântări și scrisori, three volumes [București: Göbl, 1909], Volume I, pp. 24-26.

[17]Carol, Memoirs, pp. xli-xlii of the preface.

[18]Carol, Memoirs, 7 July 1866.

[19]The contrast is made by P P. Panaitescu in "Urcarea în scaun a Principelui Carol de Hohenzollern," Revista Funaţiilor Regale, Vol. 6 (1939), p. 266. Also useful on Carol's election is P. C. Georgian, Intemeierea dinastiei Române [București: Cartea Românească, 1940].

[20]Papadopol Calimah, a Cuza partisan, in his Amintiri, Mss. Rom. 864, folio 458, comments that Carol's election "saved the country from sure catastrophe...otherwise civil war, foreign occupation, and distruction of the union" would have followed. See also Titu Maiorescu, Istoria, 1925, pp. 14-16.

[21]Cited in Xenopol, Partidelor politice, 1910, p. 470.

[22]See Văcărescu, "Memorii," (1916), pp. 608-613 for information by a contemporary concerning the split in the coalition's ranks over this question.

[23]The draft, debates, and final texts are found in Alexandru Pencovici, Desbaterile adunarei constituante din anul 1866 asupra constitutiunei și legei electorale din Romania [București: Tipografia Statului, 1883]. Comparisons and parallel texts are given in the useful study by Filitti, Izvoarele, 1934. For some of the implications of the new constitution, see V. Russu, "Constituţia de la 1866 și ideea de independenţă" Analele Ştiinţifice ale Universităţii Al. I. Cuza. Istorie, Vol. 22 (1976), pp.11-18.

[24]Carol, Memoirs, 21 May 1866.

[25] Carol, **Memoirs**, 2 June 1866.

[26] See D. A. Sturdza to Ion Ghica, 8 June 1866, BAR București, Mss. Rom. 5315, folios 199-202 verso on cooperation between his people and Brătianu's group. Two attempts to defeat the senate proposal failed by one vote.

[27] **Românul**, 28/29 May 1866. Rosetti, even in 1848, had opposed universal suffrage, though Brătianu had favored it. See N. Bălcescu, **Opere**, Volume IV: **Corespondența**, Gh. Zane, ed. [București: Editura Academiei, 1964], pp. 281-282.

[28] This is the estimate of Émile Picot in 1866 (see É. Picot to Mme. Cornu, 2/14 November 1866, in Georgescu-Tistu, **Correspondance Picot**, 1927, pp. 13-14.

[29] See for example its 18 June 1866, editorial denouncing the proposed voting system.

[30] The Moldovan declaration was somewhat more restricted than the Muntenian. See Filitti, **Izvoarele**, 1934, p. 26, for a summary comparison.

[31] Crémieux (see below) actually believed the conservatives to be more "enlightened" toward the Jews than the liberals. See his letter to **Le Siècle**, 16/28 July 1866, reprinted in Isidore Loeb, **La Situation des Israélites en Turquie en Serbie et en Roumanie** [Paris: Joseph Baer et Cie., 1877], p. 148.

[32] Carol, **Memoirs**, 2 June 1866. The mention of a loan, curiously enough, is deleted from Romanian texts of the **Memoirs**. See especially Loeb, **La Situation**, 1877, pp. 146-158, which contains much documentary material.

[33] From the debate of 18 June 1866, Pencovici, **Desbaterile**, 1883, p. 49. See also Carol, **Memoirs**, 15 June 1866: "a cry of Horror passes through Moldova."

[34] Debate of 18 June 1866, quoted in Pencovici, **Desbaterile**, 1883, p. 58.

[35] D. A. Sturdza to Ion Ghica, 19 June 1866, BAR București, Mss. Rom. 5315, folios 205-208 verso. Police reports are in A. S. București, MAI/Ad/198/1866.

[36] Carol, **Memoirs**, 18, 19, 20 June 1866.

[37] See Loeb, **La Situation**, 1877, for some of the foreign reaction.

[38]The government took a number of steps to prevent and punish subsequent anti-Jewish acts during 1866. See A. S. București, MAI/Ad/187/1866 and 203/1866.

[39]Carol, **Memoirs**, 26 June 1866.

[40]A move by the liberals to get them declared "natural rights" failed.

[41]See, for example, E. C. Decusara, **Les Délits de presse dans la législation Roumaine** [Paris: Arthur Rousseau, 1912].

[42]**Românul**, 7 July 1866; Xenopol, **Partidele politice**, 1910, p. 546, concurs.

[43]**Acte Brătianu**, Volume I, Part 2-a, p. 103.

[44]As some post-1948 historiography asserts. The statement by Dionisie Ionescu, et. al, **Dezvoltarea constituțională a statului Român** [București: Editura Științifică, 1957], pp. 160-174, that "tho constitution of 1866 [was a] model of reactionary law," is simply absurd. [This conclusion from my 1975 thesis corresponds to the subsequent analysis of V. Russu, "Teoria alianței," (1978), pp. 455-456.]

[45]Titu Maiorescu expresses the conservative view that the constitution of 1866 was "premature liberalism." **Istoria**, 1925, p. 12.

[46]R.W. Seton-Watson, **A History of the Roumanians** [Hamden, Conn.: Archon Books, 1963], p. 319.

[47]D. P. Marțian, "Privire generală 1861," in: Slăvescu, **Marțian**, 1944, Volume II, p. 160. French influence on Romania is the subject of: Mathieu Fotino, **L'Influence française sur les grands orateurs politiques Roumains de la seconde moitié du XIXe siècle** [București: Cartea Românească, 1928]; Paul Desfeuilles and Jacques Lassaigene, eds., **Les Français et la Roumanie** [București: Naționala, 1937], an excellent anthology; and John C. Campbell, **French Influence and the Rise of Roumanian Nationalism** [New York: Arno Press, 1971].

[48]**Românul**, 30 June/ 1 July 1866; and Carol, **Memoirs**, 30 July 1866. The reference to "more absolutist regime," interestingly enough, is omitted from the Romanian versions. Mme. Cornu seconded this view in a letter to Carol in October

(Carol, **Memoirs**, undated portion preceeding entry for 23 October 1866). Carol's secretary É. Picot had little good to say about the constitution either (see his letter to Cornu in November, 1866, in Georgescu-Tistu, **Correspondance Picot**, 197, pp. 13-14).

[49]Carol, **Memoirs** for 23, 31 May, and 1 June 1866. See also D. A. Sturdza to Ion Ghica, 1 June 1866, BAR Bucureşti, Mss. Rom. 5315, folios 190-191 verso.

[50]See V. Mihordea, **Răscoala grănicerilor de la 1866** [Bucureşti: Editura Academiei, 1958], pp. 14-16. The consular reports of Green (PRO London, FO/78/1920) contain numerous mentions of these rumors.

[51]Golescu to I. Ghica, 2/14 May 1866, nr. 120, telegraphic, BAR Bucureşti, Arhiva Ion Ghica, VIII.varia.12. The date on the telegraph is 14 May but this is likely new style. The actual date is not crucial to this point.

[52]Golescu to I. Ghica, 4/16 May 1866, nr. 133, telegraphic, BAR Bucureşti, Arhiva Ion Ghica, VIII.varia.12. Tulcea commands the Danube delta.

[53]Details in Polihroniade and Tell, **Carol I**, 1937, pp. 104-111, and C. Fărcăşanu, "Schiţă istorică a transformărilor în organisarea armatei de la 1866-1906, " **România Militară**, Vol. I (1906), pp. 629-633.

[54]D. Lecca to the government, 19 March 1866, nr. 1747, in **Monitorul**, 22 March 1866.

[55]Fărcăşanu, **România Militară**, Vol. I (1906), p. 631.

[56]See for example, sub-prefect of Calafat to M.A.I., 13 May 1866, telegraphic, A. S. Bucureşti, MAI/Ad/182/1866, folios 17-18 verso.

[57]E.g. by Mihordea, **Răscoala**, 1958, especially p. 24. A better perspective is in Cristea,"Manifestări antidinastice,"(1967), pp. 1073-1091.

[58]See also Green to Clarendon, nr. 94, 21 May/2 June 1866, and nr. 102, 4/16 June 1866, PRO London, FO/78/1921.

[59]Carol, **Memoirs**, 22 May 1866.

[60]See the account by Văcărescu, "Memorii," (1916), p. 613.

[61]See especially the report of the Romanian delegation which

visited Napoléon III on 19/30 June. The French emperor promised continual French insistance on direct negotiations. The report is in A. S. București, Casa Regală/48/1866.

[62]Prokesch to Mensdorff, nr. 26, 22 May 2 June 1866, telegraphic, reprinted in Henry, **Cuza**, 1930, as document 322.

[63]Carol, **Memoirs**, 4 June 1866. On the hopes for Ghica's mission, see D. A. Sturdza to C. Hurmuzaki, 2 June 1866, BAR București, Fond. D. A. Sturdza, coresp. 131316.

[64]Türr's report on his activities gives a summary. See Stefania Türr, **L'Opera di Stefano Türr nel Risorgimento Italiano (1849-1870)**, two volumes, [Firenze: Tipografia Fascista, 1928], Volume I, pp. 97-100.

[65]On the Bulgarian issue, see the excellent works of Constantin N. Velichi: **La Roumaine et le mouvement révolutionnaire bulgare de libération bulgare de libération nationale (1850-1878)** [București: Editura Academiei, 1979]; **România și renașterea Bulgară** [București: Editura Științifică și Enciclopedică, 1980]; "C. A. Rosetti și Comunitatea bulgară," in: Condurachi, ed., **Constantinescu-Iași**, 1965, pp. 527-532; "Relațiile romîno-turce în perioada februarie-iulie 1866. Înființarea Comitetului Central Secret Bulgar de la București și legăturile acestuia cu guvernul romîn," **Studii**, Vol.16 (1963), pp. 843-867. For Romanian involvement in general with Southeast European revolutionaries, see Nicolae Ciachir, **România în sud-estul europei (1848-1886)** [București: Editura Politică, 1968], passim.

[66]These measures are elaborated in a document from the ministry of interior, A. S. București, MAI/Ad/143/1866, folio 5.

[67]This measure had been defeated in 1862 on similar grounds.

[68]See Xenopol, **Partidele politice**, 1910, pp. 488-500; and N.A. Bogdan, **Regele Carol I și a doua sa capitală** [București: C. Sfetea, 1916], pp. 20-29 for discussions.

[69]Green to Stanley, 8/20 July, nr. 120, PRO London, FO/78/1921.

[70]See the letters of J. Gradowicz to Ion Ghica, 17 June and 1 July 1866, BAR București, Mss. Rom. 5315, folios 230-236 verso.

[71] Lascăr Catargiu to prefect of Iaşi, 16 July 1866, nr. 14873, A. S. Iaşi, Primariu Iaşi/105/1866. The date is incorrect.

•CHAPTER EIGHT: pp. 147-159

[1] D. A. Sturdza to Ion Ghica, 22 June 1866, BAR Bucureşti, Mss. Rom. 5314, folios 209-213 verso. On this Ghica ministry, see V. Russu, "Din activitatea politică a lui Ion Ghica în perioada instabilităţii guvernamentale şi parlamentare (iulie 1866-februarie 1867)," **Anuarul Institutului de Istorie şi Arheologie A. D. Xenopol**, Vol. 14 (1977), pp. 191-210. Russu stresses that Ghica's relative political neutrality was more important in his selection than his diplomatic ties to the Ottomans.

[2] **Românul**, 17 July 1866.

[3] See Green to E. Hammond, 20 July/1 August 1866, private, PRO London, FO/78/1922.

[4] On this and subsequent programmatic aims, see Ion Ghica's circular to all prefects, 19 July 1866, printed in **Monitorul**, 20 July 1866.

[5] Radu D. Rosetti to ministry of interior, 19 July 1866, BAR Bucureşti, Arhiva Ion Ghica, VIII.varia.11. This chatty file, a kind of intelligence report on the activities of non-governmental political gatherings and leaders, is an excellent and unusual source for politics during the Ghica ministry. Its very existence reveals that, while Ghica favored decentralization and a free society, he was still going to keep close tabs on things.

[6] Details in **Românul**, 2 August 1866.

[7] **Românul**, 6 August 1866.

[8] C. A. Rosetti to Paul Bataillard, 8 August 1866, BCS Bucureşti, Fond. St. Georges, Pach. LXI/D.7.

[9] See Carol's **Memoirs** for his impressions. On Carol and Moldova, complete—though uncritical—coverage is given by Bogdan's **Carol I**, 1916, passim.

[10] From an article in a moderate Iaşi newspaper, **Constituţiunea**, cited by Xenopol, **Partidelor politice**, 1910, p. 487.

[11] Maiorescu, **Istoria**, 1925, pp. 16-18 emphasizes this point. Basic information about the Romanian railroads may be found in the bulky, chronicle-like C. C. Mănescu, **Istoricul căilor ferate din România**, one volume in two, [București: Socec, 1906], which only goes up to 1869; Bucur Țincu, "Contribuții la istoria căilor ferate din România. Idei și probleme în perioada 1859-1869," **Studii**, Vol. 24 (1971), pp. 951-962; C. Botez and L. Eșanu, **Uzina mecanică de material rulant Pașcani, 1869-1969** [Iași: Institutul de Studii Istorice și Social-Politice de pe lingă CC al PCR, 1970]; and the recent and thorough C. Botez, D. Urmă, and Ion Saizu, **Epopeea feroviară românească** [București: Editura Sport-Turism, 1977].

[12] See St. Clair (Iași) to Green, 22 August/3 September 1866, nr. 20, copy, in Green to Stanley, 2/14 September 1866, nr. 137, PRO London, FO/78/1922.

[13] Bogdan, **Carol I**, 1916, pp. 30-62.

[14] Letter to the editor, **Românul**, 13 August 1866.

[15] See Green to Clarendon, 5/17 October 1866, nr. 145, PRO London, FO/78/1922.

[16] See, for instance, **Românul**, 8 September 1866.

[17] See C. A. and Maria Rosetti to Bataillard, 17/29 September 1866, BCS București, Fond. St. Georges, Pach. LXI/D. 7.

[18] This is clear in a letter from Ghica to his associate A. G. Golescu, 26 September 1866, BCS București, Fond. Kogălniceanu, Pach. LXXXV/D.14.

[19] A. S. București, MAI/Sanitar/601/1866, Volume I, folio 25.

[20] A useful commentary is N. Suțu's "Aperçu sur l'état economique du pays et sur les besoins les plus presents," written in 1866, published for the first time in Slăvescu, **Vieața Suțu**, 1944, pp. 579-591.

[21] Napoléon III to Carol, in Carol, **Memoirs**, 23 August 1866.

[22] Details in Carol, **Memoirs**, passim.

[23] Carol's notes to Ghica, 8 October 1866 and 25 October 1866, BAR București, Mss. Rom. 5315, folios 602-603, 606, on the matter are unambiguous and typical. Picot, a fairly impartial source, wrote "L'autorité a strictment respecte la Constitution, qui lui fait un devoir absolu de s'abstenit." Picot to Cornu, 2/14

November 1866, in Georgescu-Tistu, **Correspondance Picot**, 1927, p. 14. Documents on the election are in A. S. București, MAI/Ad/201/1866.

[24]Carol, **Memoirs**, 23 October 1866.

[25]N. Iorga, **Istoria Românilor**, ten volumes in 11, [București: n.p., 1936-1939], Volume X, p. 38.

[26]The dispatch of Green to Stanley, 7/19 November 1866, nr. 151, PRO London, FO/78/1922, is an excellent report on these matters.

[27]**Monitorul** carried all these results. Among the elected were two of those arrested in April, the separatists N. C. Aslan and N. Rosetti-Rosnovanu.

[28]Carol, **Memoirs**, 13 November 1866.

[29]R. Rosetti to minister of interior, 14 November 1866, BAR București, Arhiva Ion Ghica, VIII.varia.11, in a report to the government on this meeting.

[30]Carol, **Cuvântări**, 1909, Volume I, pp. 55-59.

[31]Gh. Știrbey to A. G. Golescu, 6/18 October 1866, BCS București, Fond. Kogălniceanu, LXIX/D.6. The date should be December.

[32]Green to Stanley, 9/21 December 1866 and 16/28 December 1866, nrs. 157 and 159, PRO London, FO/78/1922.

[33]See the interesting analysis of this situation carried by **Constituțiunea** (Iași), 22 October 1866, in an article called "Partidele la noi," pp. 2-3.

[34]Radu Rosetti's police reports kept close tabs on these meetings. See BAR București, Arhiva Ion Ghica, VIII.varia.11, passim.

[35]Details in Dobrovici, **Desvoltării economice**, 1934, pp. 86-91; and Slăvescu, "Vieața Mavrogheni," (1939), pp. 594-596. Mavrogheni, himself, recognized the loan as a disaster, but saw no alternative.

[36]Carol, **Memoirs**, 28 October 1866. The date should be 31 October.

[37]Carol to Ion Brătianu, 10/22 December 1866, BCS București, Fond. St. Georges, Pach. LI/D.5.

[38]Reported by R. D. Rosetti to I. Ghica, 27 December 1866,

BAR București, Arhiva Ion Ghica, VIII.varia.11.

[39] Carol, **Memoirs**, 19 December 1866.

[40] Green to Stanley, 30 December 1866/11 January 1867, nr. 3, PRO London, FO/78/1971.

[41] This unsettling allusion was made by Gh. Știrbey to A. G. Golescu, 3 January 1867, BCS București, Fond. Kogălniceanu, LXIX/D.6.

[42] Published by N. Georgescu-Tistu, "Émile Picot et ses travaux relatifs aux Roumains," **Mélanges de l'École Roumaine en France**, Vol. 3 (1925), Part 1, pp. 181-278; Georgescu-Tistu, **Correspondance Picot**, 1927; and Marcel Emerit, "Une ingérence française dans la politique intérieure roumaine au début du règne de Charles I-er," **Revue Historique du Sud-Est Européen**, Vol. 16 (1939), pp. 53-73. There are some additional letters in A. S. București, Casa Regală.

[43] Picot to Cornu, 15/27 January 1867, in Georgescu-Tistu, **Correspondance Picot**, 1927, pp. 32-36.

[44] Avril to Drouyn, 22 June/4 July 1866, quoted in M. Emerit, "Le dossier de la première mission militaire française en Roumanie," **Revue Roumaine d'Histoire**, Vol. 5 (1966), p. 584.

[45] Carol, **Memoirs**, 12 February 1867. See the warning by Cornu on rising French sentiment against Prussia, Cornu to Picot, 6/18 January 1867, in Georgescu-Tistu, "Picot," (1925), pp. 265-267.

[46] See especially Slăvescu, "Vieața Mavrogheni," (1939), pp. 589-609.

[47] See Picot to F. Aubert, 6/18 February 1867, in Georgescu-Tistu, **Correspondance Picot**, 1927, pp. 36-38; Bogdan, **Carol I**, 1916, pp. 68-76; Carol, **Memoirs**, passim; and I. Minea, "Opinia publică din Iași și Regele Carol I în 1867," **Buletinul Institutului A. D. Xenopol**, Vol. 2 (1942), nr. 3, pp. 54-66.

[48] Rosetti-Rosnovanu, for one, was on top of this ploy. Cf. A. S. București, Fond. Petre Carp, 80/1867, folio 1,a declaration of protest on the court issue.

[49] Green to Stanley, 23 December/4 January 1867, nr. 1, PRO London, FO/78/1971.

⁵⁰Text in **Din scrierile Brătianu**, 1903, Part I, pp. 416-425. See also R. D. Rosetti's report to I. Ghica, January, 1867, BAR Bucureşti, Arhiva Ion Ghica, VIII.varia.11.

⁵¹R. D. Rosetti to I. Ghica, 2 and 4 February 1867, BAR Bucureşti, Arhiva Ion Ghica, VIII.varia.11.

⁵²These previously-ignored negotiations have been brought to light by V. Russu, "Din lupta politică în anii instabilităţii guvernmentale: înţelegerea de la Concordia (Februarie 1867)," **Analele Ştiinţifice ale Universităţii Al. I. Cuza. Istorie**, Vol. 17 (1971), pp. 73-91, on which the following is based together with the R. D. Rosetti reports.

⁵³Radu D. Rosetti includes Ionescu as a drafter [report to I. Ghica], n.d., February 1867, BAR Bucureşti, Arhiva Ion Ghica, VIII.varia.11; Russu does not.

⁵⁴R. D. Rosetti to I. Ghica, 6 and 14 February 1867, BAR Bucureşti, Arhiva Ion Ghica, VIII.varia.11.

⁵⁵The text of this program is reprinted in **Istoricul liberal**, 1923, pp. 84-89.

⁵⁶This question is discussed in the following chapter. Certainly Ion Ghica's relative lack of interest in the Transilvanian problem was a contributing factor in the fall of his ministry.

⁵⁷Ghica to Golescu, 17 February 1867, BCS Bucureşti, Fond. Kogălniceanu, Pach. LXXXV/D.14.

⁵⁸Carol, **Memoirs**, 24 February 1867.

⁵⁹Carol regarded Brătianu as the most capable and personally likeable Romanian politician of the day and stated this directly in his **Memoirs**, 24 and 27 February 1867.

⁶⁰See Green to Stanley, 1/13 March 1867, nr. 29, PRO London, FO/78/1971.

●CHAPTER NINE: pp. 160-176

¹Carol, **Memoirs**, 13 March 1867.

²Rosetti was viewed as the evil genius of the Muntenians by the British consul. See Green to Stanley, 1/13 March 1867, nr. 29, PRO London, FO/78/1971. Green saw Creţulescu as "well informed...even...learned," but eccentric; Golescu and Dumitru

Brătianu "are reputed honest, but...devoid of intelligence, whilst Jon Bratiano, who is not unintelligent, is frequently unwise."

[3] The Brătianu-Rosetti group will often be referred to as "the liberals" below. Other liberal groups or factions will have some associated modifier to distinguish them.

[4] The Iași Fraction was another liberal group that had an ideology and leadership, but it is doubtful that they really constituted a political community, the key element of our definition of "party".

[5] Text in **Istoricul liberal**, 1923, pp. 85-89. They refer to themselves in the text as "the liberal party."

[6] While the conservatives and the Ion Ghica liberals did not lack sympathy for the Transilvanian Romanians, they believed the situation was inopportune and favored a policy of caution.

[7] Soton Watson, **A History**, 1963, p. 306.

[8] Green to Stanley, 1/13 March 1867, nr. 29, PRO London, FO/78/1971.

[9] This opinion was shared by Carol's father, who was his closest and most trusted advisor.

[10] Cited in Carol, **Memoirs**, 10 July 1867.

[11] Cornu was also convinced that "our branch of the Hohenzollern is not well loved by the Cadet [i.e. Prussian] branch..." She believed Bismarck would be none too hesitant about sacrificing Romania to Russia if needed. See Cornu to Picot, 21 February/5 March 1867, in Georgescu-Tistu,"Picot," (1925), pp. 268-271.

[12] Ion Brătianu to all prefects, 2 March 1867, nr. 4422, A. S. București, MAI/Ad/77/1867, folios 1-1 verso.

[13] Carol, **Memoirs**, 3, 5, 9, and 13 March 1867. See also É. Picot to J. Wechsler, 15 March 1867, in Georgescu Tistu, **Correspondance Picot**, 1927, pp. 57-58. Picot specifically denied that Krenski had any political mission.

[14] Additional details are provided in some notes by Picot, April 18//30, 1867, published in Georgescu-Tistu, **Correspondance Picot**, 1927, pp. 82-86.

[15] See Carol, **Memoirs**, 13 March 1867.

[16] Opponents included Dimitrie Ghica and C. Boerescu. Also

opposed was the Fraction, led by N. Ionescu, because of the large Jewish population of Iaşi. See Bogdan, **Carol I**, 1916, p. 80.

[17]Ion Brătianu to the mayor of Iaşi, 30 March 1867, reprinted in Bogdan, **Carol I**, 1916, p. 81. Carol planned to keep pressing the issue, see his speech to the parliament, 13 April 1867, in Carol, **Cuvântări**, 1909, Volume I, p. 75.

[18]See Picot to Cornu, 5 April 1867, in Georgescu-Tistu, **Correspondance Picot**, 1927, p. 77.

[19]See Appendix Two on money for background. V. Slăvescu, **Recunoaşterea dreptului de a bate monetă** [Bucureşti: Fundaţia Regele Carol I, 1941]; Constantin Moisil, "Renaşterea monetei Româneşti," **Arhiva Românească**, Vol. 4 (1940), pp. 37-71; and G. Zane, et al., **Crearea sistemului monetar naţional la 1867** [Bucureşti: Editura Academiei, 1968], deal with the monetary negotiations between 1866-1870

[20]Texts in Băicoianu, **Istoria**, 1932, Volume I, Part 2, pp. 231-300.

[21]Carol, **Memoirs**, 4 April 1867.

[22]Picot to Bălăceanu, 29 April 1867, in Georgescu-Tistu, **Corresondance Picot**, 1927, p. 93.

[23]Carol, **Memoirs**, 20 December 1867.

[24]Cooperation with the I. Ghica group was of course impossible. A letter from Ghica to A. G. Golescu (14 May 1867, BCS Bucureşti, Fond. Kogălniceanu, Pach. LXXXV/D. 14) expresses very strongly the former minister's bitterness against "Brătianu and Co."

[25]See Damé, **Histoire**, 1900, p. 182, and Maiorescu, **Istoria**, 1925, pp. 18-19. Damé mistakenly lists the Court of Cassation issue as another part of the Moldovan group's demands; erroneous since they opposed the move.

[26]Carol, **Memoirs**, 2 April 1867. The wrong date is given here.

[27]**Monitorul**, 14 September 1866, for the Ghica order. See also BAR Bucureşti, Arhiva Ion Ghica, VIII.varia.11, for R. Rosetti's 24 November 1866 report on the roundup of 500 vagabonds.

[28]The treatment here is based largely on the folowing: two

works generally unsympathetic to the Jews, their authors are Romanians, Verax [Radu Rosetti], **La Roumanie et les Juifs** [București: Socecu, 1903], and N. Petrescu-Comnene, **Étude sur la condition des Israélites en Roumanie** [Paris: Pedone, 1905]; three works favorable to the Jewish view, their authors are Jewish, Isidore Loeb, **La Situation**, 1877, Bernard Stambler, **L'Histoire des Israélites Roumains et le Droit d'Intervention** [Paris: Jouve, 1913], and Joseph Berkowitz, **La Question des Israelites en Roumanie** [Paris: Jouve & Cie., 1923]. A balanced but brief, contemporary account is Ernest Desjardins, **Les Juifs de Moldavie** [Paris: E. Dentu, 1867]. Additional studies on this question include: S. Bernstein, **Die Judenpolitik der Rumänischen Regierung** [Copenhagen: Trykt I Martius Truelsens Bogtrykkeri, 1918]; G. Bogdan-Duică, **Românii și Ovreii** [București: Tipografia Românească, 1913]; Enric F. Braunstein, **L'Oligarchie Roumaine et les Juifs** [Paris: Beresniak, n.d.]; J. B. Brochiner, **Chestiunea Israeliților Români** [București: Carp and Marinescu, 1910], covering to 1848; Anastase N. Hâciu, **Evreii în Țările Românești** [București: Cartea Românească, 1943]; M. A. Halevy, **Monografia istorică a tempulului Coral din București** [București: Cartea de Aur, 1935];

[29]Stambler, **Histoire**, 1913, pp. 66-69.

[30]This point is a matter of some controversy, but the arguments (among others) of J. C. Blüntschli, **Der Staat Rumänien und das Rechtsverhältniss der Juden in Rumänien** [Berlin: W. &. S. Loewenthal, 1879] and Stambler, **Histoire**, 1913, pp. 75-82 seem conclusive.

[31]For the period under consideration, the problem was largely a Moldovan one. In Muntenia before 1860 there were fewer than 10,000 Jews or about four in a thousand. Rosetti, **Les Juifs**, 1903, pp. 48.

[32]Rosetti, **Les Juifs**, 1903, pp. 6-7.

[33]Rosetti, **Les Juifs**, 1903, p. 32.

[34]Statistics in A. C. Cuza, **Despre poporație**, 2nd revised edition, [București: Independența, 1929], pp. 542-546, 649. The urban Romanian population of the thirteen Moldovan județs (i.e.

excluding Moldova on the left bank of the Prut) all showed a net deficit between 1870-1879, totaling 19,687, while the Jewish population grew 14,153. Iaşi between 1866 and 1875 showed an excess of 6,092 deaths over births for the non-Jewish population, while the Jews showed an excess of 2,940 births. Since A. C. Cuza was a notorious anti-Semite and careless plagiarizer, these statistics have to be taken with some degree of uncertainty.

[35] See A. S. Bucureşti, MAI/Sanitar/60/1866, Volume I, folio 13 and elsewhere. This is the view of Desjardins, **Moldavie**, 1867, pp. 16-17, as well.

[36] Rosetti, **Les Juifs**, 1903, p. 29.

[37] See Rosetti, **Les Juifs**, 1903, pp. 101-111.

[38] Rosetti, **Les Juifs**, 1903, p. 95.

[39] Rosetti, **Les Juifs**, 1903, pp. 98-99, 276. Desjardins, **Moldavie**, 1867, also supports this idea.

[40] Desjardins, **Moldavie**, 1867.

[41] Desjardins, **Moldavie**, 1867, p. 6 This was partly a result of hostile legislation.

[42] I. C. Codrescu, **Cotropirea Judoveasca in Romania**, [Bucureşti: Noua Typographia a Laboratorilor Romanî, 1870] p. 34, citing Alliance sources.

[43] This is stressed by Desjardins, **Moldavie**, 1867, pp. 6-7. See also the less convincing B. P. Hasdeu, **Istoria toleranţei religiose în Romania**, 2nd revised edition, [Bucureşti: Typographia Lucrătorilor Associaţi, 1868].

[44] Already some Romanian anti-Semites were advancing the theory that the Jewish presence and competition automatically meant decline and enfeeblement of the Romanian "race." B. P. Hasdeu, **Industria naţională, industria streină, şi industria Ovreească faţa cupprincipiulu concurenţei** [Bucureşti: Lucrătoriloru Associaţi, 1866] is the first exposition of this theory which later became the staple of intellectual Romanian anti-Semitism. See A. C. Cuza, **Despre poporaţie** [Iaşi: Naţionala, 1899]. The actual validity of these highly dubious theories is irrelevant since the hypotheses were adduced and accepted as explanations at the time.

[45] Most of the Jews in Romania at this time were likely

immigrants according to Desjardins, **Moldavie**, 1867, p. 8.

[46]This is spelled out in **Note sur la situation des Israélites en Roumanie au point de vue des relations internationales** [Paris: Charles Maréchal, 1875], passim.

[47]Adolf Stern notes this ironic point in his **Din viaţa unui Evreu-Român** [Bucureşti: Progresul, 1915], pp. 80-85.

[48]Solomon Posener, **Adolphe Crémieux** [Philadelphia: The Jewish Publication Society of America, 1940], p. 137.

[49]See Desjardins, **Moldavie**, 1867, pp. 17-18 for a discussion of Brătianu's aims.

[50]Or even a mere gesture, since the order was not really enforceable. See Desjardins, **Moldavie**, 1867, p. 18.

[51]Summaries in Loeb, **La Situation**, 1877, pp. 218-219, 272.

[52]Loeb, **La Situation**, 1877, p. 118; **Note sur la situation**, 1875, pp. 9-20; and Berkowitz, **La Question**, 1923, pp. 358-359.

[53]Great Britain, Foreign Office, **British and Foreign State Papers**, Volumes 48-62, [London: William Ridgway, 1865-1877], Volume 58, pp. 887-888.

[54]Desjardins, **Moldavie**, 1867, pp. 18-21. Documents relating to this affair are printed in Great Britain, **State Papers**, 1873, Volume 58, pp. 887-897; 1877, Volume 62, pp. 689-710; Great Britain, Parliament, **Correspondence respecting the Persecution of Jews in Moldavia** [London: Harrison, 1867]; Great Britain, Parliament, **Further Correspondence respecting the Persecution of Jews in Moldavia**, two broshures, [London: Harrison, 1867]; and Loeb, **La Situation**, 1877, pp. 272-296.

[55]Carol, **Memoirs**, 11 May 1867, Cornu had written in March to warn Carol of Napoléon's growing hostility. See Cornu to Picot, 28 February/12 March 1867, in Georgescu-Tistu, **Mélanges France**, Vol. 3 (1925), p. 271.

[56]Desjardins to Cornu, 19/31 May 1867, in Emerit,"Une ingérence,"(1939), pp. 58-59. Desjardins also believed that Carol's Prussian counterpart to Picot, Friedlander, was a definite obstacle to French policy.

[57] Carol, **Memoirs**, 14 May 1867.
[58] Carol, **Memoirs**, 14 May 1867.
[59] Green to Stanley, 14/26 May 1867, telegraphic, in Great Britain, **Correspondence**, 1867, document 5.
[60] Carol to Napoléon III, 14 May 1867, telegraphic in Carol, **Cuvântări**, 1909, Volume I, p. 79.
[61] See Bogdan, **Carol I**, 1916, p. 85, and Carol, **Memoirs**, 18 May 1867.
[62] St. Clair to Green, 15/27 May 1867, telegraphic in Great Britain, **State Papers**, Volume 58 (1873), pp. 884-885.
[63] Green to Stanley, 14/26 May 1867, in Great Britain, **State Papers**, Volume 58 (1873), p. 843. This is a typical human rights evasion.
[64] St. Clair to Green, 17/29 May 1867, in Great Britain, **State Papers**, Volume 58 (1873), pp. 889-890.
[65] Carol, **Memoirs**, 12 May 1867; Loeb, **La Situation**, 1877, pp. 282-284. Among the signers were D. A. Sturdza, V. Pogor, M. C. Epureanu, and P. P. Carp. At least D. A. Sturdza seems genuinely distressed by the matter, however. See D. A. Sturdza to Ion Ghica, 15 June 1867, and to C. Hurmuzaki, 9/21 July 1867, BAR București, Fond, D. A. Sturdza, coresp. 83934 and 131322.
[66] Green to Stanley, 15/27 May 1867, in Great Britain, **Correspondence**, 1867, document 6.
[67] See the warning of P. Bataillard to Rosetti, 12/24 June 1867, BCS București, Fond. St. Georges, Pach. LXI/D.7.
[68] Details on this aspect are taken from Emerit, "Une ingérence," (1939), pp. 53-73, which is based on correspondence between Carp, Bălăceanu, and Cornu. Also useful were two long telegrams by Carp to Picot, 10/22 May and 17/29 May 1867, A. S. București, Casa Regală, 44/1867 and 47/1867; and some notes by Bălăceanu in BAR București, Arhiva Ion Bălăceanu, I.Mss.14.
[69] Carol to Cornu, 20 May 1867, resume in Carol, **Cuvântări**, 1909, Volume I, p. 80.
[70] This was the task assigned Eugeniu Carada, who published three pamphlets in Paris to unavail, as part of a propaganda mission. The pamphlets were **La Propaganda russe en Orient**

[Paris: Dentu, 1867]; **Intrigues de la Russie en Roumanie** [Paris: Luxembourg, 1867];and **Les Israélites, le vagabondage et le ministère Bratiano** [Paris: Serviere, 1867]. The aid of Paul Bataillard and others was also enlisted (see C. A. Rosetti to Bataillard, 17/29 July 1867, BCS București, Fond. St. Georges, Pach. L/D.3).

[71]St. Clair to Green, 16/28 June 1867, in Great Britain, **State Papers**, Volume 58 (1867), pp. 896-897.

[72]Carol, **Memoirs**, 12 June 1867.

[73]On 2 June, Carol had, in fact refused a request for permission to return by Cuza. Cuza's letter and Carol's reply are found in A. S. București, Casa Regală, 4/1867 folios 1-3. On Cuza after his ouster, see: Bobango, **Emergence**, 1979, pp. 208-212; C. C. Giurescu, "Alexandru Ioan Cuza la Viena," **Revista Arhivelor**, Vol. 9 (1866), pp. 139-143; M. Ionescu, "Contribuții privind exilul lui Alexandru Ioan Cuza," **Studii**, Vol. 22 (1969), pp. 531-538; D. Vitcu, "Alexandru Ioan Cuza—anii exilului (1866-1873)," in: Platon, **Cuza Vodă**, 1973, pp. 551-567; and Grigore Ploeșteanu, "Alexander J. Cuza im exil (1866-1873).Innerer Nachklang und diplomatische implikationen," **Revue Roumaine d'Histoire**, Vol. 22 (1983), pp. 47-58. On Cuza's death, see Grigore Chiriță, "Presa, opinia publică din România la moartea lui Cuza Vodă," **Studii**, Vol. 26 (1973), pp. 545-554.

[74]Bogdan, **Carol**, 1916, pp. 93-94.

[75]Green to Lyons, 4/16 July 1867, in Great Britain, **State Papers**, Vol. 58 (1873), p. 898. **Le Siècle**, in Paris published a defense of the Romanian government's policy in its 15/27 June 1867, issue.

[76]The conflicting stories are printed in Berkowitz, **La Question**, 1923, pp. 376-379. A.S. București, MAI/Ad/46/1867, and Great Britain, **State Papers**, Volume 62 (1877), pp. 689-715, have various documents on the question. See also the report of **Le Siècle**, 28 July/9 August 1867.

[77]Carol, **Memoirs**, 10 July 1867. At the same time Picot was apparently in Paris trying to mollify Crémieux. See Georgescu-Tistu, **Correspondance Picot**, 1827, pp. 100-102.

Crémieux was adamant that the only step was for Carol to "strike Brătianu with an absolute dismissal..." (Posener, **Crémieux**, 1940, p. 187).
[78] Carol, **Memoirs**, 29 July 1867.
[79] Carol, **Memoirs**, 29 July 1867, and Picot to Crémieux 2/14 August 1867, in Georgescu-Tistu, **Correspondance Picot**, 1927, pp. 97-98.
[80] See Green to Stanley, 15/27 May 1867, in Great Britain, **State Papers**, Volume 58 (1873), pp. 883-884.
[81] For these appeals and on the Montefiore mission see Sir Moses and Lady Montefiore, **Diaries of Sir Moses and Lady Montefiore**, two volumes, [Chicago: Belford-Clarke Co., 1890], Volume II, pp. 193-212; 361-363.
[82] The assessment of Montefiore's visit given in Carol, **Memoirs**, 13 August 1867, is highly inaccurate.

●**CHAPTER TEN: pp. 177-189**

[1] Despite the fact that Carol characterized him as lacking in energy, **Memoirs**, 3 August 1867.
[2] Transilvania had been a constant preoccupation of Rosetti and his associates.
[3] Green to Stanley, 9/21 August 1867, nr. 93, PRO London, FO/78/1972.
[4] Early in the year, the Austrians had been disturbed by the travels of Candiano-Popescu in Transilvania, whom they arrested for irredentist agitation. Candiano-Popescu, **Amintiri**, 1944, pp. 137-140.
[5] Carol, **Memoirs**, 30 August 1867. Napoléon adds, hypocritically, "...je ne me suis jamais cru autorisé à influencer votre décision quant au choix de vos ministres."
[6] Picot to Cornu, 14/26 August 1867, in Emerit,"Une ingérence," (1939), pp. 63-66. Cornu's disgusted reply of 8/20 September 1867, [Georgescu-Tistu,"Picot," (1925), pp. 272-274], bluntly abandoned Carol; she was now "completely disinterested in the affairs of Romania."
[7] Green to Stanley, 21 August/2 September 1867, nr. 88, PRO

London, FO/78/1972.

[8]Picot to Cornu, 3/15 October 1867, in Emerit, "Une ingérence," (1939), pp. 66-69. See also BCS Bucureşti, Fond, St. Georges, Pach. LXI/D.7 and Pach.L/D.3.

[9]Posener, **Crémieux**, 1940, p. 187.

[10]See D. A. Sturdza to I. Ghica, 5 and 9 November 1867, BAR Bucureşti, Fond. D. A. Sturdza, coresp. 83935 and 83836, for the negative view. Brătianu's correspondence reads for 25 September/7 October 1867, "Today I see Napoléon," but subsequent letters do not mention if he did or not. One would suppose he would have mentioned it if he had. However, the files are incomplete. See Ion Brătianu to Pia Brătianu during September-October, 1867, in Nistor, **Corespondenţa Brătianu**, 1933, Volume I, pp. 87-93.

[11]Ion Brătianu to Pia Brătianu, 9/21 October 1867, in Nistor, **Corespondenţa Brătianu**, 1933, Volume I, pp. 91-92. Brătianu also published anonymously a pamphlet defending his ministry, **La Question d'Orient et la nation roumaine** [Paris: Luxembourg, 1867].

[12]Quoted in Seton-Watson, **A History**, 1963, pp. 324-325.

[13]Carol, **Memoirs**, 16 October 1867.

[14]See Carol's speech opening the session, Carol, **Cuvântări**, 1909, Volume I, pp. 85-87.

[15]Green to Stanley, 23 October/4 November 1867, nr. 91, PRO London, FO/78/1972.

[16]See Carol, **Memoirs**, 16 October 1867.

[17]Carol, **Memoirs**, 16 October 1867.

[18]Green to Stanley, 1/13 November 1867, nr. 94 and 95, PRO London, FO/78/1972. An indictment of the chamber as unrepresentative and unreasonably obstructive is found in Carol, **Memoirs**, 1 November 1867. Cp. also Nicolescu, **Parlamentul**, 1903, Volume I, pp. 26-30.

[19]Green to Stanley, 4/16 November 1867, nr. 96, PRO London, FO/78/1972.

[20]See D. A. Sturdza to I. Ghica, 4/16 November 1867, BAR Bucureşti, Fond D. A. Sturdza, coresp. 83937. Sturdza believed a European intervention was near, which would be fatal for

Romania considering how antagonistic nearly all the powers now were. He made a substantial appeal against Brătianu to Karl Anton (see D. A. Sturdza to C. Hurmuzaki, 20 December 1867, BAR Bucureşti, Fond. D. A. Sturdza coresp. 131323, and Carol, **Memoirs**, 1 November 1867).

[21] Carol, **Memoirs**, 13 December 1867.

[22] See J. Gradowicz to A. G. Golescu, 4/16 January 1868, BCS Bucureşti, Fond. St. Georges, Pach. VI/D.3.

[23] Green to Stanley, 14/26 November 1867, nr. 98, PRO London, FO/78/1972.

[24] Bolintineanu, **Domnii regulamentarii**, 1869, pp. 92-94.

[25] Green to Stanley, 8/20 December 1867, nr. 106, PRO London, FO/78/1972.

[26] Text in Carol, **Cuvântări**, 1909, Volume I, pp. 91-100.

[27] Carol saw a rail link between Iaşi and Bucureşti as the means of finally eliminating separatism and cementing union. See Carol to Karl Anton, 13 January 1868, in Carol, **Cuvântări**, 1909, Volume I, p. 102.

[28] Carol, **Memoirs**, 16 January 1868.

[29] See Carol, **Memoirs**, January-March, 1868, passim.

[30] C. A. Rosetti to P. Bataillard, 14 April 1868, BCS Bucureşti, Fond. St. Georges, Pach. L/D.3.

[31] This Bulgarian matter is the primary subject of Green's dispatches to London in 1868. See PRO London, FO/78/2030, 2031, and 2032. See also Dalyell, consul at Ruščuk, to Stanley, PRO London, FO/78/2035.

[32] See Carol to Karl Anton, 24 February 1868, in Carol, **Cuvântări**, 1909, Volume I, p. 106. "Moustier is more Turkish than the Sultan....Brătianu shows himself more and more as a daring statesman, but he is a thorn in the eye of the French government." See also Cornu's letter to Carol in Carol, **Memoirs**, 14 February 1868.

[33] This was seen clearly by Émile Picot, who characterized Brătianu's policy as "insane." Picot to Mme. Cornu, 28 February /11 March 1868, in Georgescu-Tistu, **Correspondance Picot**, 1927, pp. 112-115.

[34] Carol, **Memoirs**, 25 and 29 January 1868.

[35] Carol, **Memoirs**, 14 February 1868.

[36] Text in **Proictu de lege pentru Regularisarea stării Jidoviloru in România** [n.p.: n.p., n.d. (1868)]. Also in Loeb, **La Situation**, 1877, pp. 301-313. The proposal is a concise statement of the Fraction's anti-Jewish position.

[37] [Antoine Lévy], **Réponse aux attaques dirigées contre les Israélites** [Bucureşti: Weiss, 1868]. My copy is enscribed "de la part de l'auteur Antoine Levy."

[38] Carol, **Memoirs**, 18 March 1868.

[39] Karl Anton wrote to Carol that at all costs the Jewish issue must cease discussion. "This question is a noli me tangere because the Jews have money and the entire press." Reprinted in Carol, **Memoirs**, 25 March 1868.

[40] Carol, **Memoirs**, 5-8 April 1868. Carol was on a visit to Iaşi where he found separatism almost completely gone. The coincidence between this and friendly contacts with Russia is noteworthy! Carol was a guest of both Metropolitan Calinic and Rosetti-Rosnovanu, leaders in the 1866 revolt.

[41] See D. A. Sturdza to Ion Ghica, 20 and 21 April 1868, BAR Bucureşti, Fond. D. A. Sturdza, coresp. 83939 and 83940, and Carol, **Memoirs**, 11 and 14 April 1868.

[42] Relevant documents in Loeb, **La Situation**, 1877, pp. 323-328, and 334; and Austria. Foreign Office, **Correspondenzen des Kais.Kön.Gemeinsamen Ministeriums des Äussern, Nr. 2: Jan. bis Nov. 1868** [Vienna: K.K. Hof und Staatsdruckerei, 1868], pp. 47-74. See also Şt. Golescu to A. G. Golescu, April, 1868, in Fotino, **Boierii Goleşti**, 1939, Volume IV, pp. 421-422.

[43] Carp's speech is reproduced in his **Discursuri**, 1907, Volume I, pp. 1-19; Brătianu's in **Din scrierile Brătianu**, 1903, Part I, pp. 433-446.

[44] See his speech of 30 April to the chamber in **Din scrierile Brătianu**, 1903, Part I, pp. 447-464, passim, especially p. 458.

[45] Green to Stanley, 31 May/12 June 1868, in Great Britain, **State Papers**, Volume 62, pp. 743-745.

[46] Carol, **Memoirs**, 9 May 1868.

[47] Carol, **Memoirs**, 31 May-3 June 1868.

[48] D. A. Sturdza to C. Hurmuzaki, 30 July 1868, BAR București, Fond. D. A. Sturdza, coresp. 131326.
[49] See Carol's comments, **Memoirs**, 1 June 1868.
[50] Carol, **Memoirs**, 12 June 1868.
[51] Carol wrote sarcastically to his father on 1 August, "I think it would be more important for there to be a change of ministry in France rather than Romania." Carol, **Cuvântări**, 1909, Volume I, p. 117.
[52] Carol to Adrian, 2 August 1868, A.S. București, Casa Regală, 17/1868.
[53] Carol, **Memoirs**, 13 August 1868.
[54] Texts in **Din scrierile Brătianu**, 1903, Part I, pp. 473-490.
[55] See Ion Brătianu to division commanders, 12 August 1868, in **Din scrierile Brătianu**, 1903, Part I, pp. 471-473. A thorough review of this issue is Maria Georgescu, "Politica militară a guvernării liberale din anii 1867-1868," **File din Istoria Militară a Poporului Român**, Vol. 3 (1975), pp. 120-138. Constantin Căzănișteanu discusses the post-Cuza decade in military development in "Un deceniu de realizări militare: 1866-1875," **File din Istoria Militară a Poporului Român**, Vol. 7 (1980), pp. 96-128; see also Olteanu, **Armed Power**, 1982, pp. 145-154.
[56] See Carol, **Memoirs**, 6 August 1868.
[57] Carol, **Memoirs**, 19-27 October 1868.
[58] Carol, **Memoirs**, 2 November 1868.
[59] Carol, **Memoirs**, 11 November 1886.
[60] Joachim Pepoli to Carol, 12/24 November 1868, A. S. București, Casa Regală, 43/1868, folios 3-6 verso.
[61] See his correspondence in Perticari-Davila, **Corespondența Davila**, 1935, pp. 234-244. The quotation is on p. 241.
[62] **Din scrierile Brătianu**, 1903, Part I, p. 312.
[63] D. A. Sturdza to C. Hurmuzaki, 30 July 1868, BAR București, Fond. D. A. Sturdza, coresp. 13126.
[64] Carol, **Memoirs**, 26 October 1868.
[65] Details in Carol, **Memoirs**, 1,2,6, and 11 November 1868.
[66] Text in Carol, **Cuvântări**, 1909, Volume I, pp. 130-136.

⁶⁷V. Russu and D. Vitcu, "Frămîntări politice interne în vremea guvernării D. Ghica—M. Kogălniceanu (1868-1870), Pt. I," **Anuarul Institutului de Istorie și Arheologie A. D. Xenopol**, Vol. 7 (1970), pp. 143-147 for details.
⁶⁸? to ?, 2/14 De 1868, "confidential" from Paris, A. S. București, Casa Regală, 72/1868.
⁶⁹This is spelled out in Carol's reply to Marquis Pepoli, 3 December 1868, A. S. București, Casa Regală, 43/1868, folios 8-10, copy.

●CHAPTER 11: pp. 190-200

¹The assertion [e.g., Russu and Vitcu,"Framîntări...1868-1870," (1970), p. 146] that Carol did so simply to concentrate more power in his own hands does not appear substantiated by the evidence or events. The 29-year-old prince had learned a lot in three years, but not enough to be such a Machiavellian. However, in this article, its companion part II (published in the same journal, Vol. 8 (1971), pp. 61-98), and their shorter article (cited below in note 15), provide first rate coverage of the period. On the new cabinet's foreign policy, see N. Corivan, "Apecte din politica externă a Principatelor Unite in timpul guvernării D. Ghica—M. Kogălniceanu (16 noiembrie—2 februarie 1870," **Cercetări Istorice**, Vol. 6 (1975), pp. 141-159.
²Carol, **Memoirs**, 19 November 1968.
³**Monitorul**, 20 November 1868.
⁴See a series of undated notes by D. Ghica on this period in BCS București, Fond. St. Georges, Pach. L/D.10, and also Ion Ghica to D. A. Sturdza, 30 January/12 February 1869, BAR București, Mss. Rom. 5316, folios 234-244.
⁵See the debates in **Monitorul**.
⁶**Acte Brătianu**, 1935, Volume I, Part 2-a, pp. 1-13.
⁷Carol, **Memoirs**, 8 January 1869.
⁸There were some liberal legislative activities in 1868 in connection with "explaining" the electoral law more clearly that contributed to this possibility. See Russu and Vitcu, "Framîntări...1868-1870," (1970), pp. 159-161.
⁹A typical summary of this situation is in Ion Strat to D. A. Sturdza, 10/22 February 1869, BAR București, Mss. Rom. 5316, folios 276-282 verso. See also Carol, **Memoirs**, entry following

[10]D. Ghica to D. A. Sturdza, 7/19 January 1969, BAR București, Mss. Rom. 5316, folios 139-143 verso, spells out this policy in detail. It is a constant theme of Ghica's dispatches in the same series. See also Kogălniceanu's 24 January 1869, chamber speech (**Monitorul**, 30 January 1869).

[11]See D. A. Sturdza to D. Ghica, 11 January 1869, very confidential, nr. 5, BAR București, Mss. Rom. 5316, folios 154-161, for favorable reaction of British, French, and Russian diplomats at Constantinople; and L. Steege to D. Ghica, 9/21 February 1869, nr. 12, BCS București, Fond. St. Georges, Pach. LVII/D.1 for Vienna's promise of aid. See also N. Iorga, **Politica externă a Regelui Carol I**, second edition [București: Luceafărul, 1923], pp. 76-79.

[12]D. Ghica to Sturdza, January 7/14, 1869, BAR București, Mss. Rom. 5316, folios 139-143 verso.

[13]D. Ghica to I. Strat, L. Steege, and D. A. Sturdza, 15/27 February 1869, draft in BCS București, Fond. St. Georges, Pach. LVII/D.1.

[14]See also D. Ghica to Constantinople, 10 June 1869, very confidential, copy in BCS București, Fond. Kogălniceanu, Pach. XLIX/D.10, "after we have been so to say the gendarmes of Turkey...after having rendered...the most valuable service, what has she done to boost our internal prestige?...I have profound regret that Turkey does not see on this point its true interests;" and D. Ghica to D. A. Sturdza, 26 July 1869, confidential, BAR București, Mss. Rom. 5317, folios 340-341, which expresses surprise that those governments which have the most to gain by stability in București aid the least, despite the fact that only his cabinet stood between Europe and the "incendiary contagion" waiting to be sparked in the Balkans.

[15]See above, pp. 157-158, and Kogălniceanu's speech in **Monitorul** for 26 February 1869. For Kogălniceanu's motives and activity in this cabinet, see V. Russu and D. Vitcu, "Date noi referitoare la activitatea politică a lui Mihail Kogălniceanu (1869)," **Anuarul Institutului de Istorie și Arheologie A. D. Xenopol**, Vol. 17 (1980), pp. 617-622.

[16]Brătianu told D. Ghica, "Before 2 months you will be obliged to arrest me." Cited in D. Ghica to D. A. Sturdza, 26 January 1869, nr. 74, draft, BCS București, Fond St. Georges, Pach. LVII/D.1.

[17]See Brătianu's speeches for these issues in: **Acte Brătianu**,

1935, Volume I, Part. 2-a, pp. 60-93; and D. Ghica's report to D. A. Sturdza, 2 February 1869, nr. 100, BAR București, Mss. Rom. 5316, folio 235.

[18] I Cantacuzino to D. A. Sturdza, 11 April 1869, telegraphic, BAR București, Mss. Rom. 5317, folio 49. A sampling of Kogălniceanu's "methods" may be found in letters reprinted in M. Kogălniceanu, Scrisori. Note de călătorie, edited by A. Z. N. Pop and Dan Simonescu [București: Editura pentru Literatura, 1967], pp. 78-80; 137-140. Another index is the fact that for the period 1 March-9 April 1869, there remain over 300 confidential messages sent by Kogălniceanu relating to the elections. See A. Z. N. Pop, ed., Catalogul corespondenței lui Mihail Kogălniceanu [București: Editura Academiei, 1959], pp. 197-252. One of the most interesting of these messages was to the prefect of Argeș requesting his agents to refrain from their normal "excess of zeal" in Ion Brătianu's district because Brătianu had always refrained from "intervention" against Kogălniceanu when the liberals "conducted" elections. See Kogălniceanu to Prefect of Argeș, 3 March 1869, copy in BCS București, Fond. St. Georges, Pach. VIII/D.12.

[19] See Carol, Memoirs, 3 February 1869.

[20] See D. A. Sturdza to D. Ghica, 1/13 Feb 1869, very confidential, nr. 10, BAR București, Mss. Rom. 5316, folios 229-234: "Ali Pasha has been enchanted" by the dissolution of the liberal chamber; and L. Steege to D. Ghica, 4/16 February 1869, nr. 9, BCS București, Pach. LVII/D.1, reporting the "great relief" in Vienna.

[21] See Carol to Karl Anton, 2 February 1869, in Carol, Cuvântări, 1909, Volume I, pp. 140-148.

[22] See Damé, Histoire, 1900, p. 200, for details.

[23] Russu and Vitcu, ,"Frămîntări...1868- 1870," (1971), pp. 66-73. They also argue that Kogălniceanu was attempting to resurrect his pre-1866 social program, but the actions of "his" chambers fail to reflect any such program.

[24] The letters of Ion Strat, the government's agent in Paris, to D. A. Sturdza are quite illuminating on this aspect. See for example the letter of 4/16 May 1869, BAR București, Mss. Rom. 5317, folios 199-203. Sturdza in turn wanted to resign if his efforts at the Porte were only to bolster the position of Kogălniceanu whom he despised. See D. A. Sturdza to Al. G. Golescu, 29 July 1869, BAR București, Mss. Rom. 5317, folios 400-402 verso.

[25] Carol, **Cuvântări**, 1909, Volume I, pp. 158-159. In fact, many deputies never showed up at all because of agricultural duties on their estates.

[26] Carol, **Memoirs**, 3 June 1869.

[27] The larger implications fo this futility were spelled out in a letter by the Bucovinian leader E. Hurmuzaki to D. A. Sturdza. How, he asked, could Romania's political situation possibly be attractive to Romanians outside her present borders (e.g. under Austrian and Russian domination)? How could they be asked to accept "a national state" that was backward and more disorganized than the empires in which they now lived? Romanian politics were neither "rational or national." See Hurmuzaki to Sturdza, 30 May/11 June 1869, BAR Bucureşti, Mss. Rom. 5318, folios 256-258 verso. This was a problem into the twentieth century.

[28] Carol to Karl Anton, 22 March 1869, in Carol, **Cuvântări**, 1909, Volume I, pp. 153-155.

[29] See also Maiorescu, **Istoria**, 1925, p. 19.

[30] These are collected by Russu and Vitcu, "Framîntări...1868-1870," (1971), p. 91.

[31] See I. Strat to D. Ghica, 2/14 September 1869, BCS Bucureşti, Fond St. Georges, Pach L/D.1; and Strat to D. Ghica, 3/15 September 1869, nr. 202, copy in BAR Bucureşti, Mss. Rom. 5318, folios 4-9 verso.

[32] In December, 1869, as a result of a year-long struggle, Napoléon III installed a liberal cabinet under Émile Ollivier.

[33] Napoléon had told Strat in January/February that "if your government enters into the conservative path which is the only good one for the interests of Romania, then our sympathies will be with you." Strat to D. Ghica, 29 January/10 February 1869, copy, BAR Bucureşti, Mss. Rom. 5316, folios 294-295 verso.

[34] Details in Carol, **Memoirs**, passim, and Văcărescu, "Memorii," (1916), pp. 287-298.

[35] The original announcement of the engagement is in Carol to D. Ghica, 5/17 October 1869, BCS Bucureşti, Fond. St. Georges, Pach. L/D.2.

[36] See Radu R. Rosetti, "Corespondenţa maiorului D. Giurescu," **A.R.MSI**, Seria III, Vol. 29 (1946-1947), pp. 81-82, quoting a contemporary account.

[37] Carol's letter to Karl Anton, 8 December 1869, in **Cuvântări**, 1909, Volume I, pp. 196-198, gives a clear picture of the situation.

[38] Bolintineanu, **Domnii regulamentari**, 1869, pp. 112-115. Pp. 124-141 of this book is a catalogue of abuses on the part of the Ghica-Kogălniceanu regime, especially the latter.
[39] See I. Ghica to D. A. Sturdza, 6 April 1869, BAR București, Mss. Rom. 5317, folios 190-193 verso on relations between Kogălniceanu and the liberals.

•CHAPTER 12: pp. 201-214

[1] Carol, **Memoirs**, 2 February 1870.
[2] Carol, **Memoirs**, 28 January 1870. It was the first time in nearly a year that they had spoken.
[3] See Brătianu's remarks, at yet another București banquet, designed to serve as a liberal sounding board, on 2 February 1870, reprinted in: **Acte Brătianu**, 1935, Volume I, Part 2-a, pp. 160-174.
[4] D. Ghica to Carol, [1 February 1870], draft, BCS București, Fond. St. Georges, Pach. LVI/D.4.
[5] See the acid remarks of I. Strat to D. A. Sturdza, 19 February/3 March 1870, BAR București, Mss. Rom. 5319, folios 213-220. Compare Polihroniade and Tell, **Carol I**, 1937, p. 250.
[6] Carol, **Memoirs**, 30 January 1870.
[7] Al. G. Golescu to D. A. Sturdza, 20 March 1870, circular, BAR București, Mss. Rom. 5319, folios 331-332; and Carol, **Memoirs**, 11 March 1870.
[8] This was a resolution of the negotiations begun under Brătianu in 1867 to gain acceptance of the reform from the Porte. See Constantin Moisil, "Alexandru G. Golescu și acțiunea pentru restabilirea monetei naționale," **Arhiva Românească**, Vol. 10 (1945-1946), pp. 101-120 as well as the works cited above in note 19 of Chapter Nine.
[9] BCS București, Fond. St. Georges, Pach. LVII/D.4, contains numerous telegrams on this matter.
[10] See Carol to Cuza, 18 February 1870, in Carol, **Cuvântări**, 1909, Volume I, pp. 205-206.
[11] Al. G. Golescu to D. A. Sturdza, 25 February 1870, BAR București, Mss. Rom. 5319, folios 277-278.
[12] Strat to Foreign ministry, București, 23 February/7 March 1870, personal and confidential, BCS București, Fond. St. Georges, Pach. LVII/D.4. The name of the sponsor of "occult propaganda" is given in cypher and is not known.
[13] Foreign Ministry, București, to D. A. Sturdza, 27 March

1870, BAR București, Mss. Rom. 5319, folios 333-334 verso.

[14]See Carol, **Memoirs**, 18 March 1870: "The most agitated place in the whole country is Ploești; we need to take energetic measures to prevent the digging there of a mine that could menace the whole country." Coverage of the "radical" tradition of Ploești is given in M. Sevastos, **Monografia orașului Ploești** [București: Cartea Românească, 1937]. See also N. I. Simache, "Mișcările din Ploiești 1869-1870," **File din Trecutul Istoric al Județului Prahova**, Vol. 1 (1971), pp. 127-148.

[15]? to Ion Brătianu, 12 June 1870, BCS București, Fond. St. Georges, Pach. LVI/D.4.

[16]I. Strat to D. A. Sturdza, 19 February/3 March 1870, BAR București, Mss. Rom. 5319, folios 213-220, believed that the army's support was the main barrier to revolt.

[17]See Carol, **Memoirs**, 23, 27 February, 11, 12, and 18 March 1870.

[18]See Maiorescu's biting remarks in his 1868 article, "Against the Direction of Today in Romanian Culture," reprinted in Titu Maiorescu, **Critice 1866-1907**, completed edition, three volumes [București: Minerva, 1915], Volume I, pp. 151-164, especially p.160: "We have politics and science, we have journals and academies...we even have a constitution. But in reality all these are dead productions, without foundations..." See also my "Romanian Perspectives," (1981-1982).

[19]The history of Junimea as a political group gets first-rate treatment in Z. Ornea's **Junimea și Junimismul**, second edition [București: Editura Eminescu, 1978].

[20]See Karl Anton to Carol, quoted in Carol, **Memoirs**, 30 April 1870.

[21]Spelled out in P. P. Carp to L. Steege, 29 April 1870, nr. 2812, copy, BCS București, Fond. St. Georges, Pach. LVII/D.4.

[22]Polihroniade and Tell, **Carol I**, 1937, p. 252.

[23]Speech of 5 July 1870, quoted in Gane, **Carp**, 1935, Volume I, p. 135. Cf. Beatrice Marinescu and Șerban Rădulescu-Zoner, "Le peuple roumain et la guerre franco-prussienne de 1870-1871", **Revue Roumaine d'Histoire**, Vol. 10 (1971), pp. 329-342; Gh. Cristea, "Date privind ecoul și aniversarea comunei din Paris în Romînia," **Studii**, Vol. 14 (1961), pp. 659-685; Dan Berindei, "L'écho des événements de France dans la vie politique de la Roumanie durant les années 1870-1871," **Revue d'Histoire Moderne et Contemporaine**, Vol. 19 (1972), pp. 362-375; and Al. Porțeanu, "La Commune

de Paris et le mouvement révolutionnaire démocratique de Roumanie," **Revue Roumaine d'Histoire**, Vol. 10 (1971), pp. 343-368.

[24] See Carol, **Memoirs**, 30 June 1870.

[25] Polihroniade and Tell, **Carol I**, 1937, p. 253. See also Damé, **Histoire**, 1900, pp. 208-212.

[26] These matters as well as the Ploeşti events are given excellent amplification in Gh. Cristea, "Conspiraţia 'republicana' din August 1870," **Studii**, Vol. 22 (1969), pp. 231-247. The article does not include one important source, the unpublished second part of Al. Candiano Popescu's memoirs, **Amintiri**, 1944, which are in the Mss. section of the BAR Bucureşti.

[27] Cited in Carol, **Memoirs**, 24 June 1870.

[28] Carol, **Memoirs**, 30 June 1870.

[29] See L. Steege to P. P. Carp, n.d. [July, 1870], copy, BCS Bucureşti, Fond. St. Georges, Pach. LVII/D.4; P. P. Carp to I. Strat, 10 July 1870, telegraphic, copy, BCS Bucureşti, Fond. St. Georges, Pach. LVII/D.4: and Gh. Ştirbey to P. P. Carp, n. d. [received 21 July 1870], telegraphic, BCS Bucureşti, Fond. St. Georges, Pach. LVII/D.4.

[30] Not a republic as later often assumed.

[31] Besides Cristea, "Conspiraţia," (1969), passim; see Caton Theodorian, "Ploeşti-Craiova. Scrisori din timpul răscoalei dela 1870," **Arhiva Olteniei**, Volume 16 (1937), pp. 22-35; Gh. Duzinchevici, "Un document sur l'émeute de 8-20 Août 1870," **Revue Historique du Sud-Est European**, Volume 14 (1937), pp. 69-72; Mircea Alexandrescu and Gabriel Mihăilescu, "Un veac de la mişcarea revoluţionară antidinastică. Cîteva documente inedite privind mişcarea revoluţionară din august 1870 de la Ploieşti," **Valachica**, Vol. 2 (1970), pp. 279-284; Radu Dan Vlad,"Procesul de la Tîrgovişte al mişcării antidinastice din 8 august 1870," **Revista de Istorie**, Vol. 35 (1982), pp. 903-916; a key account is Romaşcanu, **Carada**, 1937, pp. 152+. A very interesting contemporary source is N. Fleva, **Apararea făcută celor 41 acusaţi. Procesul lui 8 August**. [Bucureşti: Typographia curţii, 1871], the defense statement at the later trial of the conspirators.

[32] Cited in Cristea, "Conspiraţia," (1969), p. 240.

[33] See D. Giurescu to wife, 20 August 1870, reprinted in R. R. Rosetti, "Corespondenţa Giurescu," (1946-1947), pp. 83-84, for a contemporary report by a soldier who participated in the pacification. Little or no resistance was encountered.

[34] See for example P. P. Carp to all agents, 12 August 1870, copy, BAR București, Mss. Rom. 5320, folios 44-46; and Carp to I. Strat, 14 August 1870, telegraphic, draft, BCS București, Fond. St. Georges, Pach. LVI/D.4.

[35] Carp to D. A. Sturdza, 17 August 1870, draft, BCS București, Fond. St. Georges, Pach. LVI/D.4.

[36] Carol's reactions are in his **Memoirs**, 8 and 9 August 1870.

[37] Brătianu is said to have asked the police, sent to arrest him and search his country home, if they thought such "a practiced conspirator" would leave compromising papers around. See Carol, **Memoirs**, 9 August 1870.

[38] See Fleva, **Apararea**, 1871.

[39] Typical is the report of J. Locusteanu to Carol, 4 November 1870, telegraphic, on liberal maneuverings, in BCS București, Fond. St. Georges, Pach. LVI/D.4.

[40] The defense argument was that the Ploești leaders had merely been loyally proclaiming the regency which they had been informed had been set up in București (Fleva, **Apararea**, 1871, pp. 22-23.)

[41] See Carol, **Memoirs**, 17 October 1870.

[42] Maria Rosetti to Pia Brătianu, 5/17 September 1870, BCS București, Fond. St. Georges, Pach. LVI/D.4.

[43] C. A. Rosetti to P. Bataillard, 21 September/4 October 1870, BCS București, Fond. St. Georges, Pach. LXI/D.7.

[44] Carol, **Memoirs**, 17 October 1870: "The acquittal of those who endangered the very existence of Romania firmed the decision of the prince to abdicate."

[45] Maiorescu called it "the most confused and most unbridledly violent" Romanian parliamentary session (**Istoria**, 1925, p. 24).

[46] See Carol, **Memoirs**, passim.

[47] Carol, **Memoirs**, 25 Nov 1870.

[48] Bismarck to Carol, 27 November 1870, reprinted in Carol, **Memoirs**, 17 November 1870, which concluded: "The prince cannot count for a second even on our moral support."

[49] Details in Polihroniade and Tell, **Carol I**, 1937, pp. 255-260. Cf. Fritz Stern, **Gold and Iron** [New York: Vintage, 1979], pp. 350-393, which explores the case from the German banker side; and Hans Petri, "Ludwig Steege als Finanzminister Rumäniens und der Strousbergsche Eisenbahnbau (1867-1871)," **Südostdeutsches Archiv**, Vol. 4 (1961), pp. 92-104.

[50] Carol to Karl Anton, 10 December 1870, in Carol, **Cuvântări**, 1909, Volume I, pp. 225-226.

[51] Carol, **Memoirs**, 15 and 16 December 1870.
[52] Carol, **Memoirs**, 16 December 1870.
[53] There was in fact some negotiation toward that end as well. See Apostol Stan, "O acţiune politică pentru cucerirea independenţei naţionale în timpul războiului franco-prusian (1870-1871)," **Studii**, Vol. 26 (1973), pp. 749-765.
[54] Damé, **Histoire**, 1900, p. 223.
[55] Polihroniade and Tell, **Carol I**, 1937, p. 261.
[56] As shown in some caustic notes made by Ghica or an associate after a meeting of Brătianu and Ghica on 5 May 1870, found in BAR Bucarest, Mss. Rom. 5319, folios 406-407.
[57] See P. P. Carp to D. A. Sturdza, 7 September 1870, draft, BCS Bucureşti, Fond. St. Georges, Pach. LVI/D.4, which charges "abandoning his principles and his old friends he [Ghica] has thrown his support to the Reds."
[58] I. Bălăceanu, a Ghica adherent, asserts that there was no Ghica-liberal collusion (**Memoirs**, p. 148).
[59] See pp. 104-105 above.
[60] The majority on the committee was from the Fraction and by definition both anti-dynastic and anti-Semitic (Strousberg was Jewish).
[61] Text in Carol, **Cuvântări**, 1909, Volume I, pp. 226-228.
[62] This is the view of Maiorescu, **Istoria**, 1925, p. 28.
[63] See issues of 8, 9, and 11 March 1871.
[64] Contemporary accounts are found in Carol, **Memoirs**, 10 and 11 March 1871; Bălăceanu, **Memoirs**, p. 149; Văcărescu, "Memorii," (1915), pp. 1108-1109; and Maiorescu, **Istoria**, 1925, pp. 30-33. See also Gh. Cristea, "La Guerre Franco-allemande et le mouvement républican de mars 1871 à Bucarest," **Revue Roumaine d'Histoire**, Volume 3 (1984), pp. 277-291, and V. Russu, "Constituirea partidului conservator, (1972), pp. 117-146; V. Russu and Mihai Timofte, "Împrejurările şi semnificaţia instaurării guvernării conservatoare Lascăr Catargiu (martie 1871)," **Anuarul Institutului de Istorie şi Arheologie A. D. Xenopol**, Vol. 16 (1979), pp. 359-384.
[65] Ion Ghica to prefects, 11/23 March 1871, draft, in BAR Bucureşti, Arhiva I. Ghica, VII. Acte. 113.

●CHAPTER 13: pp. 217-226

[1] Xenopol, **Partidelor politice**, 1910, pp. 539-545 argues

this case well.

[2]See Mihail Kogălniceanu's funeral oration for Cuza, 7 June 1873, reprinted in: Mihail Kogălniceanu, **Opere**, G. Penelea, ed. [București: Editura Academiei, 1982], Volume IV, Part 3, pp. 496: "We are obliged to say that it was not his mistakes that overthrew him, but his great achievements." Kogălniceanu's double-meaning here is, first, that Cuza's reforms caused his foes to unify and oust him, and, second, that his reforms succeeded so well that his enemies could oust him without great risk to Romanian autonomy or loss of the gains already made.

[3]Lovinescu, **Istoria**, 1924, Volume I, pp. 195-196.

[4]See Platon, "1866," (1984), pp. 439-452, on 1866 as a turning point or new stage in modern Romanian history.

[5]Desjardins, **Moldavie**, 1867, pp. 21-22.

[6]Iași Jewish Committee to A. Crémieux, 4/16 June 1867, printed in Great Britain, **Correspondence**, 1867, nr. 11.

[7]Russu and Vitcu, "Framîntări (1868-1870)," (1970), p. 140.

[8]Nicolescu, **Parlamentul**, 1903, Volume I, p. x.

[9]See pp. 20-21 above.

[10]N. Iorga, "Statuia lui Cuza-Vodă," **Oameni cari au fost** [București: Fundația Pentru Literatură și Artă Regele Carol II, 1934], Volume I, p. 125.

[11]Cp. Berindei, "Antécedents," (1979), p. 802:"If Cuza was a 'mandatory,'...Prince Carol and his successors were instinctively considered by the nation...useful for a historical period..."

Appendix One:

A Note on Names and Orthography

One of the tedious chores for scholars using other than major European languages is providing a rationalization for whatever peculiar usages they adopt in spelling. Since Romanian has a Latin alphabet, there is very little justification for the often bizarre transliterations used by English publications, any more than to use them for French or German. Hence, this study has endeavored to use Romanian orthography with its diacritical marks as consistently as possible. The single exception to this is to use "Romania" instead of "România," since to use the latter would be more of an affectation than an attempt at accuracy. The reader will probably notice most the use of the Romanian forms "Moldova" instead of "Moldavia," and "Muntenia" instead of "Wallachia" for the names of the two provinces of Romania; and "Iași" instead of "Jassy," and "București" instead of "Bucharest" for their respective capitals.

Certain names may cause confusion in that their owners themselves have departed from standard orthography (i.e. Kretzulescu rather than Crețulescu); the form preferred by the owner is used. For works listed in the bibliography, titles are generally given as they appear on title pages; this often involves orthographical peculiarities. For authors who have varied the orthography of their names, only the most common form is given.

Appendix Two:

Money[1]

There are considerable difficulties in giving and using monetary equivalents in the period under discussion. The primary reason for this is that until 1867, Romania had no monetary system of its own. Prior to that time, various European monies circulated in the area and were considered legal tender. To assist in governmental financial transactions and in establishing some unity of measure, the device of a fictitious calculation unit was adopted. This unit, the "leu,"[2] unfortunately did not represent any fixed weight or value of gold or silver. It was subject, therefore, to wild fluctuations based on an extensive range of factors too complicated to mention here. Even within the country there were enormous variations depending on local conditions: for example, in 1865, a pound sterling was worth 68 lei on the official course, 68 1/2 lei in București, 72 lei in Iași, and 88 1/2 lei in Brăila.

Because taxes could be paid in a variety of currencies and because currency speculation was rife, considerable administrative confusion resulted. The same problem exists for the statement of precise figures for budgets, and other financial matters during the period. An effort has been made to state all figures in this study in new lei, that is the course established by the reform of 1867.

The following table gives the official course of the new lei in contemporary monies:

	Francs	Old lei	New lei
1 Napoléon	20.00	54.00	20.00
1 Pound sterling	25.20	68.00	25.00
1 Austrian ducat	11.85	32.00	11.75
1 Turkish pound	22.68	61.10	22.70
1 Russian pol	20.77	55.00	20.40
1 Franc	--.--	2.28	1.00
1 New leu	--.--	2.70	--.--

---

[1] The basic sources for this note are: C. I. Băicoianu, **Istoria**, 1932; C. C. Kirițescu, **Sistemul bănesc**, 1964, Volume I; and Gh. Zane, **Crearea sistemul monetar**, 1968.

[2] Romanian for "lion"; plural="lei"

Appendix Three:
Romanian Prime Ministers, 1862-1871[1]

1. Barbu Catargiu, 22 January-8 June 1862
2. Apostol Arsache, 8 June-24 June 1862 [interim]
3. Nicolae Kretzulescu, 24 June 1862-11 October 1863
4. Mihail Kogălniceanu, 11 October 1863-26 January 1865
5. Constantin Bosianu, 26 January-14 June 1865
6. Nicolae Kretzulescu, 14 June 1865-11 February 1866
7. Ion Ghica, 11 February-10 May 1866
8. Lascăr Catargiu, 11 May-14 July 1866
9. Ion Ghica, 15 July 1866-28 February 1867
10. Constantin A. Crețulescu, 1 March-16 August 1867
11. Ștefan Golescu, 17 August 1867-30 April 1868
12. Nicolae Golescu, 1 May-15 November 1868
13. Dimitrie Ghica, 16 November 1868-1 February 1870
14. Alexandru G. Golescu, 2 February-19 April 1870
15. Manolache Costache Epureanu, 20 April-14 December 1870
16. Ion Ghica, 18 December 1870-11 March, 1871

[1]Sources: Dimitrie Costescu, **Fazele ministeriale în România, 1862-1930** (București: Universul, 1930); Dan Berindei, "Guvernele lui Alexandru Ioan Cuza (1859-1866). Liste de miniștri," **Revista Arhivelor**, n.s., Vol. 2 (1959), pp. 147-163; Mioara Tudorică and Ioana Burlacu, "Guvernele României între anii 1866-1945. Liste de miniștri," **Revista Arhivelor**, Vol. 32 (1970), pp. 429-476; the **Monitorul Oficial**; and a compilation covering 1866-1888 found in A. S. București, Casa Regală, 7/1866.

Appendix Four:
A Note on Sources

This essay is designed to be a bibliographical supplement to accompany the text above. The first part contains materials of a primary nature, that is, archives, published documents, memoirs, and similar items used as the documentary basis for this study. The second part contains secondary materials used in the preparation of this study, some of which are not directly mentioned in the notes above. These include works of a general nature and reference works.

PART I: Primary Sources

A. ARCHIVES

The archival materials for this study came from the following depositories:

1. The Public Record Office, London, for the consular reports of British agents in București, Iași, Galați, and Ruščuk;
2. The Arhivele Statului in București, for the records of the ministry of interior (MAI), the Royal Archives (Casa Regală), and several minor fonds, including private papers;
3. The Arhivele Statului in Iași, for the records of the city of Iași (Primaria Iași);
4. The Biblioteca Academiei, București, Manuscript Section, for the Romanian Manuscript Collection (Mss. Rom.), for a wide range of personal archives, and for some Royal Archives (Arhiva Palatului);
5. The Biblioteca Centrală de Stat, București, Manuscript Section, for the Kogălniceanu and St. Georges [Brătianu Family] archives, for numerous correspondence files, and several minor fonds.

B. PUBLISHED DOCUMENTS

The following sources of a documentary nature contain materials related to this study: **Archives Diplomatiques** [Paris], Volume 1(1861)-Volume 13(1873); Austria—Foreign Office, **Correspondenzen des Kais. Kön. Gemeinsamen Ministeriums des Äussern**, four volumes [Wein: Druck and Verlag der K.K. Hof-und Staatsdruckerei, 1868-1871]; Alexandru Balintescu, ed., **Arhiva Generalului Gheorghe Magheru** [Bucureşti: D. G. A. S., 1968]; Marin Bucur, ed., **Documente inedite din arhivele franceze privitoare la Români în secolul al XIX-lea**, Volume I [Bucureşti: Editura Academiei, 1969]; Teodor Codrescu, ed., **Uricariul**, twenty-six volumes [Iaşi: Buciumul Român, 1852-1895]; Paul Cornea and Elena Piru, eds., **Documente şi manuscrise literare**, two volumes [Bucureşti: Editura Academiei,1967-1969]; Great Britain—Foreign Office, **British and Foreign State Papers**, Volumes 46-62 [London: William Ridgway, 1865-1877]; Great Britain—Parliament, **Correspondence respecting the Persecution of Jews in Moldavia** [London: Harrison, 1867]; Great Britain—Parliament, **Further Correspondence respecting the Persecution of Jews in Moldavia**, two broshures [London: Harrison, 1867]; N. Iorga, ed., **Correspondance diplomatique Roumaine sous le roi Charles I-er (1866-1880)**, second edition [Bucureşti: Au Siege de l'Institut, 1938]; Mihail Kogălniceanu, **Documente diplomatice** [Bucureşti: Editura Politică, 1972]; Vasile M. Kogălniceanu, ed., **Acte relative la 2 maiu 1864** [Bucureşti: Göbl, 1894]; D. A. Sturdza, ed., **Charles Ier. Roi de Roumanie**, two volumes [Bucureşti: Göbl, 1899-1904]; D. A. Sturdza, **Insemnătatea europeană a realizărei definitive a dorinţelor rostite de divanurile ad-hoc in 7/19 şi 9/21 Octomvrie 1857 şi authoritatea faptului indeplinit executat in 1866 de cei indreptăţiţi** [Bucureşti: Göbl, 1912]; D. A. Sturdza, ed., **1866-1896. Trei-deci de ani de domnie ai Regelui Carol I**, two volumes [Bucureşti: Göbl, 1897]; D. C. Sturdza-Şcheeanu, ed., **Acte şi legiuiri privitoare la chestia ţărănească**, Seria I: **Dela Vasile Lupu până la 1866**. Volume II: **1856-1866** [Bucureşti: Socec, 1907]; Gh. Petrescu, et al., eds., **Acte şi documente relative la istoria renascerei Romaniei**, ten volumes in eleven, [Bucureşti: Göbl, 1888-1909).

C. MEMOIRS

For the period under consideration, there is a fairly rich memoirialistic literature. It varies widely in quality, of course. See the following: Al. Candiano-Popescu, **Amintiri din viaţa-mi** [Bucureşti: Universul, 1944], recollections by one of the leading military participants in the ouster of Cuza; Sabina Cantacuzino, **Din viaţa familiei I. C. Brătianu 1821-1891**, second edition, [Bucureşti: Universul, 1934], useful, but less interesting than it could have been; Carol I, **Aus dem Leben König Karls von Rumänien**, four volumes [Stuttgart: Cotta, 1894-1900], the recollections of Carol for the period 1866-1881. They appeared in a number of translations; only the Romanian edition of 1939 is faithful to the German original, the others omit various passages. On the other hand, the Romanian editions contain some additions, presumably inserted later by Carol himself, and therefore need to be consulted. For a commentary on their provenance and merits, see N. Iorga, "Opera de istoric a Regelui Carol," **A. R. MSI**, Seria II, Vol. 37 (1914), pp. 179-188;

Marcel Emerit, "Memoires inédits de Madame Cornu," **Revue de Paris** (1 August 1938), pp. 583-605, has insights concerning Prince Carol's French sponsor; Ferrero della Marmora, **Un po' piu di luce**, second edition, [Firenze: Barbèra, 1873], deals with the Italian revolutionary connection; N. Gane, **Amintiri** [Craiova: Scriusul Românesc, n.d.], from a leading Moldovan cultural and political figure; Ion Ghica, **Scrisori către V. Alecsandri** [Bucureşti: Cultura Românească, 1940], these are actually memoirs in letter form. They are very interesting and outstanding from a literary point of view, but not always reliable. For Ghica's personality and pre-1859 thought, see his **Amintiri din pribegia după 1848. Noui scrisori către V. Alecsandri**, Olimpiu Boitoş, ed., three volumes [Craiova: Scrisul Românesc, n.d.]; Nicholae Kretzulescu, **Amintiri istorice** [Bucureşti:Universul, 1940], for his youth only, but useful for his thinking; Radu Crutzescu, ed., **Amintirile Colonelului**

Lăcusteanu [București: Fundația pentru Literatură și Artă Regele Carol II, 1935], rather pedestrian, but interesting for their conservative, Russophile perspectives; Lord Augustus Loftus, **The Diplomatic Reminiscences of Lord Augustus Loftus**. Second series: **1862-1879**, Volume I [London: Cassell, 1894], a diplomat with Romanian experiences; Titu Maiorescu, **Insemnări zilnice**, Volume I: 1855-1880 [București: Socec, 1937], the diaries of the Junimea leader; Moses and Lady Montefiore, **Diaries of Sir Moses and Lady Montefiore**, two volumes, [Chicago: Belford-Clarke, 1890], Volume II deals with his visit to Romania; Émile Ollivier, **L'Empire libéral**. Volume VIII: **L'Année fatale. Sadowa (1866)** [Paris: Garnier Frères, 1903], contains important details on Carol's arrival in Romania; Émile Ollivier, "Napoléon III," **Revue des Deux Mondes**, Volume 146 (1898) fourth series, pp.. 48-89 and Émile Ollivier, "La premiere candidature Hohenzollern," **Revue des Deux Mondes**, Volume 9 (1902) fifth series, pp. 768-802, contain some significant differences from what he published in **L'Empire** and need to be consulted for French activity relative to Carol's selection. C. A. Rosetti, **Note intime, 1855-1859**, two volumes, [București: Lucrătorilor Asociați, 1902-1903], are essential for understanding Rosetti's personality; Radu Rosetti, **Amintiri**. Volume II: **Din copilarie** [București: Fundației Culturale Principele Carol, 1925]; Vintila C. A. Rosetti, **Amintiri istorice. Scrieri adunate și anotate și programele liberale de la 1848 pêne astă-di** [București: Românul, 1889], very important for the Muntenian liberals; C. D. Severeanu, **Din amintirile mele**, two volumes, [București: Bucovina and Voința, 1929], somewhat pompous, but helpful on events in the capital; Adolph Stern, **Din viața unui Evreu-Român** [București: Progresul, 1915], a leader of the București Jewish community describes major events and personalities; Gh. Știrbey, **Feuilles d'automne et Feuilles d'hiver**, two volumes, [Paris: Calman-Lévy, 1916], the recollections of a leading conservative; Nicolae Suțu, **Memoires du Prince Nicolas Soutzo** [Wien: Gerold, 1899], pungent observations directed against Romanian liberals of all stripes;

M. Theodorian-Carada, **efimeridele** [sic], Volume I,

[Bucureşti: Capitalei, 1930], a good source on conspiratorial activities of the liberals; Theodor Văcărescu, "Doue episode din viaţa mea," **Convorbiri Literare**, Volume 25 (1892), pp. 125-134, Volume 26 (1892), pp. 61-74; Theodor Văcărescu, "Memorii," **Convorbiri Literare**, Volume 49 (1915), pp. 54-60, 141-149, 393-398, 546-558, 666-682, 775-789, 996-1010, 1159-1172; Volume 50 (1916), pp. 31-48, 149-160, 286-298, 418-436, 488-492, 608-616; and, "Venirea în ţară a Regelui Carol," **Convorbiri Literare**, Volume 48 (1914), pp. 955-1032, an extensive recounting of key events from this period by an insider.

D. CORRESPONDENCE

Vasile Alecsandri, **Opere**, Volume 8:Corespondenţă, 1834-1860; Volume 9: Corespondenţă, 1861-1870, Marta Anineanu, ed. [Bucureşti: Editura Minerva, 1981-1982], his **Scrisori, însemnări**, Marta Anineanu, ed. [Bucureşti: Editura pentru Literatură, 1964], and Marta Anineanu, ed., **Catalogul corespondenţei lui Vasile Alecsandri** [Bucureşti: Editura Academiei, 1957], and Marta Anineanu, ed., **Scrisori către Vasile Alecsandri** [Bucureşti: Editura Minerva, 1978], provide a very useful collection and annotated listing; Al. Cretzianu, ed., **Din arhiva lui Dumitru Brătianu**, two volumes, [Bucureşti: Independenţa, 1933-1934], letters for 1840-1870 with a biographical sketch; Ion Nistor, ed., **Din corespondenţa familiei Ion C. Brătianu**, Volume I, [Bucureşti: Independenţa, 1933]; Victor Slăvescu, "Scrisori inedite ale lui Barbu Catargui, ianuarie-octombrie 1861," **Arhiva Românească**, Vol. 7 (1941), pp. 263-290; Dumitru Ivănescu and Virginia Isac, eds., **Alexandru Ioan Cuza. Acte şi scrisori** [Iaşi: Junimea, 1973]; Alexandru Ioan Cuza and Costache Negri, **Corespondenţă**, Emil Boldan, ed. [Bucureşti: Editura Minerva, 1980], highly interesting correspondence between Cuza and his chief diplomatic advisor; E. Perticari-Davila, **Din viaţa şi corespondenţa lui Carol Davila** [Bucureşti: Fundaţia pentru Literatură şi Artă Regele Carol II, 1935]; Radu R. Rosetti, ed., **Corespondenţa Generalului Iancu Ghica** [Bucureşti: Cartea Românească,

1930]; Victor Slăvescu, "Corespondenţa lui Ion Ghica cu Dimitrie Sturdza (1860-1880)," **A. R. MSI**, Ser. III, Volume 25 (1943), pp. 1247-1358; Victor Slăvescu, **Corespondenţa intre Ion Ionescu dela Brad şi Ion Ghica** [Bucureşti: Naţionala, 1943]; N. Liu, ed., **Catalogul corespondenţei lui Ion Ghica** [Bucureşti: Editura Academiei, 1962]; Radu R. Rosetti, "Corespondenţa Maiorului D. Giurescu," **A. R. MSI**, Ser. III, Volume 29 (1946), pp. 77-112; George Fotino, **Din vremea renaşterii naţionale a Ţării Româneşti. Boieri Goleşti**, four volumes, [Bucureşti: Naţionala, 1939], first volume is text and next three volumes are correspondence; Mihail Kogălniceanu, **Scrisori. Note de Călătorie**, A. Z. N. Pop and Dan Simonescu, eds. [Bucureşti: Editura pentru Literatură, 1967]; A. Z. N. Pop, ed., **Catalogul corespondenţei lui Mihail Kogălniceanu** [Bucureşti: Editura Academiei, 1959], as with the Ghica and Alecsandri catalogues, this is a very useful instrument; G. Potra, et al., eds., **Ion Heliade Rădulescu. Scrisori şi acte** [Bucureşti: Minerva, 1972]; Victor Slăvescu, "Corespondenţa Petre Mavrogheni--D. A. Sturdza. Treisprezece scrisori din 1860-1863," **Revista Istorică Română**, volumes 11-12 (1943), pp. 1-34; Marcel Emerit, ed., **Lettres de Napoleon III à Madame Cornu**, two volumes, [Paris: Presses Modernes, 1938]; N. Georgescu-Tistu, **Correspondance d'une secrétaire princier en Roumanie: Émile Picot (1866-1868)** [Paris: Gamber, 1927]; C. A. Rosetti, **Corespondenţă**, Marin Bucur, ed. [Bucureşti: Editura Minerva, 1980].

E. PRINTED SPEECHES

Basile Boerescu, **Discursuri politice, 1858-1883**, two volumes, [Bucureşti: Socec, 1910]; C. Boerescu, **Discursuri politice, 1866-1891** [Bucureşti: Socec, 1903]; [V. Brătianu, et al., eds.], **Din scrierile şi cuvîntările lui Ion C. Brătianu**, Partea I:1848-1868 [Bucureşti: Göbl, 1903]; G. Marinescu and C. Grecescu, eds., **Ion C. Brătianu. Acte şi cuvântări. Volume I, Pt. 1 (Iunie 1848-Decemvrie 1859)** [Bucureşti: Cartea Românească, 1938]; and G. Marinescu and C. Grecescu, eds., **Ion C. Brătianu. Acte şi cuvântări. Volume I, Pt. 2**

(**1 Ian 1869-Aprilie 1876**) [București: Cartea Românească, 1935]; I. C. Brătianu and M. Kogălniceanu, **Discursurile...spre responsu la discursulu tronului** [București: Rosetti, 1868]; Carol I, **Cuvântările și scrisori**, three volumes [București: Göbl, 1909], very useful; Carol I, **Cuvântările Regelui Carol I**, C. C. Giurescu, ed., two volumes, [București: Fundația pentru Literatură și Artă Regele Carol II, 1939], a better edition of the speeches, but omits the letters; P. P. Carp, **Discursuri**. Volume I: **1868-1888** [București: Socec, 1907]; Barbu Katargiu [sic], **Discursuri parlamentare (1859-1862 Iunie 8)**, P. V. Haneș, ed.[București: Minerva, 1914]; Mihail Kogălniceanu, **Opere**. Volumes III, IV, V: Oratorie, Georgeta Penelea, ed [București: Editura Academiei, 1977-in progress], covering all of Kogălniceanu's speeches for 1857-1891 along with extensive notes and first rate commentary; Al. Lahovary, **Discursuri parlamentare 1868-1872**, Volume I, [București: Cucu, 1909]; Titu Maiorescu, **Discursuri parlamentare**, Volume I, [București: Socecu, 1897]; B. Mangâru, ed., **Discursurile Generalui Th. Văcărescu (1868-1906)** [București: Göbl, 1915].

PART II: General Bibliography

A. REFERENCE

The following reference works are of value: C. Diaconovich, ed., **Enciclopedia Română**, three volumes, [Sibiu: Krafft, 1898-1904]; D. Gusti, ed., **Enciclopedia Romaniei**, four volumes, [București: Editura Națională, 1938-1943]; I.-A. Candrea and Gh. Adamescu, eds., **Dicționarul Enciclopedic Ilustrat Cartea Românească** [București: Cartea Românească, 1931]; Lazăr Șăineanu, **Dicționar Universal**, seventh edition, [Craiova: Scrisul Românesc, n.d.]; C. C. Giurescu, ed., **Chronological History of Romania** [București: Editura Enciclopedică Română, 1972]; O. G. Lecca, **Dictionar istoric, arheologic și geografic al României** [București: Universul, 1937]; G. I. Lahovary, et al., **Marele dicționar geografic al**

Romîniei, five volumes [Bucureşti: Socecu, 1898-1902]; and Dimitrie Frunḑescu, **Dictionaru topograficu şi statisticu alu României** [Bucureşti: Tip. Statului, 1872].

The following are important for biographical information; the Predescu volume is a unique resource: Lucian Predescu, **Enciclopedia Cugetarea** [Bucureşti:Cugetarea-Georgescu Delafras, 1940]; D. R. Rosetti, **Dicţionarul contimporanilor din Romania (1800-1898)** [Bucureşti: Populara, 1898]; Ion Simionescu, **Oameni aleşi**.Volume II: **Românii**, sixth edition, [Bucureşti: Cartea Românească, 1944]; Iosif Vulcan, **Panteonulu Românu** [Pest: Kocsi, 1869]; and O. G. Lecca, **Familiile Boereşti Române** [Bucureşti: Minerva, 1899].

B. BIBLIOGRAPHY

1. General Bibliographies

The most useful brief introduction to historical reference works is Ştefan Lemny's "Instrumentarul cercetării istorice din ţara noastră. Scurt istoric," **Anuarul Institutului de Istorie şi Arheologie A. D. Xenopol**, Vol. 19 (1982), pp. 461-477. Along the same lines, but more extensive is Nicolae Bocşan, et al., eds., **Ghidul studentului în istorie. Istoria României** [Cluj- Napoca: Biblioteca Centrală Universitară/Catedra de Istorie, 1980. There are a considerable number of general bibliographical resources for the study of Romania, including the following: Ioachim Crăciun, "Bibliografia la Români," **Anuarul Institutului de Istorie Naţională din Cluj**, Vol. 4 (1926-1927), pp. 483-513; N. Georgescu-Tistu, **Bibliografia literară Română** [Bucureşti: Imprimeria Naţională, 1932]; Barbu Theodorescu, **Istoria bibliografia Romane** [Bucureşti: Fundaţia Regele Mihai I, 1945], second edition, [Bucureşti: Editura Enciclopedică Română, 1972]; and two works by and about Romanians in French: Georges Bengesco, **Bibliographie Franco-Roumaine depuis le commencement du XIXe siècle jusqu'a nos jours**, second edition [Paris: Leroux, 1907], and Alexandre and Getta Hélène Rally, **Bibliographie Franco-Roumaine**, two volumes, [Paris: Leroux, 1930]; and a similar one for English: Octav

Păduraru, **Anglo-Roumanian and Roumanian-English Bibliography** [Bucureşti: Imprimeria Naţională, 1946].

2. Historical Bibliography

The appearance since 1970 of the series **Bibliografia istorică a România [BIR]**, published by Editura Academiei, has immensely eased the task of the student of Romanian history. Four volumes covering the work of Romanian historians from 1944 to 1984, and constituting a kind of national historical bibliography since World War II, have appeared in the year of the international historical congresses: Ştefan Pascu, et al., eds. **Bibliografia istorică a României** [Bucureşti:Editura Academiei, 1970-1984], Volume I, **1944-1969**; Volume IV, **1969-1974**; Volume V, **1974-1979**; Volume VI, **1979-1984**.

A second series, dealing with the 19th century, and including publications relating to the 19th century published prior to 1944, constitutes Volumes II and III of the **BIR** thus far: the first covers general publications dealing with the 19th century and was edited by Cornelia Bodea, **Bibliografia istorică a României**, Volume II: **Secolul XIX: Cadrul General. Ţara şi locuitorii** [Bucureşti: Editura Academiei, 1972]; the second provides a bibliographical dictionary of biographies for 19th century personalities and was edited by Vladimir Diculescu, **Bibliografia istorică a României**, Volume III. **Secolul XIX: Biografii** [Bucureşti: Editura Academiei, 1974]. Both volumes are superlative aids. Bodea gives a useful discussion of Romanian bibliography as well as a précis of the 19th century series.

Other historical bibliographies, listed in chronological order are: I. C. Băcilă, **Bibliografia domniei Regelui Carol I al României** [Bucureşti: Fundaţiei Universitare Carol I, 1916]; T. G. Bulat, **Încercare de bibliografie a istorii Românilor**, two volumes, [Râmnicu-Vâlcea: Tip. Poporului [I] and Tip. şi Libr. Matei Basarab [II], 1919]; N. Georgescu-Tistu, "Pubblicazioni storiche Rumene dalla guerra in poi," **Archivio storico italiano**, N.S. VII, Vol. 13 (1930), pp. 115-136; Paul Henry, "Histoire Roumaine," **Revue historique**, Vol. 176 (1935), pp. 486-537;

Mario Ruffini, "Introduzione bibliografica allo studio della Romania," **L'Europe Orientale**, Vol. 15 (1935), pp. 236-289; P.P. Panaitescu, "Rumänische Geschichtsschreibung, 1918-1942," **Südost-Forschungen**, Vol. 8 (1943), pp. 69-109; Paul Henry, "Histoire de Roumanie," **Revue historique**, Vol. 194 (1944), pp. 42-65; 132-150; 233-252; Paul Simionescu, "Contribuţii la o bibliografie a bibliografiilor istorice romîneşti," **Studii şi Cercetări de Bibliologie**, Vol. 2 (1957), pp. 213-230; Stephen A. Fischer-Galati, **Rumania, A Bibliographic Guide** [Washington, D. C.: USGPO, 1963]; Paul Cernovodeanu and Paul Simionescu, "Essai de bibliographie sélective concernant l'histoire de Roumanie," **Revue Roumaine d'Histoire**, Vol. 4 (1965), pp. 641-663, and "Supplément," Vol. 5 (1966), pp. 547-572; Sanda Cândea, **Istoria României. Ghid bibliografic** [Bucureşti: Biblioteca Centrală Universitareă, 1968]; Paul L. Horecky, ed., **Southeastern Europe. A Guide to Basic Publications** [Chicago: University of Chicago Press, 1969], pp. 329-448 deal with Romania; Robert Deutsch, **Istoricii şi ştiinţa istorică din România 1944-1969** [Bucureşti: Editura Ştiinţifică, 1970]; Paul Simionescu,"Un guide bibliographique pour l'histoire du Moyen Âge et des temps modernes de la Roumanie," **Rumanian Studies**, Vol. 1 (1970), pp. 173-225; Hugo Weczerka, "Literaturbericht uber die Geschichte Rumaniens (bis 1945): Veroffentlichungen 1944-1970," **Historische Zeitschrift**, Sonderheft 5 (1973), pp. 324-420.

C. GENERAL WORKS

There are relatively few general narrative treatments of modern Romanian history, and they must be used with care either because they argue some thesis or contain careless mistakes: F. Damé, **Histoire de la Roumanie contemporaine** [Paris: Alcan, 1900]; A. D. Xenopol, **Istoria Românilor din Dacia Traiană**, third edition, I. Vlădescu,ed., fourteen volumes, [Bucureşti: Cartea Românească, 1925-1930] volumes XIII-XIV; N. Iorga, **Istoria Românilor**, ten volumes in eleven, [Bucureşti: n.p., 1936-1939], volumes IX-X; P. Constantinescu-Iaşi, ed., **Istoria Romîniei**. Volume IV: **Formarea şi consolidarea** orînduirii capitaliste (1848-1878) [Bucureşti: Editura Academiei, 1964]; and Vasile Maciu, De la Tudor Vladimirescu la Răscoala din 1907 [Craiova: Scrisul Românesc, 1974]. A stimulating and controversial interpretive work is E. Lovinescu's Istoria civilizaţiei Române moderne, three volumes [Bucureşti: Ancora, 1924-1925], which focus on the period 1821-1866. L. Pătrăşcanu's Un veac de frământări sociale 1821-1907 [Bucureşti: Cartea Rusă, 1945] is a sometimes provocative Marxist interpretation, but unbalanced. Good summary treatments are D. Onciul, Din istoria României [Bucureşti:Alcalay, 1908], and I. C. Filitti, "Viaţa politică a Ţării Româneşti şi a Moldovei," in D. Gusti, ed., Enciclopedia României [Bucureşti: Naţionala, 1938], Volume I, pp. 808-862. A rather marginal work which nevertheless has a little material is B. Mangâru, România sub Vodă Cuza, Regii Carol I şi Ferdinand I [Bucureşti: Cartea Românească, 1932].

General histories of Romania which touch on this period and are of some usefulness are: R. W. Seton-Watson, A History of the Roumanians, reprinted edition, [Hamden: Archon, 1963]; Ioan Lupaş, Istoria Unirii Românilor [Bucureşti: Fundaţia Culturală Regală Principele Carol, 1937]; Gh. I. Brătianu, Origines et formation de l'unité roumaine [Bucureşti: Institut d'Histoire Universelle N. Iorga, 1943]; C. C. Giurescu, Istoria Românilor [Bucureşti: Cugetarea-Georgescu Delafras, 1943]; Ioan Lupaş, Istoria Românilor, fifteenth edition [Sibiu: Dacia Traiană, 1944]; M. Roller, ed., Istoria României, third edition, [Bucureşti: Editura de Stat, 1947]; Andrei Oţetea, ed., Istoria poporului Român [Bucureşti: Editura Ştiinţifică, 1970]; C. C. and Dinu C. Giurescu, Istoria Românilor, second edition [Bucureşti: Editura Albatros, 1975]; Dinu C. Giurescu, Illustrated History of the Romanian People [Bucureşti: Editura Sport-Turism, 1981]; Mircea Muşat and Ion Ardeleanu, De la statul dac la statul român unitar [Bucureşti: Editura Ştiinţifică, 1983].

The following works were of importance to this study as noted: For the history of the city of București, Constantin Bacalbașa, **Bucureștii de altă dată**, four volumes, second edition, [București: Universul, 1935-1936]; F. Damé, **Bucarest en 1906** [București: Socec, 1907]; N. Iorga, **Istoria Bucureștilor** [București: Naționala, 1939]; Dan Berindei, **Orașul București** [București: Editura Academiei, 1963]; C. C. Giurescu, **Istoria Bucureștilor** [București: Editura pentru Literatură, 1966]. For the history of the city of Iași, N. A. Bogdan, **Orașul Iași**, second revised edition, [Iași: Naționala, 1913-1915]. For literary history and for intellectual history in general, the indispensable work is G. Călinescu's outstanding **Istoria Literaturii Române** [București: Fundația Regală pentru Literatură și Artă, 1941]. Nerva Hodoș and Al. Sadi Ionescu, **Publicațiunile periodice Românești**. Volume I: **1820-1906** [București: Socec and Sfetea, 1913] provides the necessary orientation to the maze of periodical publications appearing in the 19th century; their work is completed by George Baiculescu, et al., **Publicațiile periodice Românești** (Ziare, gazete, reviste). Descriere bibliografică, Volume II, [București: Editura Academiei, 1969].

D. GEOGRAPHY/STATISTICS

There is a wealth of material of a descriptive nature on 19th century Romania. There is no up-to-date synthesis on this subject however. The best general geography of Romania, with an ample bibliography, is V. Mihăilescu, **România** [București: Socec, 1936]. Also useful is Simion Mehedinți, **România**, thirteenth edition {București: Socec, 1935. An excellent book on Muntenia is Emmanuel de Martonne's **La Valachie** [Paris: Armand Colin, 1902]; no similar treatment exists for Moldova. A useful descriptive study for the mid-nineteenth century is C. C. Giurescu, **Principatele Romîne la începutul secolului XIX** [București: Editura Științifică, 1957]. A survey published by the government to commemorate the fortieth anniversary of Carol's reign is Ion Popa-Burcă, **România, 1866-1906** [București: Socec, 1907], which was also published in French and German.

N. Xenopol's **La Richesse de la Roumanie** [Bucureşti: Socec, 1916] is a valuable book; as is Ion Simionescu, **Ţara noastră** [Bucureşti: Fundaţia pentru Literatură şi Artă Regele Carol II, 1937].

Contemporary geographical accounts which were found to be helpful are: three books by Ion Ionescu [de la Brad]: **Argicultura romăna din judeţiulu Dorohoiŭ** (Bucureşti: Imprimeria Statului, 1866], **Agricultura Română în judeţul Mehedinţi** [Bucureşti: Impremeria Statului, 1868], and **Agricultura Română din Judeciulu Putna** [Bucureşti: Imprimeria Statului, 1869]; P. S. Aurelian and Al. Odobescu, **Notice sur la Roumanie**, second edition [Paris: Dentu, 1866]; Ulisse de Marsillac, **De Pesth à Bucarest** [Bucureşti: Ouvriers Associés, 1869]; H. Filek von Wittinghausen, **Das Fürstenthum Romanien** [Wien: Carl Gerold's Sohn, 1869]; M.-G. Obédénare, **La Roumanie économique** [Paris: E. Leroux, 1876]; and P. S. Aurelian, **Terra noastră**, second edition, [Bucureşti: Academia Română, 1880]. A helpful anthropological work is Eugene Pittard, **La Roumanie** [Paris: Bossard, 1917]. Statistical information may be found in **Analele Statistice şi Economice ale României**; N. A. Alescandrini, **Statistica României dela unirea Principateloru până în presentu**, two volumes, [Iaşi: Goldner, 1895-1898]; Ioan G. Bibicescu, **Mişcarea poporaţiunii în România de la 1870 pêne la 1878** [Bucurest: Göbl, 1880]; and in the various works of Nicolae Suţu reprinted in Victor Slăvescu, **Vieaţa şi opera economistului Nicolae Suţu, 1798-1871** [Bucureşti: Naţionala, 1941].